Bulleid of the Southern

BULLEID
of the Southern

H. A. V. BULLEID

LONDON
IAN ALLAN LTD

First published 1977
Reprinted 1978

ISBN 0 7110 0689 X

Published by Ian Allan Ltd, Shepperton, Surrey,
and printed in the United Kingdom by
John G Eccles Printers Ltd, Inverness.

Contents

Introduction

Why another Bulleid biography? Because there is enough new material to fill a book and enough published material that needs re-telling in the perspective of today. What couldn't be told in 1963 can be told in 1976.

Much background information was given in the 1963 Day-Lewis Biography and I have not repeated this, concentrating rather on the direct Bulleid story in terms of his railway work. To map out the extensive arena I have partitioned it into separate chapters. This also saves the sensitive reader from coming unexpectedly face-to-face with diesels and such.

The kind interest and response of the many people who helped me with information and verification for this book made my work unexpectedly pleasurable. They have enabled me to colour accurately the outline and detail of the achievements many of them shared with O.V.B.

So my grateful thanks go to H. W. Attwell, H. Bailey, A. G. Baker, E. R. J. Barnes, R. C. Bond, Lord Brooke of Cumnor, H. L. Butler, K. Cantlie, G. W. Carpenter, R. L. Curl, H. M. Dannatt, M. J. Devereux, W. Durban, Sir John Elliot, P. Ellis, L. J. Granshaw, R. H. N. Hardy, G. Harrison, M. S. Hatchell, A. E. Hooker, C. P. Hopkins, Mrs E. Howell (née Anderson), W. H. Hutchinson, R. G. Jarvis, Miss J. Johnston, J. G. Jones, J. Kirk, W. Marsh, A. B. MacLeod, R. Metcalfe, G. L. Nicholson, G. F. Parrinder, A. R. Pocklington, S. Richardson, R. A. Riddles, R. F. Simpson, S. W. Smart, D. Smith, S. G. Smith, E. N. Soar, S. C. Townroe, J. R. Tugwood, F. J. R. Watts, A. A. Wilton.

Cordial thanks also to British Railways, C.I.E., the Institution of Mechanical Engineers, *The Railway Gazette, The Engineer, The Times, Modern Transport, The Illustrated London News* and the *Brighton Evening Argus* for supplies of information and permission to use it; and to several resourceful Librarians and Archivists, particularly R. T. Everett and S. G. Morrison of the I.Mech.E.

I am indebted most, for wide-ranging information and discussions, for locating and preparing drawings and diagrams, for checking drafts with a very keen eye for accuracy, and for supplying some admirable photographs, to J. G. Click.

Ifold, Sussex, 1976   *H. A. V. Bulleid*

1

Overture

Generations of Bulleids lived around North Tawton, Devon; and of them two orphaned brothers, William and John, left the care of their uncle Samuel Snell Lee in 1875 and emigrated to Invercargill, New Zealand. Generations of Pughs lived around mid-Wales and one of them, Oliver Vaughan Pugh, had two daughters Janet and Marian ("Doll"). Everyone is said to have been astonished when William, on a business trip to England in 1878, met and fell for Marian and married her at Llanfyllin on July 31st.

They were back at Invercargill in November and their first child, a son, was born on 19th September 1882. Naturally they christened him Oliver Vaughan after Grandpa Pugh, and Snell after the rescuing uncle. He turned out to be hearty, adventurous and of quick intellect. Because he got into everything his mother for a time nicknamed him "Plunger." Quite soon after he could talk he extricated himself from this infra-dig title and was thereafter Oliver. No abbreviations. He first really made the news, with kudos to himself and slight panic to parents and headmistress, when he switched himself from the kindergarten to the Middle (grammar) school aged 6 and went to the top of the entry class.

Then suddenly in 1889, aged only 43, William Bulleid died of pleurisy. Since he and his wife were both immigrants with no local roots, the young widow, now with three children, sadly made the arduous journey back to Llanfyllin. Welcomed by her widowed mother she settled in at "Pen-y-bryn" and Oliver started at the local school. Welcoming visits also came from her married sister Janet Sandeman, who lived with her four children in a large house "The Chestnuts" at Church by Accrington.

In September 1893 Janet sent her son Vaughan to the Spa College, Bridge of Allan, Stirlingshire, the headmaster's wife being an old friend of the Pugh sisters. During that term it became blindingly obvious that Oliver had outgrown the limitations of the local school at Llanfyllin, and despite the parting and the extra strain on their limited finances, Marian agreed to Janet's suggestion that Oliver should join Vaughan. It was a ghastly journey in January 1894 for the two 11-year-olds, and when they got there it was a school of tough discipline in a cold climate, with far more emphasis on accuracy than on communication, both in composition and translation. The boys became and remained fast friends, the reserved and brainy Oliver offsetting the boisterous extrovert Vaughan.

They left the Spa College rather unexpectedly in December 1895 for a variety of reasons. The new Municipal Technical School at Accrington already had a very good reputation and would take them in January. Then again it would be far cheaper in fees and travelling. Besides, both mothers were cross with the Spa College because they had sent the boys home on the long cold December journey with their overcoats packed in their trunks. It was Janet who then had the idea that henceforth Oliver should live at "The Chestnuts" at least during the school terms, and in exchange her two younger daughters should live at "Pen-y-bryn." Marian had little choice but to agree to this one-sided plan, though it largely deprived her of her elder son and placed six souls in her smaller house (with servant but without bathroom or running water, h. or c.) compared with five at the larger, bathroomed "Chestnuts." She decided to grin and bear it as being in Oliver's best interests. He too was a stoic and did the same, recognising the advantages and welcomed by his always well-meaning Uncle Will and Aunt Janet and with brotherly love for cousins Ve and Olive. But he was a bright and thinking and even rather introspective 13-year-old, and he knew he already had some small responsibility as "head of" the fatherless family; so he resented being deprived of giving this support to his mother.

Oliver found the school work harder but much more interesting than at the Spa College and had only two worries. One was persistent nagging from the grown-ups about picking up the Lancashire accent. The other was an

Fig 1 John Pugh's dinner ticket, bearing his Seal. He was Bulleid's great-grandfather and set about getting a railway to Llanfyllin in 1860, unwisely subscribing £3,000 from which the family derived scant dividends and a final buy-out for £200.

8

obvious but annoying variant of his name Snell, used by some of his school fellows. He removed this annoyance with characteristic independence by substituting the name Pugh, signing himself thereafter O.V.P.B.

The train journey from Llanfyllin, Montgomeryshire, to Church-and-Oswaldtwistle, Lancs, was by Cambrian Railway to Whitchurch via Oswestry, LNWR to Crewe and Manchester, and then the L & Y. It was about 90 miles — and there could be delays. But the Pughs and Bulleids and Sandemans were hardy travellers and close families, and they were normally all together at "The Chestnuts" for Christmas, at "Pen-y-bryn" in the summer, and at the seaside for their summer holiday. There were also plenty of parties though Oliver was sometimes missing — a prey to bilious attacks, particularly when he did not want to go.

Uncle Will Sandeman was a formidable figure, a Scottish accountant but with his main interest as a colonel in "the Volunteers." His drill-hall manner of addressing the children scared them when young, but he taught them more than many a father and laughed at their escapades when they were out of hearing. Things were naturally freer and easier on holiday at Llanfyllin, though occasionally Grandma Pugh was driven to exclaim "Whatever have I done to deserve such grandchildren?" Oliver and Ve roamed far and wide together, and once when Oliver ventured right to the edge of the old quarry at Grave Hill it crumbled and he was very lucky to catch and hang on to a sapling, a few feet down. Ve, rushing for help, was equally lucky to find a farmer a few fields away. With a rope they hauled the badly shaken Oliver to safety from an 80-foot drop, incidentally providing a cautionary tale for the local paper.

His mother took things philosophically. What she liked least were the periods of humdrum, circumscribed life at Llanfyllin, and she relished her annual six-week job of helping out her friend Connie Sprague by taking over the running of the Hautboy Hotel at Ockham, near Guildford.

Oliver and Ve both made good progress at the Technical School and Uncle Will offered them a prize each if they passed the London Matriculation in July 1899. But Ve failed while Oliver passed in the First Division, and in this tricky situation no more was said about a prize, giving Oliver further practice in stoicism.

More seriously, however, rose the question of what profession to enter. Oliver's interests were decidedly catholic and gave no clue. But he was seen to be brainy and so it was decided he should take the competitive examination for the Civil Service in 1900. He therefore remained at "The Chestnuts" cramming for this, and duly sat it, but during an attack of influenza, failing to get a high enough mark to win one of the few places.

After an uneasy hiatus an offer came from Uncle John Bulleid in New Zealand for Oliver to go there to be articled to a barrister cousin, Ernest Lee. This offer reached Marian Bulleid while she was doing a stint at Ockham, and was obviously more attractive than an opening she was exploring for him in London. It would keep him close to the family and in the traditional legal profession of the Pughs. But it was yet another wrench to part with her elder son just when she hoped she might get closer to him. He was at "The Chestnuts" when she wrote to him from Ockham.

"My dearest Oliver, I have sent the letter from Aunty Fanny (Uncle John's wife), I think you must go. I am very sorry to part with you but it seems I must. You must go and say good-bye to Granny and the children and then come to me and I will rig you out and send you off. I was going up to London to fix things up with Mr Clark, but I do not think we should give up such a good chance. I know you will not forget me. With best love I remain, Your loving Mother."

Aunt Janet luckily agreed and suggested the good-byes should include Oliver's cousin, the Rev. Edgar Lee, Vicar of Christ Church, Doncaster. And so it came about that, in November 1900, Oliver and his mother stayed for a few days at Christ Church vicarage, en route to Tilbury and with a single passage booked with the New Zealand Shipping Company.

If Aunt Janet liked to run things, so did Fr. Lee. He did not think much of his sister in New Zealand, Aunt Fanny, though admittedly this would not really affect Oliver's progress. He saw the pain of another separation for Marian Bulleid, though she had herself made the same journey. He thought the vacillations were having a bad effect on Oliver, who seemed to have no strong feeling about what he should do but clearly wanted to get started. And of course the good Vicar had seen several keen and competent-looking young men such as J.R. Bazin settling down excellently to an engineering career at the Railway Plant Works under his esteemed parishioner H.A. Ivatt, whose brother added the respectability of the cloth. Furthermore he had grown out of the inhibitions, which now affected only the remoter gentry, about engineering being a rude and common occupation ("Really! One could scarcely call it a *profession*.")

So when Mrs Bulleid said doubtfully that there was really no alternative to the New Zealand plan the Vicar heartily exclaimed: "Rubbish! Of course there is. He can stay in England and train to be an engineer." And getting sharply off the mark he arranged for Oliver to see H.A. Ivatt at the GNR Works on November 13.

Ivatt was a kindly interviewer, like Ramsbottom, and recognised the mutual importance of selecting suitable and compatible young men for the premium apprenticeships. He was the first important industrialist Oliver had met, and as he asked a few questions to assess his education and intellect and outlook, he gave a lasting impression of a man to be admired and trusted. He found Bulleid's replies fully satisfactory and agreed there and then to accept him for a four-year premium apprenticeship starting in January 1901.

2

With the Great Northern Railway

It was not uncommon for "superior young men" to start their premium apprenticeship aged about 18, corresponding to their normal school-leaving age. They usually made better progress and learned more widely once they had made a good start by mucking in and not putting on airs. So there was nothing unusual when 18¼-year-old Bulleid started at Doncaster on January 21, 1901 and was shown the ropes in the machine shop by an older apprentice, R. Talbot.

Impressed by Ivatt and the Works, furnished at last with a definite career ahead, and discovering the depth of his delight with things mechanical, Bulleid really waded into his apprenticeship and into its peripheral involvements, including evening classes. On March 7th, after the usual trial period, he was formally accepted as an apprentice, so Fr. Edgar Lee paid the balance of the premium and Bulleid left the vicarage and moved into digs, sharing with Talbot. This gave him more time for technical reading and more scope for technical talk, and by the end of April he had acquired a drawing-board and tee-square. On holiday at Accrington in May, he spent a day in Bullough's textile machinery works. In June he got an application form to join the Institution of Mechanical Engineers and the foreman advised him to ask Ivatt about filling it in. When he duly returned it for signing Ivatt not only obliged on June 18 but got the Works Manager Marsh and the Loco Running Supt. Webster to sign as seconder and referee. The form got back to the Mechanicals on June 21 and O.V.P. Bulleid became a Graduate member in October.

In July the Ivatts asked him to a bicycling picnic followed by supper; their four daughters ranged in age from 22 to 12, and George was away at Uppingham, aged 15. Thereafter Bulleid was a constant visitor to the Ivatt home in Regent Square, where he also met a kindred technical spirit in J.R. Bazin, who had started his premium apprenticeship in 1897, also aged 18, and was currently in the Running shed as a fitter. Bazin also fuelled his interest in photography.

Another advantage to the older apprentice is his more enquiring and less easily appeased mind. To the question "Why are we doing it?" there are commercial and costing answers as well as the technical answer. Sometimes Bulleid got incomplete answers when he asked the foreman, so he got permission to ask Ivatt, who was pleasantly surprised, did a bit of explaining

11

himself, and arranged for him to see the accounting procedures. The foremen were equally patient with his technical quests; the American technical press was full of the pioneer brazing of cast iron. "An impossibility," said Doncaster Works. So apprentice Bulleid got a local chemist to make up the advised fluxes and coaxed the foreman to experiment. Success! (But not to be risked in actual use!)

Christmas Eve 1901 was not an exceptionally busy day for energetic Bulleid. George Ivatt called for him in the morning and they spent the day going round the whole works, including the new Crimpsall. They then walked back to the Ivatts for tea. Afterwards Bulleid wrote and posted four letters in time for delivery next day, Christmas day. Later he went back to the Ivatts, accompanying them to Midnight Mass and getting back to his digs at 2 am.

Thanks to contributions from Fr. Lee, his mother, and sundry well-wishers, Bulleid could just about pay his way without his weekly apprentice earnings of around 7 shillings. This, coupled with his life-long minor disability from periodic headaches and bilious attacks, and perhaps fanned by love of travel at the privelege quarter-fare, led to the only criticism one could make about his apprenticeship — that he lost a great deal of time. In addition to late starts and early leavings, he missed 70 working days in his first year, comforted of course by always asking permission and by knowing that his absence would not stop the Works. One jaunt was a long week-end with the Talbots at Acton. He started as he meant to continue, far more concerned to learn all he could than merely to clock up attendance. And he kept it up; a typical postcard to his cousin Celia from Crewe on December 29, 1902, read: "I have come here to go over works. Seen a good deal of them and am just going to finish. Rather tiring. Yours O.V.P.B." But he also kept remembering that all work and no play could make him a dull boy and another postcard from Newark on April 25, 1903 read: "Just come down here on a quadricycle. Yours O.V.P.B." This apparatus was an unreliable bicycle-framed four-wheeler with four-stroke engine hired from Brown's bicycle shop. They had just reached the horseshoe pond (near the race course tram terminus) on the way home at midnight when it broke down and had to be dumped for the night.

A move to the Drawing Office and staff hours in September 1903 enabled Bulleid to switch his studies to three evenings a week at Sheffield University; and at last he could properly compare his technical reading with the facts of GNR design. He was quite surprised to find that Dr. Goss's theoretical shape for petticoat and chimney were virtually the same as those on the drawings of the big Atlantics, which Ivatt himself had sketched empirically but based on long experience. The Drawing Office was not short of bright ideas, by no means all of which were accepted by Ivatt; and once when Bulleid grumbled about this ages-old snag he got an excellent reply from the Chief Clerk, Clayton: "You should try to realize the difference between seeing something from above and from below."

The Bulleid four-year apprenticeship ended with an all-too-brief fitting spell in the Carr Running shed. There he saw the inserts in the balanced slide-valves of the Atlantics, which were so meticulously fitted under special supervision in the Works, being taken out and lavishly relieved with second-cut files "to make them work." Unfortunately and uncharacteristically he never dismantled this particular Shed/Works obstacle. Then followed the long and interesting battle with the Daimler petrol-engined carriage on the Hertford branch after which, in January 1906, Bulleid was appointed to his first job, personal assistant to Webster, the Loco Running Superintendent. Again circumstances conspired to prevent him from gaining a really intimate experience of day-to-day (and night-to-night) Running Shed maintenance problems, because Webster tended, naturally enough, to use him on technical matters, often those involving Shed/Works arguments. He began to wonder when he would get on to a more important job; he would be 24 in September. Besides, he was falling in love with Ivatt's youngest daughter, Marjorie, now eighteen and a rather exuberant charmer compared with her more distant older sisters. If he did not do something about it, she was bound to be snapped up. In mentioning marriage obliquely to his mother he was told he was far too young and earning far too little to think of it. Yet J.R. Bazin, three years older and well thought of, was earning only 55 shillings a week as Shed Foreman at Colwick.

These thoughts were sharpened on Bulleid's twenty-fourth birthday by the Grantham accident. Bazin's knocker-up shouted the terrible message "Scotch express down the bank at Grantham," and Bazin had his break-down gang from Colwick helping the main gangs by the early hours of the morning. To the relief of all at Doncaster the engine was found not to have contributed to the accident. Webster had an idea that it was travelling at an excessive speed and even got Bulleid to calculate the centre of gravity and hence overturning speed, an absurd waste of time in view of the missing data — amount of water in the boiler, state of track and trim of engine when entering the reverse curve at which it overturned.

Only Bazin, in his quiet methodical way, came up with an explanation of the accident that fitted all the reliable evidence. The signalman at Grantham South, horrified at the excessive speed of a train booked to stop, looked intently and saw both driver and fireman standing in their normal positions. The guard noticed a brake application as the train entered the platform. A regular Atlantic driver like Fleetwood would work the engine hard over Stoke summit and then allow the speed to increase to about 70mph on the 1 in 200 downgrade into Grantham. He would then shut off steam and open the blower and coast the last two or three miles. Bazin's theory, fitting the medical evidence, was that Fleetwood had a seizure but remained supported by the reversing lever and that Talbot, fairly new to firing and with no clue whatever to what had happened, only realised something was wrong when he actually sighted Grantham station. Then he had to shout to Fleetwood, to realize the implication of no response, to move the inert body and to make the brake application. He was probably only about fifteen seconds too late.

Bulleid mourned his friend but got on with his work, which was becoming his main hobby. More technical problems kept coming up, such as an outbreak of coupling failures. "These are due to the Works making a sharp-cornered undercut, acting as a stress-raiser," came Bulleid's report, which Webster at once passed to Wintour. And when, the next week, in January 1907, Bulleid was transferred to be personal assistant to Wintour, it was smoothly handed back to him for action.

Thanks to the combined efforts of Ivatt, Marsh and Wintour the prestige of Doncaster Works was very high. Overseas visitors went away impressed. S.M. Vauclain, the Superintendent of the Baldwin Locomotive Works, wrote to Ivatt in March 1906:

"Dear Sir,

   I arrived in New York on the 6th inst. after a very pleasant but hurried trip through England and the Continent of Europe.

   Your Shops at Doncaster were the most interesting and instructive of all the Shops I have seen, and I feel that you are leading other railroads in equipment facilities.

   We expect to be benefited in our own Shops by my visit to yours, and I wish to express my sincere thanks to you for the courtesies extended by yourself and staff.

   With kind regards, and wishing continued prosperity to your Road and especially to your department.

Very truly yours,

S.M. Vauclain."

Continuing with his modernising policy, Ivatt now had sanction for mechanizing the Forge and Wintour gave Bulleid a free hand in buying and laying-out the necessary drop-hammers and forging machine. He collected some credit for a good job and some venom for reduced labour requirements, that terrible and perennial halter on progress. Wintour withheld the free hand when Bulleid collaborated with the loco accountant on improved paperwork and costing, turning the scheme down and remarking that he was not going to have the Works run by the Accountant. Unabashed, Bulleid presented a paper on the subject to the newly-formed Doncaster Engineering Society.

There was no shortage of interest in the Works in 1907. The pace was hotting up with an annual building programme of 45 new engines, including a famous newcomer, the 0-6-2 suburban tank. On the Carriage side H.N. Gresley was already making his mark, the new coaching stock being accepted as the East Coast Joint Stock standard.

Bulleid enjoyed all this but was irked by his status as "assistant to." Restrictions seemed big and pay small. He noted in the technical press advertisements for engineers abroad, often at salaries around £4 per week compared with his £2. He had taken his romance with Marjorie Ivatt to the stage of an unofficial engagement in April and knew he had a powerful ally in Mrs. Ivatt. He also knew that Marjorie would as soon live in France as in England, at least for a bit. And so, backed in his gruff way by Wintour but warned by Gresley that it was easier to leave a railway than to get back on it, Bulleid accepted a job as Test Engineer with French Westinghouse at Freinville near Paris to start in March 1908 with promotion in June, if satisfactory, to Assistant Works Manager and Chief Draughtsman. He started learning French with tremendous gusto. The salary was £240 a year, adequate for marriage.

3

Europe: Westinghouse & Board of Trade

The leading British Railway Works provided the best available mechanical engineering training at this time, and they "exported" many pupils and premium apprentices who took up less secure but better paid jobs both home and abroad. These engineers naturally in their turn looked to the same source to fill vacancies — an admirable method because you got a really honest opinion on the candidate from your former colleagues. That is how E.S. Hawkins came to offer the Westinghouse job.

Bulleid enjoyed his work for Westinghouse at Freinville from the word go, but he had two big and immediate surprises. One was the difficulty of the spoken word in French despite his real proficiency at reading it. The other was the extreme precision of the work, and the amount of in-line and final inspection, and the elaborate test procedures; this applied particularly to the manufacture of electrically-driven compressors and the valves and finer parts of the Westinghouse brake and signalling equipment. With courage and the will to have a go and with evening lessons in spoken French, Bulleid rapidly got on top of the job and by April felt settled, with his move up to Assistant Works Manager and Chief Draughtsman in June confirmed. So he came over to England and called on the Ivatts to seek their permission to be formally engaged to their youngest daughter. Mrs Ivatt later confided to this daughter that his opening words were "I am determined to marry Marjorie." H.A. Ivatt also liked determination, and agreed, though after a rather searching discussion on prospects. The engagement was announced on April 27 and the marriage took place on November 18. Asked if she minded settling in France, Mrs Bulleid replied that anything would be better than being the youngest of four unmarried daughters living at home.*

Back in France, Bulleid pressed on with a major Westinghouse job and one which introduced him to railway officers as customers — the first electro-pneumatic signalling installation, at Les Aubrais outside Orleans: a nice place for a trip. As Assistant Works Manager he was responsible for manufacture and quality and as Chief Draughtsman he had to supervise the design of the intricate interlocking in the signal box. It turned out to be a straightforward if arduous job, based on applying Westinghouse know-how to the local conditions.

*In 1963, for *Master Builders of Steam*, she asked me to substitute a bowdlerised version.

16

Sometimes customer pressure caused the Managing Director to tell the Drawing Office to get out a design for a job, and to tell the Works Manager separately at about the same time. Then the Customer would urge the job and the Works would have a stab at it independently of the Drawing Office. "Often the Works got there first, and their solution was usually simpler and more straightforward," remarked Bulleid, with a show of fair-mindedness but actually revealing slight impatience with the D.O. which always insisted on boring and perhaps non-essential recording and standardisation procedures.

F. Wintour, Doncaster Works Manager, had a brother in the Board of Trade responsible for British Exhibitions Overseas who signalled that he was in need of a Mechanical & Electrical Engineer for the 1910 Brussels and 1911 Turin Exhibitions. Naturally Wintour suggested Bulleid, as a suitable man on the spot; and on being accepted he resigned from Westinghouse, after a useful and stretching 1¾ years, and joined the Board of Trade. In December 1909 the Bulleids moved into a flat in Brussels and, Mrs Bulleid being *enceinte*, quickly engaged a maid-of-all-work, Fanny Vanderkelen, daughter of a policeman.

It was a busy and hectic time for Bulleid and it gave him many useful lessons in diplomacy when he was racing against time to get the British section finished, whereas local officials had all the time in the world to tell him what had to be altered to suit local regulations and safety standards, particularly with the electric wiring. Both sides finally reckoned they did everything right, but the entire British section was burned to the ground before the end of the Exhibition.

The exhibits themselves gave Bulleid much pleasure and instruction, notably a wool-processing line from Bradford. There were also peripheral technical delights, such as the four different makes of producer-gas engines driving the dynamos. One was a Campbell engine running on open hearth producer gas and economically using lower grade fuel.

Then came a reminder from the Institution of Mechanical Engineers that he had passed the age limit of 28 for Graduate membership. So it was panic stations to put in an application for transfer to Associate member, and the panic showed in some of the dates given being a year out, a point quite unnoticed by the referees. It was lodged on November 23 1910, signed by Ivatt, Marsh, Webster, Wintour and Hawkins, and resulted in one of the contemporary parchment-mounted certificates of Associate Membership, measuring 20 by 24in, dated March 30 1911 and issued to O.V.P. Bulleid.

In December 1910 the Bulleid family, now including daughter Chrystine, maid Fanny and a cheerful mongrel named Joujou (rather like an over-sized Yorkshire terrier done in grey) moved into a villa in the country at Cavoretta outside Turin. They found it even more delightful, despite the language difficulty, than Paris or Brussels. Bulleid attacked his work at the Turin Exhibition with the full advantage of previous experience, and he minimized the language problem by taking lessons, by making some use of French, by sometimes cashing in on his admitted ignorance, and generally by making a better shot at it than most English engineers. In July 1911 he obtained his Italian driving licence and his first car, a Ford, which opened out further the warm Italian countryside.

As well as the expected technical and diplomatic experiences, Bulleid had the good fortune to obtain a considerable education in artistic values at the Turin Exhibition from the consultant architects, Lutyens and Sir Charles Allom. Both appreciated the help given by the interested young engineer and with Allom especially, who was responsible for the decorations, a long-lasting *rapport* developed.

Though the Board of Trade job was known to be temporary, and the chance of making it permanent was jettisoned when Bulleid made a fair but unwise criticism of his boss, the problem "What to do now?" was no less real when the job came to an end in December 1911. The Bulleids thought they had been long enough away from England and their families thought the same. So obviously the first thing to do was to enquire from Gresley, who had just taken over from Ivatt, whether there was a suitable job on the GNR. After consultation with Ivatt, who had stayed on in a consulting capacity till the year end, Gresley shrewdly offered a choice of jobs; District Loco Superintendent at Grantham, or Personal Assistant to Gresley at Doncaster. Bulleid always claimed this was an open choice — but what loading! Grantham town was an unknown, the boss Webster did not like innovations and Running people seldom got the top jobs. Conversely, Doncaster was still full of Bulleid and Ivatt friends and was the nerve-centre of the GNR. The Gresley job would obviously be wide-ranging and it had only the one snag; that the P.A. was a mere 6 years younger than the boss. This factor probably decided Gresley to offer a choice, while feeling confident he would succeed in signing up not only the best P.A. available in the business but one who had already proved himself well able to stand up to, and occasionally outmanoeuvre, that formidable pair Wintour and Webster. They had both felt they had some claim to the boss job now occupied by 35-year-old H.N. Gresley.

So the Bulleids, renting a house in Victorian Crescent, were back to Doncaster and its chronic fogs early in 1912, accompanied by daughter and Fanny. And the dog? In quarantine. And had it been easier to leave the railway than to get back? No. Gresley was wrong.

4

Back to the GNR

In January 1912 H.N. Gresley was consolidating his position as Boss of Webster and Wintour, who must at first have proved a bit difficult to handle, particularly when it came to improvements and innovations. So it was doubly useful to have a personal assistant in that small office just beside the Drawing Office, and incidentally one who had seen life beyond the railway, who had the knack of always exposing the true facts of a case, who liked trying to do everything better, and who was there on call when needed, but when not needed was out and about, fact-finding and job-chasing on his own.

Conversely, Bulleid enjoyed Gresley's quick blossoming to "Boss size," his clarity of thought and aim, and his leadership qualities, of which he said later that "he was always ready to adopt a suggestion, if you could make a good case. If he agreed to try anything you knew it would almost certainly be a success. He had a wonderful memory, was extremely observant, and read drawings very quickly. Disloyalty was the one thing he did not tolerate. After all, the head of a department deserves loyal, unremitting service and obedience."

Bulleid also rather liked Gresley's touch of insolence towards his General Manager and Directors, which was in the Stirling/Webb tradition and the very opposite of H.A. Ivatt's tactics. On one occasion a letter of complaint came in from the GM and in drafting a reply Bulleid put in explanations and regrets that the GM had to complain. Gresley, who had decided that the complaint was trivial, sent for him and said: "You cannot send such a reply. Wait while I do it." The GM had unwisely added a final, subsidiary paragraph to his letter, and Gresley completely ignored the main complaint but dictated a strong reply objecting to the final paragraph. As he finished dictating he looked at Bulleid and said: "That is how to deal with such letters." Nothing further on the subject came from the GM, which doubled Bulleid's appreciation of the incident.

There were plenty of interesting technical jobs in Doncaster and plenty away, for the twin reasons that the Running Sheds came under the command of Gresley and that he had good contacts on the other railways. One such was Henry Fowler on the Midland at Derby, then a recognised expert on gas lighting, from whom Bulleid collected all the necessary data for modernising the lighting in Kings Cross Shed. Another was J.A.F.

Aspinall, then GM of the Lancashire and Yorkshire at Manchester, where he had just installed the first Central Train Control system. In a lengthy collaboration with the GNR Traffic department, inspired by Gresley, Bulleid visited this and worked out details of the equipment required for the GNR scheme, using the same supplier, Western Electric. Then he and Attwood of Traffic classified all goods trains by type and speed, and worked out the appropriate engine loadings over the various routes. This resulted in a new Loading Circular for goods trains, saving 3 million train-miles a year. It involved increased engine-loadings and therefore reduced working margins at the Sheds, and some of the new loadings were hotly contested. Bulleid accordingly moved in for practical trials, and found that in some cases the Sheds were right, the reason being a number of out-of-date gradient profiles.

They also carried out corresponding braking trials, and nearly suffered a nasty accident when they saw a rake of wagons with a brake-van whose wheels had picked up disappearing in a typical Yorkshire mist down the 1 in 50 incline towards the Midland main line at Shipley. Fortunately the guard just managed to stop before reaching the catch points. This incidentally exposed the fault of Gresley's eight-wheel brake van, where inability to balance the brakes perfectly caused each lightly-loaded pair of wheels to pick up in turn, thus giving less effective braking than a conventional four-wheel van.

Bulleid found interest and relish in all these jobs, but most of all in the new design work taking shape in the Drawing office, so handy from his own adjacent office. From his own past experience in the Doncaster Drawing Office, and from his Westinghouse experience, his was often a useful opinion on a drawing problem; and his closeness to Gresley made him a useful contact between the Drawing Office and the Great White Chief.

Gresley's first design, the two cylinder Class K1 2-6-0, emerged from the Works in 1912, but Gresley's thinking was to advance to larger boilers for these mixed traffic engines and also for goods engines. Bulleid enthusiastically agreed; the effect of the advance to large boilers on the Atlantics had deeply impressed him and he had enough footplate and Shed experience to understand the frustrations of being short of steam. Besides, he saw no reason to deny mixed traffic, nor goods for that matter, the boilers now deemed essential for passenger traffic. He had also seen plenty of decent sized boilers in France. So 5ft 6in diameter boilers were designed for the Class K2 2-6-0s and the new 2-8-0s and considerable publicity, of a style typical of both Gresley and Bulleid, heralded the important event of these superior, bigger-boilered locomotives. One such publicity platform was the supplement published by *The Engineer* on November 28 1913 marking the 60th anniversary of Doncaster Works.

Both these new Atlantic-size boilers were round-topped over the firebox, and during the hydraulic test to twice working pressure the boiler shop foreman noticed a slight bulging at each side between the horizontal and vertical firebox stays. Bulleid quickly rigged up a framework from which any such movement could be measured and as a result transverse stays were fitted — a rather crude device which led him to prefer the Belpaire arrangement.

The Class K2 2-6-0s with their 5ft 8in wheels were very speedy and successful engines, but of course they had 20in by 26in cylinders compared with the 19in by 24in and 6ft 8in wheels of the Atlantics; passenger-oriented drivers were delighted by their easy starting and acceleration, but complained that they were apt to run short of steam and must therefore be under-boilered or over-cylindered. They were right back to H.A. Ivatt's picturesque description of the impossible; he said in 1900 that everyone wanted "to start with an engine of the dray-horse type, capable of exerting great tractive force and quickly getting the speed up to about 50 miles an hour, then to take that engine off and put on another of the quick trotter or high-flyer type." Bulleid got involved in the perennial and pointless argument and remarked that in a sense *all* engines with narrow fireboxes were under-boilered. Interestingly, it soon became clear that the large-boilered 2-6-0s were using less coal than the K1s.

The modern touches in this design work, such as standardising on outside Walschaerts valve gear and the use of large diameter piston valves, made the job doubly satisfying to Bulleid, who kept right up to date in his technical reading. He was also very happy on the domestic front, old friends of his and the Ivatts having warmly welcomed the returned foreigners. He took his photographic hobby quite seriously, collecting some know-how from J.R. Bazin and building a dark room in the cellar with an adjustable safe-light included in the partition, but turning his camera mainly on wife and kids and dog. There was also a good wooden garage at 10 Victorian Crescent, ideal for casual tinkering with the aging single-cylinder Cadillac, to keep it reliable for occasional spins on the dusty and bumpy but empty roads.

The first serious shadow fell across these happy domestic scenes when the old soldier reservists were called up in the late spring of 1914. Many were from the GNR Works and Bulleid was given the job of visiting their dependents. He found some heartbreak from separation and from desperate lack of money, but fortunately the GNR had decided to pay an allowance to such called-up employees pending action by the Government. Then war was declared and he realised only too clearly that his own family would miss him and his GNR salary, when he had to go.

5

World War One

Although he was very patriotic, it was as a stoic and not as an enthusiast that Bulleid volunteered for War Service in the early autumn of 1914. Naturally dramatists use the theme of young men going to war as playboys and becoming (if not returning) disillusioned, but in fact very few took any illusions with them. The essentially practical Bulleid put in some revolver practice in the attic before reporting to Aldershot, carefully placing a one-inch plank behind the target. He flattered himself, however, missing both target and plank on a few occasions. The bullets landed in the attic next door, so there was more than just the noise to explain.

Young Lieutenant Bulleid arrived in France in January 1915 and in February was appointed Railway Transport Officer in the area bounded by St Omer-Cassel-Hazebrouck-St Venant-Berguette, which were all railway junctions. His sympathetic and knowledgeable interest in railway operating and his excellent colloquial French gave him an immediate *rapport* with the local railway people at all levels; they were civilians with much to endure and if badly handled they could take refuge in impenetrable intricacies of red tape. Some of them figured, alongside churches, allies, colleagues and engines in the photos Lieutenant Bulleid so openly took with his 2¼in square folding Kodak in the early months of 1915 before greater pressures and greater discretion intervened.

In September 1915 he was promoted to captain and pressure of work correspondingly increased. He went on coaxing from the French railway people such good service that his colonel was goaded to enquire, quite testily, how he managed to do it, bribery being impracticable. But 1916 became a year of many frustrations, adding gravely to the work-load and the discomforts of working and often living in a cold railway van; and in September he was invalided back to England severely run down and suffering from carbuncles. After four weeks in a Military Hospital and four weeks convalescing back home in Doncaster, he returned to France on November 30 and the next day was promoted to Major, DADRT — Deputy Assistant Director of Railway Traffic. So started another gruelling 15 months, including the Ypres operation, relieved however by two factors which brought him lasting satisfaction. First, an exceptionally good billeting with the ageing, aristocratic Mlle. Bieswal in her fine house at Hazebrouck, sixteen miles West of Ypres. Second, characteristically fired by the best local example, conversion from High Anglican to the Catholic faith.

In May 1918 Major Bulleid became DADRT to the Fourth Army Railhead, that network of track laid specially to support the Front Line. There were other problems besides rail work; when a consignment of hand grenades was found to be exploding prematurely, killing the soldiers throwing them, he helped to avert further casualties by diagnosing a safety-catch fault. Around the railway, with steam sometimes making a target, dangerous incidents were always close; but these were less of a strain than seeing the names of friends in the casualty lists. For Bulleid this sort of bad news started all too early in the war when his cousin Ve was killed by a sniper.

However hard and hazardous the task, one likes to be in at the end; and there were real signs of an end in sight in August 1918. But others were also thinking about the peace, not to mention their commercial interests; and in particular Oliver Bury, General Manager of the GNR, wanted an up-and-coming engineer to take over as CME of the São Paulo Railway of Brazil in which he had an interest. He therefore asked his friend Sir Sam Fay, formerly General Manager of the Great Central Railway and then Director General of Movements and Railways, to get Major Bulleid back to England as soon as possible. Fay found a suitable job and lobbied and then wrote to the Director General of Tranportation at GHQ France on August 3rd:

"Dear Crookshank,
    With reference to our conversation upon the subject of Major Bulleid. I shall be very glad if you will release this officer as soon as possible for duty as Works Manager at Richborough, where he is badly wanted.
                                        Yours sincerely,
                                                Sam Fay."

On August 5th Crookshank duly wrote to his Director of Railway Traffic, Brigadier-General Murray:

"Dear Murray,
    I fear we shall have to let him go, so will you please arrange.
                                        Yours,
                                                S. D'A Crookshank."

This brought a long and anguished reply from Murray, pointing out the rarity of Officers with all Bulleid's assets, doubting the importance of the Job in England, expressing disquiet at the effect on the critical railhead duties, and concluding, with a hint of resignation:

"In any case Major Bulleid cannot be relieved until after the 18th, when Lt-Col Ditmas will be back from the GHQ (South) Area.
                                                (sgd) V. Murray."

Bulleid reported as Works Manager of the Workshops, Mechanical & Shipyard Formation, Inland Waterways & Docks, Royal Engineers, Richborough, Kent, on August 28 1918, with the rank of Major, RE. He sub-let his Doncaster house furnished and rented a furnished house at 12 St. Mildred's Road, Ramsgate. You could see the Monitor beyond the harbour from the back windows, and each morning you could see and hear the Works Manager setting off to the Works in the side-car of their Douglas motor-cycle. It made a noise and smell, said Mrs Bulleid, reminiscent of H.G. Ivatt's early motor-bike known to his sisters as the stink-wheel.

On November 8, neatly before the Armistice, the War Office circularised all Officers of the RE, seeking their demobilisation wishes. Bulleid, distracted by the Armistice and frightfully busy learning Portuguese, replied on November 28 saying that "I am going to the São Paulo Ry Co as Locomotive Engineer" and "I wish to continue to serve with the Directorate until such time that the São Paulo Ry Co ask for my release."

Christmas 1918 was a cheery time for the family though toys were scarce. But in January 1919 the São Paulo job fell through and so Bulleid was suddenly exerting every effort to get away from Richborough and back to Doncaster, and exchanging notes with his friend Edward Thompson on how best to urge the process. Success! His release was agreed for late February, and the only slight snag was having to find furnished rooms in Doncaster on account of the unexpectedly early return.

But then an unexpected and graver snag arose; Mrs Bulleid, normally of robust health, succumbed to the prevailing epidemic of virulent influenza. She got worse, and her mother came over from Haywards Heath to help. Then she got worse still and anxieties grew, and Mrs Ivatt and Fanny shared the round-the-clock nursing, and the children were temporarily boarded out at their nearby Convent School. Gloomy news of influenza deaths came in, including a close friend of Mrs Bulleid. Then the crisis mercifully passed, and the moment she was able to travel they were off to Doncaster once again.

A chapter of many peoples' lives ended with the war, and like others Bulleid wanted his AB439 (Officers' service record book) duly completed by his Service bosses. His letter to Brigadier-General Murray contained three Bulleidisms:

"8 March 1919

Dear General,

I am sending you my AB439 and shall be very pleased if you will make some entry regarding my service under you, eulogistic I hope, on page 14. Now that I am demobilised I want this book to be completed so that I may have some small record of my service.

I shall always be very sorry your efforts to prevent me being recalled home were not successful. The Home Establishment may have points, but in a place like Richborough, officered and manned to an overwhelming extent by conscripts, they were too difficult for me to find."

That certainly did it. Major General Crookshank's entry in the AB439 read:

> "Maj. Bulleid has rendered exceptionally good services under the Director Genl. of Transportation, BEF. During the Passchendale operations of the Fifth Army in 1917 especially his sound railway knowledge and experience, good judgment and temper, and thorough application and efficiency were of the greatest value to the Army and to me. I hold a high opinion of Major Bulleid as a capable and keen officer."

Brigadier-General Murray endorsed these remarks and added further eulogies.

These, and the medals, are the small record of the Bulleid service in World War One. And of course the gratuity, considerably reduced on account of the posting to Richborough.

6

Post-war GNR

Domestically, the return to Doncaster in March 1919 was rather dismal —
into furnished rooms in Thorne Road because the Bulleid's house in
Victorian Crescent was sub-let till July. This was in powerful contrast to
Bulleid's return to the GNR, where he received an exhilarating welcome from
everyone, Gresley downwards. Those who had not been to war had been
trebly harassed by pressure of work, rationing and a guilt complex which
stimulated their welcome to the returning warriors.

Gresley's satisfaction at the return of Bulleid can be easily understood:
not only would the help be forthcoming again, and attention be given to all
those peripheral jobs, but the young assistant had acquired extra wisdom
and stature from his war experiences, luckily without arrogance. There were
masses of jobs to be done and Bulleid, thankful to be back, set about them
with a will and even more sure than before of Gresley's support. He could
be found at Manchester examining the L&Y Central Train Control, or at
Gorton studying J.G. Robinson's pulverised fuel experiments: or at Swindon
discussing with Burrows a new accelerometer or just borrowing the GWR
dynamometer car, after which he would become engrossed in trials. He
coaxed cooperation persuasively from those he visited and from his own
colleagues. The more junior the colleague, or the younger the artisan, the
more polite and considerate he would be. And, of course, vice versa; to
equals (and his family) he paid the compliment of assuming they required
no wheedling nor flannel, nor for that matter automatic permissions. So
when, for example, Gresley told him to find the cause of excessive wear and
heating in side-rod bushes Bulleid acquired a French instrument with which
the angular setting of the crank pins could be read off very accurately and
discovered that the quartering machine in the Works was not accurate. As
he was leaving the shop with his tackle the Works Manager, Wintour, came
in and expressed great indignation that his permission had not been asked.
Bulleid, who rightly thought he was merely helping and wishfully thought
Gresley would have told Wintour, expressed equal indignation that his help
was not properly appreciated. A second act was played out in Gresley's office,
rather obviously leading to the machine being put right. A third act was
Bulleid's article on permissible quartering errors, leading to a $7.50 cheque
from the *American Machinist*.

The most important and probably most valued jobs done by Bulleid for

Gresley were on the new engine, the three-cylinder Class K3 2-6-0 No. 1000. This carried the simplified two-to-one gear for driving the inside valve and Bulleid gave the Drawing Office some of the design fixes, notably a maximum deflection of $\frac{1}{16}$ in at the centre pivot. Then came the balancing problem, more important with this faster mixed-traffic engine than with Gresley's previous three-cylinder job, the 1918 2-8-0 No. 461. Like all senior executives who undertake design, Gresley had to delegate most of the time-consuming and complicated jobs and calculations to the Drawing office and was displeased if they got stuck, particularly on a subject which he himself found complex and tedious. This happened in the case of the balancing and Gresley, not wanting to do the necessary deep digging and anyway too busy, called in Bulleid and said rather brusquely: "Get the balancing worked out, the Drawing Office don't know how to do it properly." Nor did Bulleid know how to do it, but he acquired and studied the recently-published paper on balancing by Professor Dalby and saw to it that it was correctly applied by the Drawing Office. Like all good chiefs, Gresley took precautions on matters in which he was not personally confident, and on balancing he duly sought the opinion of Professor Dalby, who looked over the calculations and expressed whole-hearted agreement. He couldn't have done them better himself. "H.N.G. never thought of asking me where I got my information," chuckled Bulleid.

Far less important but far more difficult was the problem posed by a porter at Bawtry, who sent in a suggestion that there should be a series of rollers in the main line and the expresses running over these rollers would operate dynamos to light the stations and operate cranes. To spare himself and perhaps to baffle his brilliant assistant Gresley handed Bulleid the suggestion with instructions to explain to the porter the impractibility of his idea. Bulleid had to admit utter failure: "I left him convinced that, had there been more intelligent and forthcoming people at headquarters, his great idea would have been introduced."

Despite rumours about the nationalisation or amalgamation of the railways those were sunny days for the GNR at Doncaster in 1920. Post-war hopes ran high, traffic was good and improving and the technical field was full of stimulating challenge. Occasionally my father took me to the Works via the station where I would admire a blue Great Eastern engine in the south bay platform more than he did, and he would point out some less obvious interest, such as the red rose of Yorkshire and the white rose of Lancashire in the crest of a black L&Y Atlantic. Then to an 0-6-0 saddle tank doing the yard shunt, where I would stay for an hour while he did some work. Once he forgot all about his 7-year-old son and dashed off to Leeds on some urgent job, after which his only comment was that I was quite old enough to find my own way home.

Golfing enthusiasm swept into the Plant about this time, affecting (in order of competence) Groom, Thompson, Peppercorn and Bulleid. They were all friendly players but utterly different. Groom was icy calm and reckoned to do every hole in what was then called bogey. Thompson was an efficient 10-ish handicap and always immaculately attired. Peppercorn played with immense vigour and Bulleid kept seeking refinements of technique, both playing to around 18 handicaps with moments of irritating brilliance as when they walked away with a flag competition at Rossington.

Doncaster always seemed perfectly all right to me, but to the Thompsons particularly York offered advantages. It was a city, was not a "railway town," was not so industrialised, had many cultural connections and facilities, and of course was the home town of Mrs Thompson, née Raven, whose father was CME of the most powerful of the East Coast lines, the North Eastern Railway. So no one was flabbergasted when Edward Thompson was asked for, to take charge of the NER carriage works at York. Conversely, Bulleid always claimed he was rather astonished when Gresley promptly appointed him to succeed Thompson as Assistant Carriage and Wagon Superintendent with a satisfactory advance of salary to £850. Thompson was a clear thinker and a good organiser, and he took pleasure in giving his friend the best possible introduction to the "Carriage side," probably sensing his intention to liven things up. Not that Bulleid was a stranger among carriages; there were foremen and men remembered from apprentice days seventeen years before and from numerous visits on sundry jobs thereafter.

Gresley was keen on the economies and the reduced train resistance offered by mounting two carriage ends on a common bogie, and by 1920 the GNR had about 130 articulated sets, mostly of two coaches but some with three and four coaches and one quintuple set of Stirling-Howlden carriages, mounted on six bogies in 1915. Among Bulleid's first jobs was the building of a new quintuple set for the Leeds express service, comprising two composites, two diners and a kitchen car in the middle. Suggested and supported by Gresley and enthusiastically carried out by Bulleid, this was the world's first all-electric kitchen car and its technical, practical and operational success combined to make a good launching pad for electrics. At that time adequate power for cooking was a problem despite the largest practicable dynamos and batteries, and power supplies were required at various stations for battery charging and for pre-cooking. This 1921 novelty flummoxed some City Electrical Undertakings and my father recorded one such tussle:

"When the all-electric kitchen car was sent to Leeds on trial the City Electrical Engineer refused to let it take current at the station until he had inspected and approved the electrical installation. So I had to tell him that this was outside his powers; we, the Railway, were the responsible authority and if he persisted in his refusal Higher Authority would be invoked and he would be overruled. I also told him that the car would have to take power in London, Doncaster, York, Bradford and in due course Edinburgh and beyond and that consequently it was out of the question for all these City Electrical Engineers to be allowed to lay down conditions. All that was wanted was to see that the ground equipment was to the local requirements and a supply of current given. He saw the point. After which I took him over the kitchen, which he found most interesting."

With the superb quality of the post-war GNR main line there was positively no excuse for bad riding and Bulleid spent much effort on what became and remained a great interest, the riding of bogies, carrying out experiments and using advice from many sources. These technical advances alongside his first efforts at standardised carriage and wagon details at the Clearing House, whose C&W Superintendents Committee he joined in 1920, were two of Bulleid's main contributions to the Carriage side: the third was, rather surprisingly, interior design.

In 1920 the rather florid Edwardian style of interior decor suddenly struck Bulleid as out-dated and he asked himself how it would look in 1940, which would still be well within its expected life. "Fussy and archaic" was the answer and he opted for the simple design with plain mouldings and panelling, but with the finest possible paintwork and veneers. Though their "starkness" was deplored at the time they looked exactly right in the contemporary Art Deco scene of the twenties and early thirties.

Bulleid did not always get away with the functionally correct. He mocked-up a tapered bed as a space-saver in the 1922 East Coast Joint Stock sleepers, but the Carriage Works verdict was sufficiently off-putting; it was chalked neatly on the mock-up — "THE COFFIN." Mrs Bulleid, on one of her rare visits to the shops, had to test the new beds for comfort, and voted them adequate. Then they rashly asked her if there was anything else of particular interest and she said yes, there was one thing she had always wanted; could she please pull the communication cord? A.H. Peppercorn, genial and courteous as ever, was among those present. "Oh, yes, of course," they all said, and watched with indulgent smiles as she grasped the chain and gave it a firm pull . . . in vain. Incredulous helping hands moved in to do it, also in vain. It wouldn't budge an inch. Even Peppercorn couldn't shift it. Laughter mingled with embarrassment and everyone was suddenly too busy with the problem to find an alternative, pullable cord. Mrs Bulleid later remarked that she never really got over her disappointment.

Gresley's competence as Chief, his interest in the Carriage side and his growing *rapport* with Bulleid, all subscribed to an enjoyable and successful posting. Gresley always came at once when Bulleid phoned to say a new carriage was ready for him to inspect. Nor did they talk exclusively about carriages, Gresley typically confiding the bit of luck which came with a complaint by a director about late-running in November 1921; the engine concerned was the Vulcan compound Atlantic no. 1300 and Gresley was able to point out that it had never been as satisfactory as the standard simple Atlantics, that he was preparing the design and cost of converting it to a simple, and that the decision to buy it had been made (please note) not by Mr Ivatt the Locomotive Superintendent but by the General Manager.

Rumours about Amalgamation filled the year 1921 and when that was settled rumours about who would get the top jobs filled the year 1922. Top people were understandably cagey: not only were there many arguments, but some jobs were interdependent and decisions had to be made seriatim. And of course the formal appointments could only be made *after* the Amalgamation. The choice of H.N. Gresley as CME of the Eastern Group was delayed because the job was first offered by seniority to J.G. Robinson of the Great Central, but he preferred to retire. Then Gresley had to do quite a bit of thinking and discussion with his superiors before deciding about the CME's supporting staff, and it was only in the autumn of 1922 that he confided to Bulleid, during one of those noisy rides home on the Avenue Road tram, that he had been appointed the overall CME. At Bulleid's enthusiastic reaction he added "What, would you like to come?"

That was a quicker and a better offer than was the lot of many, and as winter set in and there were still many decisions to make and therefore much job uncertainty, the GNR issued a circular to senior staff. O.V.P. Bulleid was sent a copy for his private information on November 17th:

PRIVATE & CONFIDENTIAL
EASTERN GROUP OF RAILWAYS: ORGANISATION
It is anticipated that the Scheme for the amalgamation of the Companies forming the Eastern Group will come into operation on the 1st January, 1923. The adoption of the Scheme will necessarily involve an extensive re-organisation of staff, particularly the Headquarters staff of the various constituent companies, but it is not possible, nor is it the intention of the Board, to introduce any general re-organisation as from January 1st 1923. Pending the preparation and introduction of a thoroughly considered scheme of re-organisation all officers are asked to co-operate in carrying on their duties until further notice, and to use their best endeavours to secure that the transfer of responsibility from their respective constituent companies to the new amalgamated company shall be carried through smoothly, and without friction or interruption of any kind.

In order to allay any uneasiness which may exist in the minds of any officers as to the effect which compliance with this request may have upon them and their rights under the Railways Act, I am authorised to say that the new Board intend at their first meeting after the amalgamation comes into operation to pass a Resolution to provide that the rights of any officer under the Railways Act or under contract shall not be prejudiced during the three years following the date of the amalgamation by reason of his continuing service in any capacity under the Amalgated Company.

In the context of this cautious circular Bulleid was very pleased to be fixed up with a job he knew he wanted, and he was even more pleased when it was formally confirmed in March 1923 with a salary increase from £950 to £1,200. He started work in London in April, bought a house overlooking Hadley Common in May, moved South in July and at once got into his drill of the daily one-mile walk to and from New Barnet station for the LNER train link with his Kings Cross office.

7

LNER — The Best Years with Gresley

When Gresley and Bulleid moved into CME's offices along platform 10 at Kings Cross in April 1923 they controlled ten Works employing over 100,000 and the maintenance and replacement of over 7,000 engines, 20,000 carriages and 300,000 wagons. For this large task Gresley wisely decided to use existing local facilities and only direct and check from Kings Cross where he therefore set up a small drawing office for scheme and checking work; he himself approved most loco drawings and Bulleid approved the remainder and all carriage and wagon drawings.

The smoothness of any merger depends on co-operation, often much aided by the retirement of older seniors who would have found it impossible not to rebel. The LNER fared well on the CME side:

Railway	CME	Location	Action	Resulting District Mechanical Engineer
NER	Raven	York	retired	A.C. Stamer
GCR	Robinson	Gorton	retired	R.A. Thom
GER	Hill	Stratford	retired	C.W.L. Glaze
NBR	Chalmers	Cowlairs	stayed	W. Chalmers
GNofS	Heywood	Inverurie	stayed	T.E. Heywood

The first three District Mechanical Engineers were unhesitating supporters of the new set-up, at least as far as one could be under the annoyance of change and diminished promotion prospects. Chalmers retired in 1925. Only at small-scale Inverurie (the GNofS had 122 engines) was there any real discord, about which my father wrote: "I never got beyond Inverness, going up Speyside which all came under Inverurie, managed by Heywood in the old Great North of Scotland days. He had the track as well and the running. He was Provost, etc, etc, etc so it was understandable he did not like the Amalgamation. Even less did he like Gresley, who disliked him equally. I tried hard to keep the peace. Heywood was a really good mechanical engineer."

Gresley was meticulous with paperwork and all the important mail was placed on his desk each morning supported by the relevant files. When he was away or the mail was exceptionally heavy it was Bulleid who decided what could go direct to himself or to Rogerson (accounts) or Richards (electrical). Preparing the mail for Gresley took a bit of time and Bulleid sometimes grumbled if he arrived early. "The chief should not come barging in until 9.30 or so when things are ready for him," he would remark, advice he himself ignored entirely after 1937. He and Gresley averaged about four of the five-and-a-half working days per week in London, the Saturday morning then being traditionally the time when you cleared your desk and got outstanding stuff into the mail, all ready for its recipient to tackle first thing on Monday.

Right from the start of the LNER Bulleid was much more a free agent than Gresley, who had to attend many meetings of directors and senior officers and who was also in demand outside the LNER on account of his increased status. So it was Bulleid who got around the vast new arena more often, who delighted to know all that was going on, who succeeded in gaining the confidence of the new District Mechanical Engineers, and who already had the knack of keeping Gresley well and succinctly informed.

With Gresley so busy, and wisely deciding not to rush into new locomotive design till he was better acquainted with the latest local designs, and with Bulleid still C&W-oriented from his last job, it is no surprise that the LNER Carriage side was quickest off the mark. Other cards in Bulleid's excellent hand were his already-accepted East Coast Joint Stock, his co-operation with other C&W Superintendents since 1920 on the Clearing House Committee, and the invaluable N. Newsome. The result was that carriage manufacture to the old local designs finished by early 1924 when the new standard LNER (really GNR) designs were fixed, including GNR standard bogies and running gear and teak bodies on steel underframes:

Type	Coupling	Length of body	Bogie centres	Width
Corridor	Buckeye	61ft 6in	43ft	8ft 9in
Non-corridor	Screw	51ft 1½in	35ft	8ft 9in

Bogie centres were fixed at 43ft for general articulated stock. The three standard bogie types were single bolster for brake vans, light compound bolster for carriages up to 35 tons, and heavy compound bolster for heavier and articulated carriages. Bulleid carried out many experiments with different swing link lengths and angles, but with little effect on riding, and he began to dislike the swing-link arrangement.

For wagons the Clearing House standards were adopted; and by 1925 it was fair to say that the LNER had not only digested its new standards but had built successfully to them in all the Carriage Works, including quadruple and quintuple suburban sets and new trains for the 'Flying Scotsman' and the 'Hook Continental' that embodied articulated restaurant car sets. They also found time to refurbish the LNER royal train, ex Gresley's 1908 production for King Edward VII. It was all very interesting but massive work for Bulleid and Newsome, not to mention the Works and Drawing Offices, and it contained innumerable detail improvements. Their latest all-electric cooking had the increased benefit of two 7¼ kW generators with

180 volt battery. On the new articulated Kings Cross suburban sets they made provision for power bogies because in October 1923 a scheme was put to the LNER Board by the Chief General Manager, Wedgwood, supported by Gresley and Richards, to electrify the suburban services as far as Welwyn Garden City and Hertford: it had to be taken into account until it was turned down on 30 September 1925.

Bulleid was full of indignation at the parlous state of the Great Eastern carriage stock at the Amalgamation and Gresley had to explain to him the rather obvious facts that when a Company is barely paying its way and is then told it is to be taken over, it lacks both the cash and the will to leave its house in perfect order. In fact the North British had stopped all locomotive building in 1921, doubtless thinking the Sassenach Amalgamators could sort out the resulting loco shortage. So most of the LNER renewals in its early years were devoted to making up back-logs. Bulleid and Newsome were fooled again by Liverpool Street, underestimating the over-crowding which caused the frames of their suburban quintuple sets to sag so that the doors would not open. A very urgent stiffening operation had to be carried out.

The year 1925 was very significant on the locomotive side. In it came the 2-8-8-2 Garratt, in which Bulleid took a rather detached interest, and the Class P1 2-8-2, in which he participated with enthusiasm and delight, keen on the wheel arrangement with its excellent adhesion and on the application of the Pacific boiler to freight work, and knowing that with its three 20in by 26in cylinders *and* a booster on the trailing truck it would silence any Traffic Department complaints about shortage of power — which it duly did.

More significant, however, were the exchange trials between a Pacific and a GWR "Castle". These engines had stood close together at the Wembley Exhibition in 1924 and positively invited comparison, the decidedly smaller *Caerphilly Castle* boasting a higher tractive effort. LNER engineers and enthusiasts derided the smaller engine and said the boiler could not support that tractive effort, while GWR supporters derided the oversized hulk of the Pacific *Flying Scotsman*. But if the "Castle" really could do all that was claimed Gresley certainly wanted to know how it was done and Bulleid always thought he had either suggested or engineered the exchange trials, as I reported in *Master Builders of Steam*. But in March 1966 E.D. Trask reported to Edward Marsden and Cecil J. Allen that he had been sent for in May 1925 by W.G. Maclure, the Southern Area Running Superintendent, and told details of the exchange as arranged by Alexander Wilson (LNER Southern Area Divisional Manager) and Sir Felix Pole (GWR General Manager); Maclure added that Gresley had known nothing about it till he read it in his newspaper. The full story is given in Cecil J. Allen's book *The London & North Eastern Railway*; but I must say my father did not believe this, strongly doubting that Pole would have got so involved with Wilson while his correct opposite number was Wedgwood, and further doubting that Wilson would have got so involved without a courtesy reference to

Gresley. He also thought it very odd that Gresley first heard of it from the press announcement in a newspaper because the LNER Press Office under Teasdale would normally confer with all interested departements. Also he thought Gresley would have grumbled to him about it, which he did not. Finally, most of the arrangements had been made before the press release appeared, and the mind boggles at trying to believe they were kept secret; they were not even *meant* to be confidential.

The LNER entered with three known disadvantages: their men had a longer and harder route to learn in the week allowed; their engine would not like Welsh coal; and they had inside big-end worries. These did not seriously affect the result, however, the GWR winning hands down. The latter used a lot less coal, maintained higher average speeds, and made less noise and fuss about doing it. All but one of Gresley's staff were horrified and put out various explanations, which I vividly recall because on the strength of them I got involved in a typical 12-year-old's school argument and was reduced to mincemeat by my GWR opponent.

Gresley (who, interestingly, never lost face at the result and gained stature by his adoption of the GWR 'secret') got involved in no so such arguments. He relished the thought that if he could locate the secret of the "Castle" and apply it to his engine, then the resulting Pacific would walk away from any future "Castle". So he sent for his one assistant who had not been astonished, the redoubtable B. Spencer, and at once agreed to apply his earlier, shelved proposal for long-travel valves. The result was a conspicuous success: coal consumption on 500 ton trains between Kings Cross and Doncaster was reduced from 50lb to 38lb per mile.

"How absurdly simple," one is tempted to say, and then to ask "Why wasn't it done years before?" After all Churchward positively advised it at an Institution of Mechanical Engineers meeting in March 1906. It is worth noting the answers: Churchward did not say it again; those who listened forgot; Hughes tried it on the L&Y 4-4-0s in 1908 but failed to notice the dramatic improvement because a second change, superheating, was made at the same time. Gresley himself used 5⅜in travel on his 1912 and 1913 2-6-0 and 2-8-0 and agreed with the 6¾in travel planned with Churchward at the ARLE for the proposed 1918 standard locomotives. But then in 1920 the Class K3 2-6-0 broke its inside steam chest cover by the inside valve over-running and this led to the Pacifics being designed with only 1¼in lap and valve travel only 4 9/16in, which incidentally aided the geometry of the conjugate gear. The merits of long lap, long travel valves were conveniently forgotten. Never was there a sharper reminder than by *Caerphilly Castle* in 1925. I estimate there was a two-to-one chance, appropriately enough, that Bulleid would have spotted the wrong decision on the Pacifics if he had not been away on the Carriage side when they were designed in 1921, because he was always deeply suspicious of seeming to solve a problem by brushing it away, and he would have nosed out the increasing support for longer travel. After all, Maunsell was already convinced. Probably Gresley only turned down Spencer's suggestion in 1924 because he had no money to spare for improvements while there was still a shortage of engines, and after all the Pacifics were certainly doing their job.

The 1925 Congress of the International Railway Congress Association was held in London, so delegates could visit the railway Centenary celebrations and incidentally see the latest LNER engines on parade with their forebears. During the Congress Bulleid complained about inaccurate translations from the French and so Sir Henry Fowler promptly signed him on as a translator.

Before 1925 was over Bulleid had shifted perceptibly closer to the locomotive side, Gresley inviting him to join the still comparatively exclusive Association of Railway Locomotive Engineers and also sending him on a high-level trip to France to discuss compounding with the leading French Railway engineers. The French were all keen, excepting Lacoin of the Paris-Orleans, and they so convinced Sir Henry Fowler that he started designing a compound 4-6-2 for the LMS. Gresley and Bulleid remained, like H.A. Ivatt, unconvinced. Gresley did feel, however, that it was time to go for higher boiler pressures than 180psi and Bulleid strongly supported this, preferring the smaller cylinders it permitted by simply strengthening the boiler. Moreover their current highest pressure of 180psi had to be compared with the 225psi of the "Castle" and the 220psi of Maunsell's 1926 *Lord Nelson*. Then in 1927 Sir Henry Fowler went to 250psi for the *Royal Scot*. Gresley and Bulleid together visited this beefy new 4-6-0 while it was on private view at Euston and both felt it should have been a Pacific. They also felt very glad when, a month or two later, they got good results from their own first trials with 220psi and increased superheater heralding the Class A3 Pacifics.

After the 60mph derailment on the Southern Railway in August 1927, involving one of Maunsell's "River" class 2-6-4 tanks near Sevenoaks, the Ministry of Transport asked Gresley to report on the suitability of the engines for high-speed passenger working. Trials were arranged between Woking and Walton, and observers included Bulleid and Sir John Aspinall; but they came to a sudden stop, Bulleid reported, "by Gresley refusing to travel on the footplate over so defective a stretch of line. Colonel Pringle poked his walking-stick through a sleeper. The trials were transferred to the S-curves on the GNR at Tempsford, laid without transitions, and over this road the engines rode well and HNG reported in favour of them." But Gresley's wording concluded ". . . and on a road well laid and well maintained are suitable for working express passenger trains." This brought considerable dismay to the Southern General Manager and to its Civil Engineer, G. Ellson who, however, persisted with his own opinion that the main culprit was the pony truck. The engines were rebuilt as mixed traffic 2-6-0s.

Gresley was President of the ARLE in 1927 and among interesting points made in discussions that year were Stamer's assurance that the boosters were satisfactory and Gresley's comment that their fitting was not justified unless they could be manufactured in England at lower cost. Beames also led a discussion on Caprotti valve gear as fitted to "Claughtons", saying he was achieving about the savings claimed by the Italians on a group of 50 engines, namely 7% saving in coal.

Of course you have to see for yourself as well as discussing, and on October 26 1927 Bulleid rode from Victoria to Dover and back on No. E850 *Lord Nelson*, with 455 tons on the down train, returning with only 277. They easily kept time on the 98 minute schedule and Bulleid jotted down his impressions, perhaps coloured a bit by the very easy return loading:

"This engine was never worked to any power, and appears to be too powerful for the work it is doing. The blast action on the fire was very steady indeed (8 exhausts per rev) and no sparks were thrown. Boiler pressure was easily maintained, in fact care was taken to prevent the boiler blowing off frequently.

The engine was driven on the regulator. The exhaust injector was used to maintain the water and was in use most of the time.

The engine is very steady. The tender rode extremely well but the design of coal space is bad — the coal not feeding forward.

Smoke and steam beat down badly. The fireman found the long grate rather difficult and had to push the fire forward four times."

This was the type of subject, outside the day's immediate business, which Gresley would discuss with Bulleid after the 5pm rush, the mail gone and now in a more leisurely period before they caught their trains home — usually the 6.19 in Bulleid's case. It was about this time that the full Gresley-Bulleid *rapport* was achieved, both communicating without notes on general matters and both clearly remembering points made by the other in the most casual discussions, so keen were they on their combined work and hobby. And of course there were entertaining asides giving scope for mock-serious description by Gresley as he stood, back to comfortable fire, sometimes reinforced at Bulleid's suggestion by an additional cup of tea. For instance, there was poor Sir Henry publishing all those bogus *Royal Scot* figures when the LMS dynamometer car was faulty. Thank goodness Newsome (and Bulleid I suppose) had kept a better eye on the calibration of *our* (ex-NER) dynamometer! Then there was Bulleid's answer, during the discussion on his Booster paper in January 1928, to a critic of wide fireboxes: "One day you will probably want an engine with 50sq ft of grate and it will be extremely interesting to see how the firebox will be arranged." This witty prophecy of wide fireboxes on the LMS greatly amused Gresley. He could equally laugh, at least in retrospect, at criticisms; as when on Darlington station he sought the views of a driver on a "Shire" class 4-4-0, the notorious rough rider, and got a frank reply which could be paraphrased as "You provided a seat but it needs a copper-bottomed driver."

Both Gresley and Bulleid got jocularly involved in the dimensions of the corridor in the tender of the non-stop *Flying Scotsman*, wanting the very minimum loss of coal and water space but dreading the thought of a driver getting jammed in it. Five Pacifics were so fitted, led by No. 4472 *Flying Scotsman*, and other small changes included enlarged oil cups in connecting and side rods for the long journey. Bulleid described as a "pleasing comment" the reply of a driver when asked how he proposed to drive: "If you want to save a little coal I will notch up as far as possible but if you want me to be sure to get to Edinburgh non-stop I will drive on the regulator." Bulleid, always a bit disdainful about saving the last bit of coal, arguing that there was more profit from one additional passenger, further commented that the driver's reply "would have pleased Mr Ivatt, who said an engine runs most sweetly in a certain position of the gear lever and that is where it should be placed and left." A new train was built for the non-stop service, with coach width increased to 9ft and decor again by Sir Charles Allom: of it my father wrote "The style was Charles II, not Louis XIV. Some industrialists on the LNER Board criticised it and Lord Grey remarked that some authority had written to him to congratulate the Board on producing such a fine piece of work."

Another feature of the Gresley/Bulleid *rapport* was that they never seemed to get in each other's way. No one ever heard of them both doing the same job, or issuing conflicting instructions, and except at Kings Cross and occasional formal events and Continental meetings they were not very often seen together. Gresley specially appreciated the Bulleid ability to communicate what he was doing and to be aware of what Gresley was doing; and both played in public their roles as scripted: Gresley . . . *the Chief* and Bulleid . . . *an Assistant*. Sometimes Bulleid played it so disarmingly that you could see the closer relationship behind the scenes, as when he presented his Poppet Valve paper to the Loco Engineers in February 1929 and said, after crediting the project to Mr Gresley, "I have, however, played a modest part in it owing to my interest in new devices." Needless to say he also credited Stamer and Glaze, who looked after the work at Darlington and Stratford.

Bulleid also credited Gresley with an outstanding ability to avoid backing failures, pulverised coal being a good example. In a 1929 discussion at the Loco Engineers Maunsell announced he would be trying out the AEG gear on the Southern. Bulleid recalled the Gorton experiments by Robinson and Thom, and recapped the attractive potential advantages: one man only on the engine, automatic firing, no smoke, no ash, no clinker, no spark-throwing, no smokebox cleaning and reduced tube cleaning. Gresley listened carefully but would not buy it: he just could not visualise anyone coping with all that coal dust on a locomotive.

In the arena of hobbies, Bulleid's keen interest in wireless receivers and in golf receded at this time, under pressure from his growing committment with the English edition of the Journal of the IRCA. Keeping his spare time available was helped by his complete disinterest in fiction and positive dislike of films which, as later with TV, he claimed tired his eyes and gave him headaches. He had a number of bad headaches and a bout of flu every year, which he accepted with gloomy resignation. Any moment of fatigue and every journey's end demanded the refreshment and relish of a cup of tea. He often hurried but never rushed and, however late at night, would always methodically lock up the house, often carrying the current Yorkshire terrier round with him. He always disliked anything vulgar or anti-establishment but was extremely patient — capable of great indignation but never loss of temper. This sometimes made a rebuke doubly effective. He had a puritanical streak and deplored the enjoyment of leisure before the corresponding task had been completed. He rarely boasted, even about golf, and only seldom recounted personal feelings and dreams — including one in which he was on an express train overtaking a goods on the same line, and wondering what to do, when suddenly his train jumped right over the other and continued on its express path. The dream of a real optimist, not deterred by obstacles.

Bulleid was more an interested onlooker than an active participator in Gresley's collaboration with Sir Alfred Yarrow on the high-pressure water-tube boilered compound 4-6-4 No. 10,000, and in Gresley's noble but unsuccessful efforts to get a locomotive testing plant built in 1931. He was in another busy and experimental spell with Newsome on the Carriage side, and many were the cost and weight-saving and comfort-improving experiments designed to tempt passengers to travel despite the prevailing slump. There were new sleeping cars, the first buffet cars for the Cambridge run, and then the 'tourist trains' — twin articulated sets of open carriages with plywood bodies painted green and cream. Popularity of the buffet car bars necessitated their enlargement within the year. An experimental aluminium-bodied carriage was built, saving 1½ tons, painted and grained to simulate the standard LNER teak exterior.

Urged by Bulleid, Gresley agreed to modify the standard 8ft 6in heavy bogie by placing the inner bolster in a sprung casting instead of on its swing links. Extensive tests were then made in bogie brake vans loaded to simulate restaurant cars, with the floors partly removed so that the behaviour of the bogies could be watched. Various celebrities accompanied Gresley and Bulleid on these noisy excursions, well described by T. Henry Turner in the discussion on Newsome's classic paper on LNER carriages to the Institution of Locomotive Engineers in March 1948. Nor were guards forgotten as they jolted along behind the fast freight trains; comfort was improved in the new vans with the wheelbase extended from 12 to 16ft. Less popular was the one-and-only, experimental, vault-like, all-concrete brake van. Other new vehicles included flat wagons for the growing container traffic, 50-ton bogie wagons — some for ICI Billingham, where Bulleid first met F.E. Smith and they formed a powerful pair of protagonists for large-capacity wagons. One mammoth was the 110-ton trolley wagon, and one line of specials was the 20-ton hopper type bottom-discharge grain wagon.

In parallel with all this Bulleid was making his first major foray into welding, recalling Richborough and stimulated by the growing news of its technical advances and by its rewards when successful (it was when, not if, to Bulleid) of a lighter product and a cheaper process than riveting. He obtained keen co-operation from the Works, but Gresley was naturally extremely cautious so that Bulleid had to stage various demonstrations before advancing to a welded carriage underframe and, soon after, by courtesy of Babcock and Wilcox, three all-welded barrels for J class 0-6-0 boilers.

Another modernising and cheapening touch was the change from the traditional passenger compartment with door flanked by two windows to a single wide window with sliding windows above. Paintwork replaced polished teak in these and the newest sleepers, again with Allom decor, till damage by scratching caused Bulleid to replace paint by the new synthetic leathercloth, Rexine. There were also gimmicks, like wireless with gramophone fill-in made available through headphones on two trains, and even a TV experiment, both in 1932.

A party of nine railway officers visited France in the summer of 1932 to examine the *Routes Nationales* and the Waterways. On the return sea crossing the party, including Riddles, Urie and Groom, enjoyed a very rare entertainment — an impersonation of some of their recent French hosts, ably put over (it is said) by the only two competent French speakers in the party, O. Bulleid and J. Elliot.

The brighter economic climate of 1933 turned traffic thoughts to higher speeds and thus found Gresley and Bulleid closely involved in a high-speed Kings Cross-Newcastle train. They visited the *Flying Hamburger* (average speed 77mph) and arranged for the makers, Maybach, to quote for an LNER train. They also travelled with Bugatti at the front of his railcar from Deauville to Paris maintaining 70 mph regardless of curves or the effect on the passengers. This outing was a perennial source of amusement to Bulleid and he reported: "HNG was alarmed and asked Bugatti how he dared put so much petrol in the vehicle, and did he not fear a fire? Bugatti replied that the vehicle travelled so fast that in the event of the tanks discharging their contents and the petrol catching fire on the line the railcar would have left the fire well behind." Bulleid admired Bugatti's method of determining the streamline form of his railcar; being, like Bulleid, convinced that wind-tunnel tests were misleading he fitted various steamline bodies on his fleet of fast road vehicles and on the long straight French roads he simply found which went furthest for a given amount of fuel. Thus he found and adopted the wedge front and rear for his railcar. It cleaved the atmosphere with minimum disturbance and Gresley adopted it.

Then the Maybach quote arrived and Gresley discussed it with his General Manager, Sir Ralph Wedgwood, who demonstrated his leadership quality by suggesting that a Pacific could put up an equally good performance, and with a better train including a dining car, and could do it more cheaply. Naturally the GM did not want to annoy his industrial customers by importing unnecessary foreign diesels. Gresley was not going to argue against this flattering instruction; he at once told Bulleid, who expressed delighted agreement, and the steam 'Silver Jubilee' was on, with plans for its introduction in the autumn of 1935. Of course there were more wind tunnel tests, not always very convincing, as when some NPL results arrived at Kings Cross showing that the LMS train models had less air resistance than the LNER. Gresley asked Bulleid what he thought about them and got the reply: "It just shows the tests aren't worth the time given to them because we all know that our trains are extraordinarily easy to haul. If you look at the LMS design with the big gap between the vehicles and square-cut ends, and then at ours with the roof and sides all brought neatly in at the ends, it doesn't make sense." "You can't say that," said Gresley, "this is the National Physical Laboratory." "I don't care who it is," said Bulleid. Gresley remained neutral and later published some NPL results showing savings in horsepower required to overcome head-on air resistance of about 42% at 100 mph with the first streamlined Class A4 Pacific, *Silver Link*.

But while these high-speed plans were cooking, Bulleid was even more taken with the big new passenger express engine for the Edinburgh-Aberdeen traffic, to be capable of hauling 550ton trains over this difficult section compared with the 480ton limit on the Class A3 Pacifics. Gresley agreed this should be a 2-8-2 after some successful passenger running with the 5ft 2in-wheeled 1925 2-8-2s. He was not going to have another failure after No. 10000 and went very carefully about his design fixes, calling on Bulleid a great deal and also, of course, on the wisdom of Spencer and the Doncaster Drawing Office. He decided on 6ft 2in wheels; three cylinders 21in by 26in stroke, all driving the second coupled axle; grate area 50sq ft; boiler extended to 6ft 5in dia. and with 220 psi pressure giving a tractive effort of 43,462lb. Bulleid was in on the Gresley-Chapelon discussions leading to large, smoothed steam and exhaust passages and Kylchap double blast pipes and chimneys. Gresley fitted the first engine, No. 2001 *Cock o' the North*, with Lentz rotary cam poppet valves and the second with 9in piston valves worked by Walschaerts-Gresley gear.

From first to last Bulleid was highly delighted by *Cock o' the North*, saying "Now, what did I tell you?" to any sceptics when, in June 1934, it sailed over Stoke summit at 57 mph with 30% cut-off taking a 650ton train of 19 carriages plus dynamometer car. He accompanied it to Vitry for a turn on the new French locomotive testing plant in December, but it showed its paces best on the Orleans run, and, one must add, on exhibition at the Gare du Nord, where the Frenchman-in-the-street considered it more *chic* than the local product. Several lessons were learned and applied from Vitry but one was not; Bulleid noted that No. 2001 always made more smoke than the French engines on test and concluded that the fire must be getting insufficient air for complete combustion. So he suggested damper and grate alterations, but Gresley, probably on account of the cost, was not interested. He and Bulleid could already see that *Cock o' the North* would have to be converted to Walschaerts gear, the Lentz gear proving unsatisfactory with limited choice of cut-offs and wasteful in coal and water due to larger clearance volumes. Also there were vexing reports from Scotland that though the new engines did the job they were wasting coal, running hot boxes and spreading the track; and their long trains were hindering station working. Bulleid tried to counter all these complaints but Gresley just got on with the next major job-in-hand, the high-speed train.

Bulleid had always been an advocate of hard driving, particularly a brisk acceleration at starting; he was also a strict realist about high-speed running and claimed it was he who got Gresley to make his well-known pronouncement that "the art of fast timing is the art of fast running uphill," to which he would then add the rider that this meant burning a lot of coal. It all arose from Bulleid pointing out that to reach 100 mph soon after breasting Stoke summit a train must approach the summit at nearly 80 mph, a speed not then normally associated with uphill running. These contentions had been well proved in November 1934 when, with Bulleid on the footplate, Class A1 Pacific *Flying Scotsman* took a four-carriage train to Leeds, 185.7 miles, in 152 minutes, average speed 73 mph, and brought back six carriages in 157½ minutes. Another test trip was made in March 1935 to Newcastle and back with Class A3 Pacific *Papyrus* and six carriages, taking just over 3hrs 50min each way and proving the feasibility of the proposed four-hour Kings Cross-Newcastle schedule. This left Gresley with quite a bit up his sleeve, as he intended to use not A3 Pacifics but a hotted-up version with improved boiler, 9in piston valves, pressure further raised to 250psi, cylinders reduced to 18½in but tractive effort slightly up at 33,730lb and with the benefit at speed of being streamlined and having a streamlined train. With all drawings ready, sanction was only received at Doncaster Works in April, and the train and the first Class A4 engine, *Silver Link*, were completed just in time for a trial run to Grantham on September 27 1935. An average speed of 100 mph was sustained for 43 miles beyond Hitchin and any doubting LNER senior officials were jolted into complete acquiescence, the track being not yet quite tailored to suit these speeds.

The public, but not all enthusiasts and purists, were sold on the stream-lined engine; and everyone was sold on the silver Rexine train with its silver fairing to within 10in of rail level, carriage joints covered and, inside, improved sound insulation. The brake power had been increased from the normal 80% to 100% of the tare weight, but with full brake applications made at 90mph and over the wheels tended to pick up on wet days and a compromise was soon made at 90%.

The speed, reliability and appearance of this first streamlined high-speed train gave a big boost to the prestige of Gresley and his staff and the LNER generally, and helped to make 1936 a golden year during which he was knighted and became President of the Institution of Mechanical Engineers. The team he led was now steeped in experience and of exceptional calibre, they in turn keeping 60-year-old Gresley and 54-year-old Bulleid mentally and physically alert. The pair worked together more as one than ever, brought closer since the strains of 1929-31, when Gresley's wife died and Bulleid was so ill that his life was despaired of, and when their daily work was often clouded by the gloom and frustrations of the long trade recession. For his part Bulleid had always extolled his Chief and could now bask in reflected glory. Besides he found great pleasures in the job itself, in the contacts it brought, and in his home and family. In 1934 he had secured Arms* for the Bulleid line and in 1935 he moved to a comfortable manor house at Mackerye End near Harpenden, feeling as well content with his lot as Gresley relished the comfort and assurance of his chief assistant. They were still just as busy but there was more certainty and less worry in their decisions and they felt under less pressure.

Bulleid often accompanied Gresley to meetings of the LNER Locomotive and Traffic Committee, held at Marylebone and attended by the General Manager and most of the Chief Officers and appropriate Board members: for example, in January 1936, when they obtained agreement for locomotive withdrawals including 20 small GN Atlantics ("35 years old, very weak, tractive effort 15,600lb, need new boilers") and 12 NB Atlantics ("heavy coal consumption, 68lb per mile"). He was also present, with Richards, when the £3½m Fenchurch Street to Shenfield electrification scheme was agreed.

Together they summarised a number of papers on "recent improvements in steam locomotives," submitted to the International Railway Congress Association by eminent railway engineers, for Gresley to present at the 1937 Congress in Paris — finding, incidentally, that the currently favoured maximum boiler pressure was 284psi (= 20 atmospheres). They were also still involved in brake improvements, including quick service valves and automatic slack adjusters, being always concerned by the problems of stopping the ever faster trains, sometimes under very adverse conditions, in places where the distant signal placings were close and the schedules demanded brisk running till they were sighted. And any new valve gear: the successful Caprotti application in 1929 to two Great Central 4-6-0s had reduced coal consumption by about 16%, but no more were converted because the performance of the engines at higher speeds was impaired. But in 1937 Caprotti introduced an improved, springless steam-operated valve, and plans were therefore made to fit two more of the class, nos. 6167 and 6164.

New engines interesting Gresley and Bulleid with their promising performance were the speedy Class V2 2-6-2s (after toying with the idea of an articulated 2-6-4-4 engine-and-tender) and the powerful Class K4 2-6-0 with 5ft 2in wheels, for the West Highland line to Mallaig.

New trains equally interesting them were the 'West Riding Limited', the

---

*For the Arms, *Sable, two Bendlets engrailed between three Plovers in bend sinister Or.* And for the Crest, *A Plover supporting with the beak a Key Or,* with motto HIC ET NVNC (see chapter decoration). The motto's dog-Latin means HERE AND NOW, Bulleid never liked waiting. The plover is known as a bullhead in the West country, source of the Bulleid surname and so furnishing a mild heraldic joke.

'East Anglian', and above all the blue-and-stainless-steel 'Coronation' for the six-hour Edinburgh service, with streamlined observation car at the rear and two all-electric kitchens, now with 10 kW generators and entirely new decor. It was probably these trains, so well publicised, that left the Public with the generally correct impression that for steam, speed and the most up-to-date outlook the really progressive railway in 1937 was the LNER.

8
Southern Railway
— the Arena

To the other three main-line Railway Companies, the Southern Railway in 1937 looked small and rather cheeky, or electric. That they were paying a fair dividend and could find capital for electrification was thought to be just their confounded luck, which was partly true as they had suffered less from freight decline in the depression of the 1930s and had prospered more from extra passengers, thanks largely to their electrics.

Much of the success and some of the brash image was due to Sir Herbert Walker, General Manager of the London & South Western since 1912 and of the Southern since 1924. He engineered the success by far sighted all-round management, including a dedication to electrification, and he engineered a better image for his railway by importing a first-class "Public Relations Officer". This was a real novelty at that time, and it was typical of Walker to recognise his own limitations opposite the Press and to take excellent curative action.

In early Southern Railway days humorists invented such items as a "Monomark" BCM/SLO and of course limericks:

A man with a death-wish design
Lay down on the Southern main line,
But he died of ennui
For the 3.43
Didn't come till a quarter past nine.

This shambling image was quickly changed when John Elliot came in 1924. Wisely, with all railway officials rather scared of publicity, he demanded and got permission to report directly to Walker, and he really set about publicising every one of the railway's many creditable items and removing all the stuffiness. Absolutely typical of John Elliot was the affair of *The Wrecker*. When in 1928 Gainsborough wanted to stage a railway accident for this film he immediately agreed. When heads were gloomily shaken he pointed out that they would film an accident anyway, that the rest of the film would have plenty of Southern Railway action, and that you couldn't always ask the film people to help your own publicity and then refuse their requests. So on Sunday August 19, 1928, the film people staged the crash at Lasham with an old SECR 4-4-0 and six carriages, and did it with such

1 Back-to-School fashions and glum looks
in 1894. O. Bulleid (left) and Ve
Sandeman.

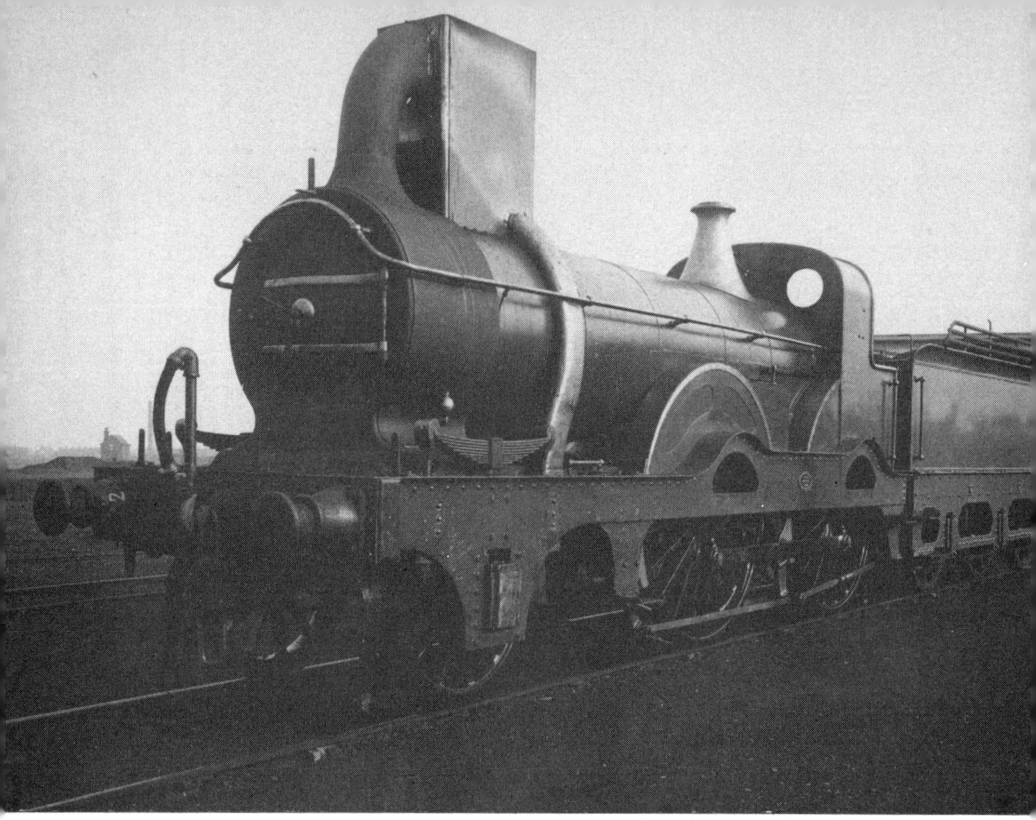

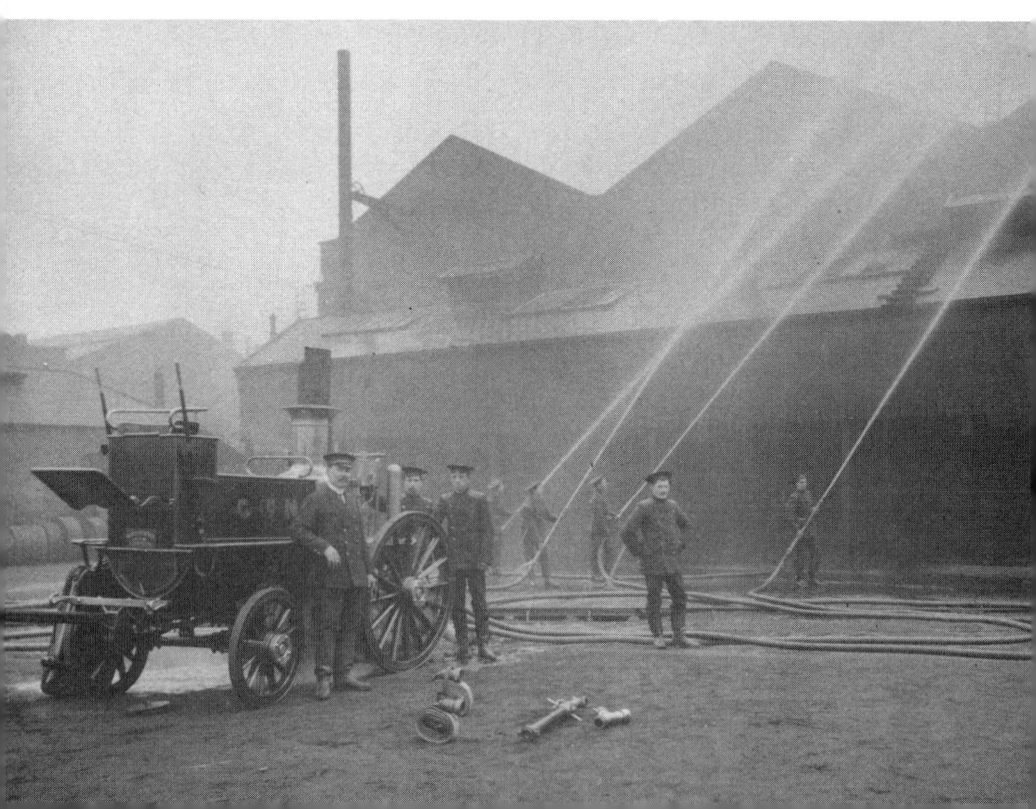

2 *Above left*: A spark arrester experiment seen by young O.V.B. Ungainly modification to Stirling 2-4-0 No. 72 in February 1905./*British Railways*

3 *Left*: Seen around Doncaster Works in 1905 — the GNR's horse-drawn Merryweather fire engine. Ivatt was very keen on fire precautions and introduced fire team cottages with electric call-out alarms./*J.R. Bazin's collection*

4 *Above*: Mr. and Mrs. Bulleid with Joujou and a local cat in their garden at 10, rue d'Eglise, Livry, August 1909./*Henrietta Ivatt*

5 *Right*: The British section of the Brussels Exhibition, 1910, after the fire./*O.V. Bulleid*

Firma del titolare _O. Bulleid_

Nome, cognome e paternità del titolare _Bullei_
Ing.re _Oliver_

Data e luogo di nascita _19 Settembre 18_
nella _Nuova Zelanda_

6 *Above*: Mrs. Bulleid in St. Mark's Square, Venice, Easter 1911. "Cerise on cream polka-dot dress of fashionable length, Liberty scarf on pale blue straw hat, fan worn on long chain, ½-hunter gold watch in clumsy leather case on strap and of course gloves," Mrs. Bulleid recalled in April 1975./*O.V.B.*

7 *Above right*: Bulleid's driving licence, Turin, July 1911.

8 *Right*: Typical H.A. Ivatt contribution to staff training — sectioned Stirling 0-6-0 photographed in the Crimpsall, 1911. The geared operating handle is at the left./*BR*

9 *Above*: Nord "3513" class du Bousquet 4-cylinder compound No. 3578 on troop train duty at St. Venant, January 29th 1915./*O.V.B.*

10 *Below*: Two slightly damaged Nord 0-6-2-2-6-0 Compounds photographed with interest by Bulleid at Cassel in March 1915. They were articulated locomotives of the Kitson-Meyer type, designed by du Bousquet, with draw gear on their power bogies./*O.V.B.*

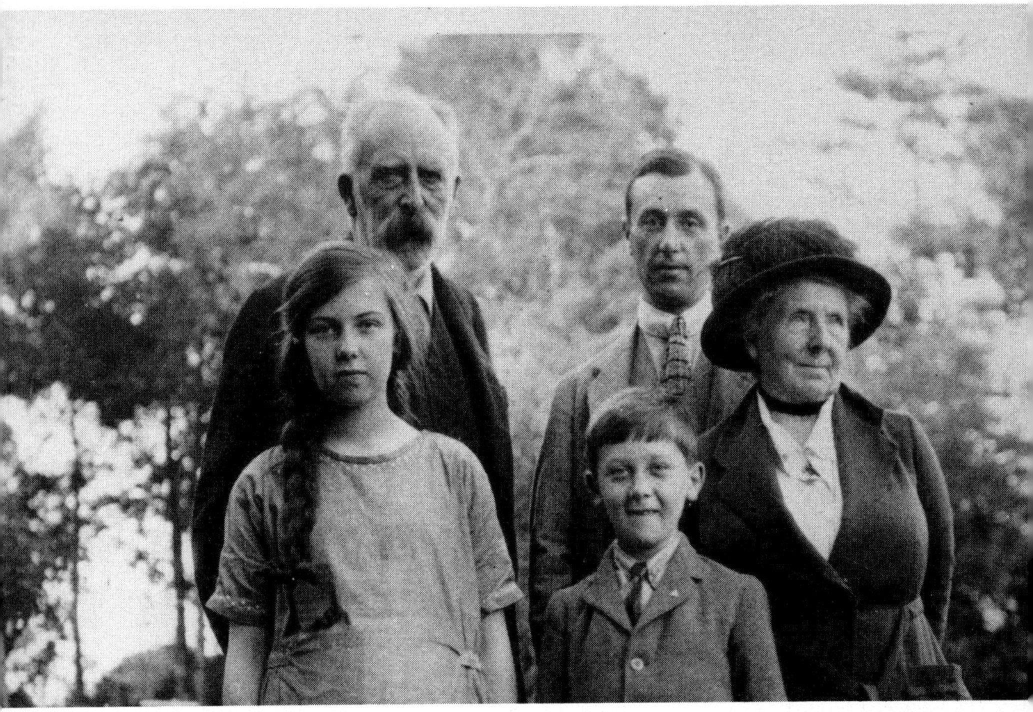

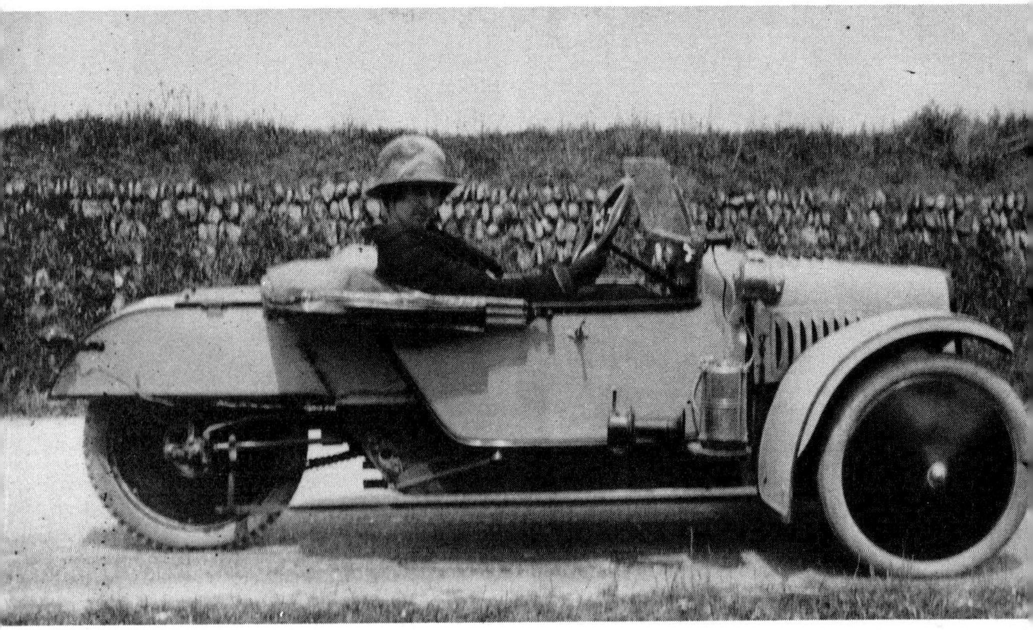

11 *Above left*: H.A. Ivatt and O.V. Bulleid with Mrs. Ivatt and the two Bulleid children at Haywards Heath, August 1920./*M.C. Bulleid*

12 *Left*: The Morgan, 1920. Driver Mrs. Bulleid, "looking a perfect fright." Note acetylene generator, Klaxon, outside lever for selecting bottom or top gear (no reverse), and hole just above it for inserting starting handle. Petrol tank under the bonnet and throttle and ignition controls clamped to the steering wheel./*O.V.B.*

13 *Above*: Peppercorn with Bulleid (holding Yorkshire terrier puppy in characteristic grip) and daughter at Hadley Common, 1924./*M.C.B.*

14 *Right*: H.N. Gresley in 1926, as best remembered by O.V.B.

15 *Above*: The Gresley/Bulleid quintuple set
of 1921 with all-electric kitchen car at
centre./*BR*

16 *Right*: Twin articulated East Coast Joint
Stock sleepers, 1922. Mrs. Bulleid tested
the beds./*Bedford Lemere*

GREAT NORTHERN
DINING SALOON

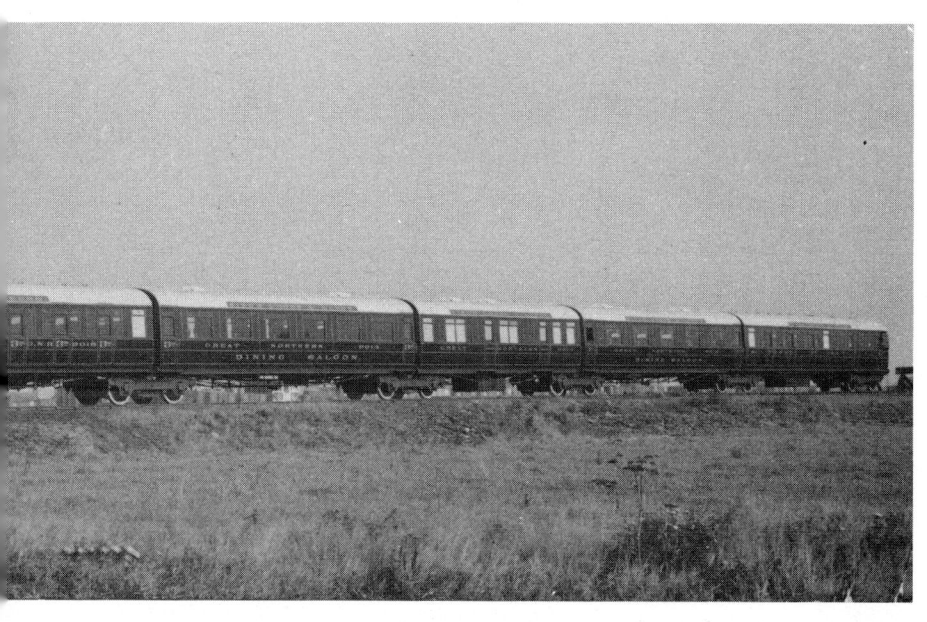

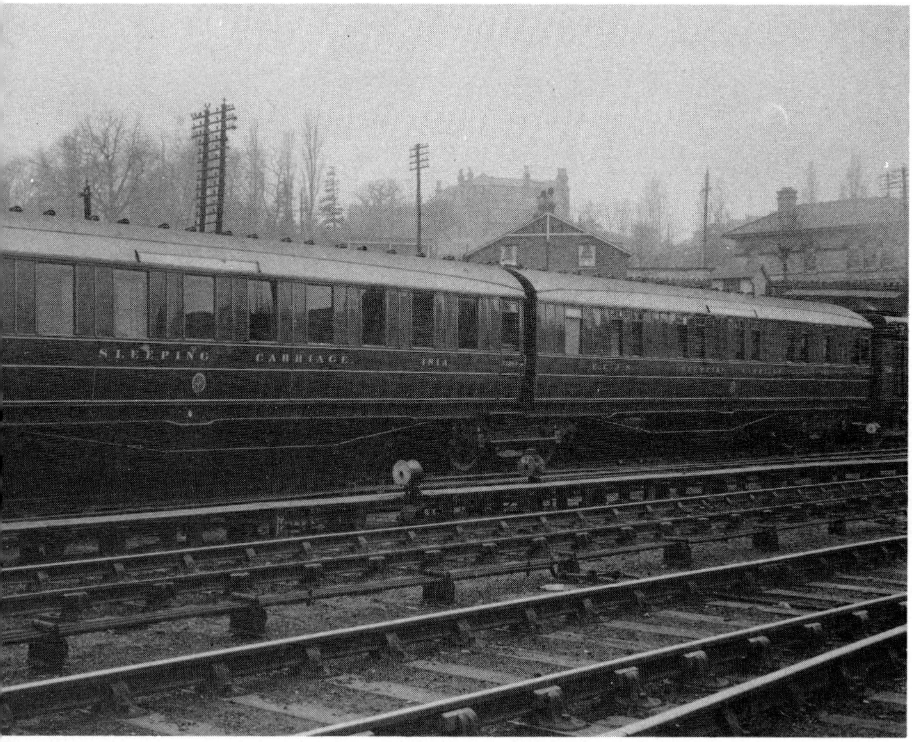
SLEEPING CARRIAGE

17 *Top*: Ivatt Atlantic No. 4419 with booster and extended cab on the Harrogate Pullman in 1924./*P. Ransome-Wallis*

18 *Above*: The second Great Central 4-6-0 to be fitted with Caprotti valve gear in 1929, No. 6168 *Lord Stuart of Wortley*. The raised footplate and casing over the cam boxes were later removed because they ran hot when enclosed./*BR*

19 *Top right*: O.V.B. liked this photo taken at Hadley Common in June 1934 of *Cock o' the North* making fast work of a heavy

down express. It felt like a typhoon on Hadley Wood station which in those days was very enclosed./*H.A.V. Bulleid*

20 *Centre right*: No. 2001 *Cock o' the North* in Amiens station, December 1934, en route to Vitry./*O.V.B.*

21 *Bottom right*: *Cock o' the North* on home ground at Inverkeithing, with the 450 tons of the 2pm Edinburgh Waverley to Aberdeen to whisk over the 9-mile climb to Cowdenbeath, August 1936./*Ian Allan Library*

22 *Above*: When the Coronation train with this heraldic effect was parked behind Doncaster station in June 1937 someone in the drawing office said "Bertram Mills Circus." This comment quickly reached Gresley and Bulleid and the lions were painted out forthwith./*BR*

23 *Below*: Not so good-looking but beefier — "Nelson" No. 30855 with the improved cylinder passages and exhaust arrangement on an easy Bournemouth train near Brookwood in 1960./*Derek Cross*

24 *Right*: Experiments to disperse the exhaust and so reduce visibility to the enemy included this November 1940 modification to No. 783 *Sir Gillemere*, with a triple jet blast pipe and three chimneys to match. Result: exhaust no less visible but cleaner tunnel ceilings./*BR*

25 *Below*: "Schools" class 4-4-0 fitted with fancy fashionable streamlining and featuring "Sunny South Sam" of the SR Advertising slogan. This was a wooden mock-up applied at Eastleigh to No. 935, *Sevenoaks* and given a spare engine number which later acquired emergency overtones./*BR*

26 *Above left*: Every 1940 comfort, and a smooth ride — the cab of the "Merchant Navy" class *Channel Packet./BR*

27 *Left*: The Bulleid/semi-Lemaitre multiple jet arrangement. The small blower steam pipe can be seen leading to the orifices in the ring round the five nozzles. The two exhaust pipes seen entering the chimney skirt are, left, from the turbo-generator and, right, from the brake ejector./*BR*

28 *Top*: First outing for 21C1 *Channel Packet*, March 1941./*Modern Transport*

29 *Above*: No. 21C5 *Canadian Pacific* after a lagging fire. This photograph was taken to help the drawing office with pipe layouts for the second ten Pacifics. Note the lagged smokebox and protective cover over trailing axlebox. The curved sides of the Bulleid tender matched engine and train and enhanced the overall modern appearance./*BR*

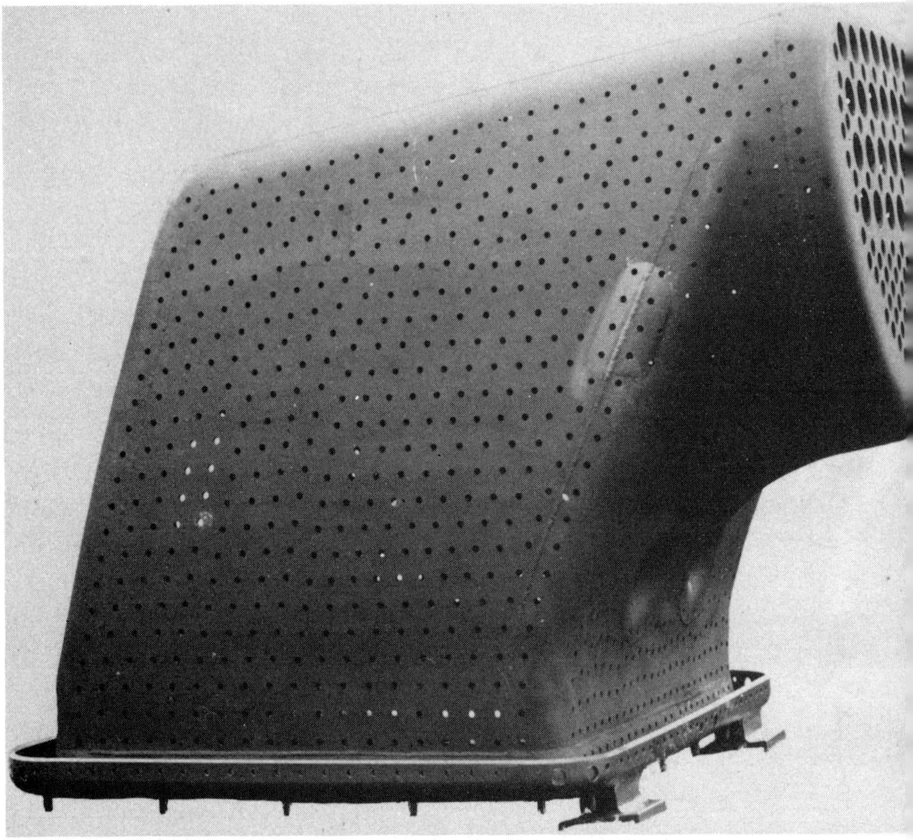

30 *Top*: A "West Country" steel firebox, showing the syphon inlets below the tubeplate, and with a small re-welded patch where the X-ray examination cast doubt on the original welding. The elegance of the welded-on U-shaped foundation ring is very evident./*BR*

31 *Above*: Austerity version of a Southern Pacific — a ½ inch scale wooden model made at Eastleigh and then firmly put aside./*J.G.C.*

ingenuity that in the film you saw four apparently quite different accidents. "Why on the Southern Railway?" I asked my father at the time and he said "We wouldn't have anything to do with it." I also asked J.R. Hind, the LNER Publicity man, and he said their policy was to refuse anything involving an accident.

Sir Herbert Walker and the SR Board were not unduly worried at steam taking second place, with the Brighton line electrified in 1933 and then the Eastbourne and Hastings in 1935. But then a new factor emerged — the other railways started a general speeding-up of passenger services. Correspondingly, they had increased the power of their express engines, the LNER with A4 Pacifics, the LMS with their first Pacifics, and the GWR with "Kings". This triple thrust of powerful steam threw into painfully sharp relief the corresponding efforts of the Southern, who had produced nothing since the "Lord Nelsons" in 1926, and even these had been pared down to an inadequate stud of 16.

Naturally Maunsell was very concerned at being left behind by the others, but both the Pacific he offered in 1933 and the 2-6-2 in 1934 were rejected by the Civil Engineer. The Dover boat trains were by then particularly in need of a more powerful locomotive, and when no suitable design materialised it must have been as frustrating to Walker as to Maunsell — not to mention John Elliot, who was by then the Assistant Traffic Manager.

Two years later, in 1937, this situation could only be described as two years worse and Walker determined to take action before he retired in October. The pending electrification to Portsmouth would emphasise the deficiencies of the remaining Southern steam. The inevitable gap till the next electrification would further emphasise them. Maunsell's age and health had militated against corrective action, and he decided to retire at the end of October, aged 69. So in seeking a new CME, Walker needed a man who would be competent on the Carriage side, able to design the mechanical parts of the electrics, able to run the four Works, but above all likely to infuse some modernity into Southern steam. Naturally he did a lot of lobbying during which he got good reports on O.V. Bulleid both from his own colleagues and Board members, notably Gilbert Szlumper and Dudley Docker, and from his opposite number on the LNER, Sir Ralph Wedgwood. He probably got the best report of all, and a strong hint to get cracking, from his Chairman, R. Holland-Martin, who held strong views on upgrading Southern steam and even stronger views on sprucing up Southern Railway carriages.

Rather typically, Bulleid was down at Bradford-on-Avon with Spencer Moultons worrying about rubber springs, when the crucial telegram reached him on May 10th 1937:

"Sir Herbert Walker wishes to see you twelve thirty tomorrow   Gresley"

It was not a lengthy interview. When Walker had made up his mind he expected others to concurr quite speedily. After explaining Maunsell's coming retirement he said "I want you to apply for the job." Bulleid was quite astonished but simply asked "What about my Chief?" He got the equally simple advice "Have a word with Sir Ralph." This he did the same afternoon, having first seen Gresley, whose comment on the job was "Yes, I think you could do it quite well." That very evening he posted his formal application to Walker. It began:

"Dear Sir,
    In accordance with our conversation this morning I wish to make formal application for the position of Chief Mechanical Engineer of the Southern Railway."

and then after a full curriculum vitae it concluded:

"I am sure Sir Ralph would be pleased to give you any information required as to my ability to satisfy the requirements needed to fill this position properly.
    I would like to thank you for the kind way in which you received me this morning, and remain
        Yours truly,
        O.V.S. Bulleid.   Mackerye End, 11.5.37."

At their meeting on May 27, the Southern Railway Board first formally heard of Maunsell's impending retirement and then approved the appointment of Bulleid as CME at a salary of £3000 to join the Company on September 20, 1937, and to take office on the day Maunsell left, October 31. An immediate press release enabled this to be announced in the *Railway Gazette* on June 4. I wish they had included a guide to pronunciation: Maunsell rhymes with *cancel* and Bulleid rhymes with *succeed*. One Eastleigh rumour had the new CME as a German, von Bulleid. Then a humorist said "Oh yes, of course — O.V.B., Otto von Bulleid" and the rumour collapsed.

Due to his age at joining, 54, a formal agreement was drawn up between Bulleid and the Southern Railway. It was mainly to assure him of pension rights not less than he would have enjoyed under comparable salary conditions on the LNER, but there was also a clause on inventions:

"Any inventions or patents made or taken out by the said Officer during the continuance of his employment by the Company shall be his sole property but the Company shall have free license without payment of any royalty to the said Officer to use the same either during the continuance of the employment of the said Officer or at any time thereafter."

When Bulleid took over as CME his colleagues included:

General Manager: G.S. Szlumper (succeeded by Missenden 25.9.39)

Asst. General Manager: J.B. Elliot
Civil Engineer: G. Ellson
Electrical Engineer: H. Jones (succeeded by A. Raworth 1.10.38)
Traffic Manager: E.J. Missenden (succeeded by R.M.T. Richards 25.9.39)
Running Superintendent: A. Cobb (succeeded by T.E. Chrimes 1.11.44)

In the Southern Railway organisation the CME was responsible for the design, construction and maintenance of all rolling stock excepting the traction equipment on electric stock, irrespective of which Department did the work; maintenance work done by the Running Superintendent was subject to the supervision of the CME. This enabled the CME to sign the annual certificate required by the Board of Trade stating:

"I hereby certify that the whole of the Company's Plant, Engines, Tenders, Carriages, Wagons, Road Vehicles, Machinery and Tools, under my charge, have, during the past year, been maintained in good working condition and repair."

The CME's Department had a Works, Shed and Depot payroll of about 10,000 and there were four Works:

Ashford, SE&CR, Maunsell's home; *Manager:* Hicks.
Eastleigh, LSWR, main Works of the SR; *Manager:* Turbett.
Brighton, LB&SCR Loco (largely closed) *Manager:* Gardiner.
Lancing, LB&SCR Carriage

There were Drawing Offices at Waterloo, Ashford, Eastleigh and Lancing. The senior technical staff was dramatically depleted by the retirements in 1938 of G.H. Pearson and J. Clayton and Bulleid appointed H. Holcroft, his Technical Assistant, to replace them. He was very well served from the start by L. Lynes as his Technical Assistant, Carriage & Wagon, and, having in mind his comparative impatience with administrative matters, excellently served by W. Marsh, previously a tower of strength to Maunsell as the Assistant for Administration and Accounts. He also retained Maunsell's personal Clerk, S. Richardson. He saw no need for a female secretary as well, so Maunsell's Miss Anderson returned to general duties. They all very soon noticed that he worked much later into the evenings than his predecessor, who had commuted from Ashford on a strictly nine-to-five basis. Just as he was getting to know them all he was asked to go with Colonel Mount on the 1938 "Pacific Committee" trip to India but refused, feeling it was wrong to leave a new job so soon, and Stanier went instead.

Bulleid got to know his Works and Works Managers by frequent visits and by continuing with two-monthly Works Managers Meetings, at which common problems and inter-Works supplies were aired for all to hear. Two of the Works Managers, Gardiner and Hicks, suffered ill-health and Bulleid moved up-and-coming M.S. Hatchell from Eastleigh to be Assistant

Works Manager at Ashford; he became Manager when Hicks died in 1938. Gardiner retired in 1940 and was succeeded by O.G. Hackett.

As on the other railways, so on the Southern there was a huge gap in salary and status between departmental heads and their principal assistants. This was one of the reasons for stodginess and technical inertia on the railways after the 1922 Grouping, even the principal assistants being mostly demoted or promotion-thwarted. The resulting absence of an energetic young "new wave" of executives allowed stagnating errors to be made, particularly on the LMS, which left scars of weak engines, slow trains and flabby time-keeping which later plagued British Rail. H. Brooke saw and started to correct this gap when he joined the Southern Board in 1943. Highly-paid young whiz assistants may be a menace at times, but they challenge errors and they keep up the tempo if the Chief starts coasting. It has even been said that curbing a young colt prevents an old driver from getting too frisky.

On the Southern in 1938, however, Bulleid soon made it clear that he would do all the necessary whizzing himself. He quickly reported on the run-down and aged state of the steam locomotive stock and by March 1938 had obtained sanction to build ten new express engines, a main duty being the Dover boat trains. That was the toughest Southern duty, with heavy trains and the hilly track and restricted loading gauge of the SE&CR and the London, Chatham & Dover, not to mention hopes of a faster schedule. But meanwhile, how about hotting up the existing engines? Was it not always said that the good engines of one CME could be made better by another? There was not much scope in the small but excellent 'Schools' class 4-4-0s, but surely the "Nelsons" had potential?

It chanced that L.J. Granshaw, in charge of the Test Section at Brighton, was in Clayton's office one afternoon in September 1937 when Maunsell and Bulleid walked in and so, of course, Granshaw was introduced. "The very man I wanted to meet," said Bulleid, adding without further preamble "What's the steaming of the "Nelsons" like?" This put Granshaw rather on the spot, but he answered "Very good with hard Yorkshire coal, but they can be a bit difficult with poor coal." Maunsell said in some irritation that he had not heard that before, but Bulleid said he had experienced the trouble on a "Nelson" that very morning. It transpired that the "Nelsons" steamed so well from the start that no tuning up had been necessary.

After more footplate runs and a good look through the drawings at Eastleigh it became a certainty that these powerful 4-6-0s of Maunsell's Swindon-rooted 1926 design would benefit from freer steam passages, larger piston valves and an improved exhaust arrangement. The last had been the subject of an unconvincing experiment with the Kylchap (Kylala-Chapelon) arrangement on No. 862 in 1936, so Bulleid decided to go for the simpler Lemaitre arrangement, arguing that if the Kylchap exhaust could go through two nozzles into two chimneys there was no reason why it should not go through multiple jets into one larger chimney. But he radically simplified the Lemaitre design by omitting the central jet and its *poire réglable*, a device which enabled the driver to sharpen the blast by partly or totally closing the central jet.

A quick but meticulous series of 17 experiments was carried out with a variety of chimneys and multiple nozzles before the final arrangement was approved — five nozzles of 2⅝in diameter on a 12in pitch circle, the total blast orifice area being thereby only marginally increased to 24½sq in but the chimney increased from 15in to 25in choke diameter.

Bulleid was already getting alarmed at talk of electrifying the Dover line and he determined to show that the 'Nelsons' with this simple improvement could knock 15min off the 1hr 35min 'Golden Arrow' schedule, riding on the footplate himself and urging things along. Once his enthusiasm exceeded the speed limit at Tonbridge, causing loss of crockery and temper to diners. Running short of steam on another trip he had the train heating turned off, the slightly chilled passengers including King Boris of Bulgaria, a steam enthusiast who had time to inspect the engine on arrival. Both trips arrived 15 minutes early. But Traffic were naturally loth to speed up the train and risk late running under adverse conditions, thereby supporting Bulleid's case for a more powerful engine.

The new cylinders with improved passages for the "Nelsons" were designed, patterns made and the first set cast before a communications error was discovered. Bulleid wanted 10in piston valves, whereas the existing 8in size had been retained. So they were re-designed pdq.

But would these engines, even with the considerable and acclaimed improvements, be strong enough to re-establish Southern steam? Late one morning a message came from Bulleid to Granshaw to get an average "Nelson" on the Boat Train at Dover that same evening and to accompany the CME on the footplate. Hectic telephoning fixed this, and 5.50 found the engine backing onto the train with Granshaw and some good coal aboard. At 6.10pm the "right-away" was given and the driver's hand was on the regulator — but no CME. He turned up briskly 45 seconds late ("I hope we can make it up") and they were off. The engine steamed well and was worked hard to maintain time up the 12-mile climb to Sandling Junction. After breasting the summit speed picked up well and the engine was quite lively, with some coal spilling on to the footplate and a great deal of noise. Bulleid looked back at the train snaking along behind them and shouted "How fast?" "70 to 75," Granshaw replied. "I knew we were not really moving," Bulleid confided after a short pause. He had already made up his mind to design a more powerful and freer-running locomotive.

Two of the "Schools" class 4-4-0s were also fitted with the semi-Lemaître multiple jet blast and big chimneys, after which they distinguished themselves on the 'Bournemouth Limited' in the summer of 1939 — so much so that the publicity boys suggested cashing in on the current streamlining craze. A full-size mock-up was prepared, but the war scotched the project.

Throughout his railway career Bulleid had seized opportunities to spur on "the Traffic" to better efforts, and one such opportunity came early in 1939 when he was suddenly struck by the extraordinary comparative emptiness of Brighton station in the late morning. So he suggested a daily fast freight service at that time to permit instant re-stocking by the busy Brighton shops. Doubt on feasibility was cast by the Traffic department, which led to an experimental demonstration. Such demonstrations are usually run well outside normal peak traffic hours, and so at 9.00pm on a clear spring evening one of the Billinton Class K 2-6-0s duly set off from New Cross with 40 fitted vans and Bulleid and Granshaw on the footplate.

They were nicely on time for the first 18 miles to the top of the bank at Merstham, on the Quarry line, when the fireman failed to get his injector working and appealed to the driver for help as he was having to bring forward sludgy coal found stuck in the tender. Nor could the driver get *his* injector to work. The business of coaxing the injectors, walking repeatedly to the tender valves, looking over the cab side for the overflow, all with correspondingly diminished attention to the look-out for signals, was filling Bulleid with a horrible fascination and he resolved to place injector controls immediately accessible to the fireman on his new engines. Then he was jerked from this line of thought by the driver suggesting that with two faulty injectors and water barely showing in the glass they should stop. "No, no. Carry on," said Bulleid, remembering that fortune favours the bold and anyway preferring to fail later rather than sooner. Sure enough, the injectors cooled off, and they reached Brighton Works sidings in the hour. Electing to cross the lines to the Works Granshaw warned about live rails. Bulleid acknowledged the warning with his usual courtesy, climbed down from the footplate — and stepped back straight on to a live rail. But not to worry, it chanced to be isolated at the time. It was witness Granshaw who got the shock.

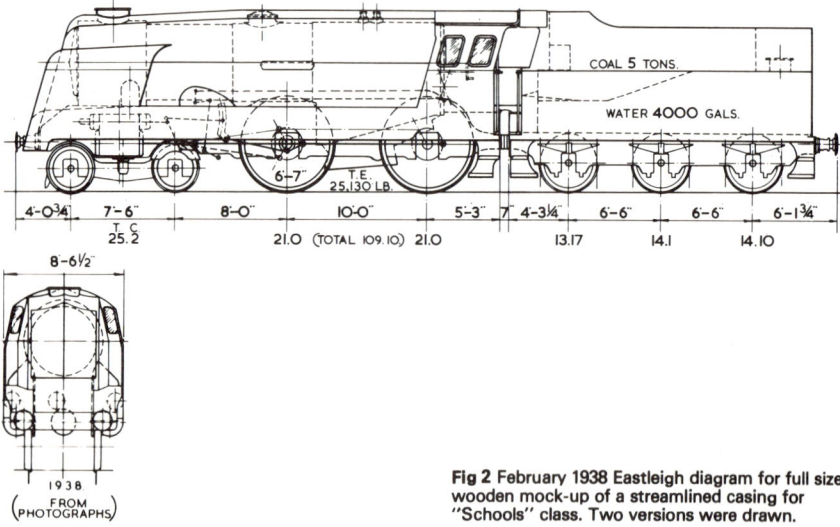

Fig 2 February 1938 Eastleigh diagram for full size wooden mock-up of a streamlined casing for "Schools" class. Two versions were drawn.

9

The SR Pacifics

By the end of 1937 Bulleid was already planning to get the most powerful locomotive he could through the cagey Civil Engineer, Ellson. Most powerful? Yes of course; all new CMEs want their prestige locomotive, and Maunsell had shown the need, and his colleagues and the Board were accepting that a dramatic steam renaissance would enhance the image of the Southern Railway.

"We must liven the place up," Bulleid repeated, and thoughts sped into the design office like quicksilver. A clutch of LNER Pacific drawings was available but for thinking about only, strictly not for copying. Then started the thinking aloud with engine diagrams. These diagrams are sometimes taken a bit too seriously by those who have never been involved in a design evolution. Remember, they range from pragmatic to fantastic, from favourite ideas to enforced practicalities, from items merely recorded before being discarded to superficial variants; moreover, they are only positive statements of fact when they have been revised in line with the engine as ultimately built — and weighed.

Bulleid and the Eastleigh drawing office flexed their muscles with engine

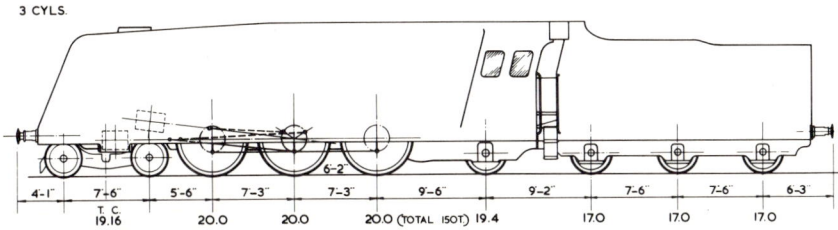

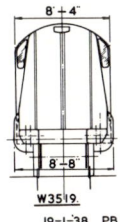

Fig 3 Eastleigh's first shot at Bulleid's new design, January 1938. With 6ft 2in wheels, but a heavy engine.

51

diagram W3519 dated January 19 1938. It looked slightly like a "Nelson" bogie leading an A4 Pacific, squeezed to clear the smaller SR loading gauge. But with emphasis on the Dover boat trains more adhesion was wanted and though there were discussions about a 4-8-2 the next diagram of note was W3630, dated June 7 1938, the first 2-8-2, with a tender evolved

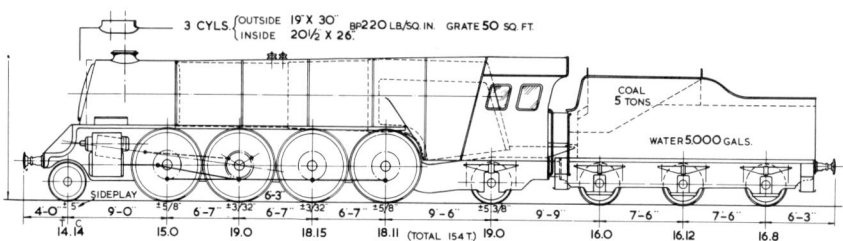

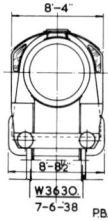

Fig 4 The first 2-8-2 proposal in June 1938, a business-like engine. Choice of chimneys.

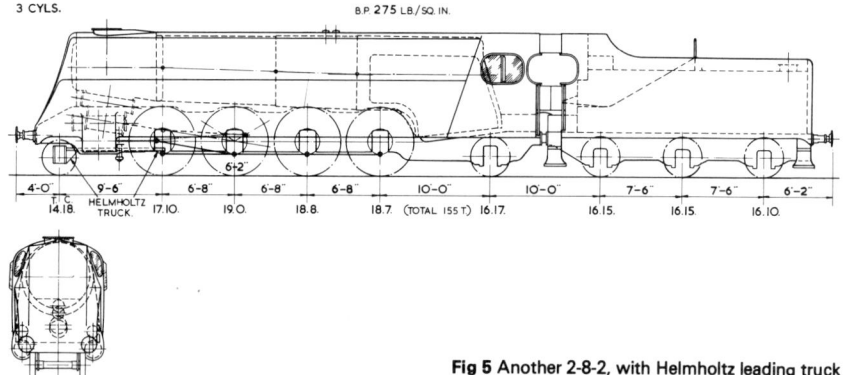

Fig 5 Another 2-8-2, with Helmholtz leading truck to please the Civil Engineer and a developing valve gear to please Bulleid.

from Maunsell's proposed Pacific. There were also thoughts of a 2-8-4 with facility for mechanical stoker, but neither would have got by the Civil Engineer, who had a rooted objection to pony trucks since the 1927 Sevenoaks accident. To clear this objection, and also to incorporate further progressive thinking, towards the end of 1938 the unlisted diagram of Fig 5 appeared, notable for the Bulleid-type tender, and more particularly for the modified type of Walschaerts valve gear comprising two inside sets with a derived 2-to-1 drive for the middle cylinder. But perhaps the outstanding feature was the Helmholtz leading truck. It was the first UK appearance of this common Continental practice, providing some articulation between the truck and the leading coupled wheels.

On this basis Ellson agreed to two 2-8-2s being built for trial; and on *that* basis Bulleid said "No thank you," foreseeing a future filled more with arguments than engines, and regretfully reverted to a Pacific. He resolved to use the very maximum axle loading permitted, but to help the Civil Engineer by minimising hammer-blow. Already worried about weight and well knowing the potential contribution of welding to weight-saving, he inspired the interest which duly made the Drawing Offices and Works of the Southern Railway the leaders in the welding field, the full effect blossoming on subsequent locomotive and carriage work. Always with one eye on safety, he kept within the range of successful international applications, and with the willing collaboration of expert companies such as Babcock and Wilcox he developed local X-ray inspection techniques to maintain welding quality.

Sanction for ten new express engines had been given by the Locomotive and Electrical Committee in March 1938, but it was not until the year's end that major decisions were cleared and design got fully under way. Some decisions were affected by shortages of materials and of manufacturing facilities because preparations for war, hotting up since 1937, were already causing restrictions approaching wartime severity by the end of 1938. In this difficult context, 1939 was the design year for the Pacifics. During the design stages "OVB" spent a deal of time at each drawing board, "discussing problems man-to-man with even the youngest draughtsman," as J.G. Jones expressed it.

Bulleid determined to ensure that his engine should never be short of steam. He chose a large grate area, he aimed at the Chapelon figure of 400°C superheat temperature, and he fixed the pressure at 280psi, or 20 atmospheres as he preferred to say, having first seriously considered 30 atmospheres. Knowing the Churchward dicta, as did his excellent drawing office boiler section under J.O.L Allott, proportions were taken which gave superb steaming, with circulation further aided by two syphons in the firebox. These connected the lower part of the rear tube plate to the firebox crown and incidentally helped to support the brick arch and to keep the firebox crown covered if water level ran low. The steel firebox was an easy decision — the duty was beyond copper. Armand's developing TIA water treatment was wanted, but had to be postponed due to the "shadows of war" situation, as had the early plan for an auto-stoker to use low-grade coal.

The boilers were an unqualified success. So were the fireboxes after the water treatment was provided, which helped them to attain the distinction of being the cheapest boilers in the country to maintain when a comparison was made in the early 1950s.

Bulleid was happy with a smaller wheel and shorter stroke than current practice, and taking a piston speed of 2,000ft per minute as a safe maximum at 110mph he came up with a 6ft 2in diameter wheel and 24in stroke. With his 280psi boiler pressure and three 18in diameter cylinders his tractive effort would be the desirable 37,000lb — as much as the adhesion would stand. But in designing the cylinders allowance was made to bore them out to 19in, ie more than the normal re-boring allowance.

Piston valves were set vertically above the cylinders and were 11in diameter. They achieved both outside admission and absence of glands by being operated from a rocking-lever in the exhaust space. Build-up of carbon was dramatically reduced.

Large, smooth, direct steam pipes and passages were provided, but the essential balance pipe between the steam inlets at the ends of the cylinders was omitted from the inside cylinder: Bulleid did not like W.H. Hutchinson's first proposal for this tricky job, with two flattened pipes to minimise the excrescence in the smokebox, and the job got forgotten. This was the main reason for fractures of components driving the piston valves in the early days, cured when the missing balance pipes were provided. I think this was the only serious worry Bulleid suffered from the early problems. Being wrongly under the impression that balance pipes were fitted to all cylinders he was at a complete loss about the rocker-shaft and allied failures and went down comparative blind alleys on lubrication and stress-raisers. At the unexpected news of the first failure he had not one but several alternatives drawn out. Then, in a casual conversation, H.L. Guy remarked that if the piston-valve drive was being over-stressed it must mean that the valves were hard to drive and this must mean a pressure imbalance. "That cannot be, with our balance pipes," thought Bulleid, but he followed it up and of course immediately spotted the omission, proving for the *nth* time that problems are more often obvious than subtle. Another design error was the stiffness of the steam pipes in relation to the flexing of the frames, causing fractures of the cylinder steam flanges. This was cured by fitting more flexible (Aiton) pipes.

In repeating his "Nelson" success by fitting a simplified Lemaître multi-jet exhaust with five 2⅜in diameter nozzles and a 29in chimney with 25in choke, Bulleid always said that there was room for further improvements in the exhaust system. He was proved right by the Giesl trial in 1962.

Bulleid was not a man to mind if piston valves over-ran slightly, but he did not like the idea of this happpening to only one of the three. Nor did he like over-heated inside big-ends, always an embarrassment during his time at Kings Cross and a horrid running sore in exchange trials. Like most mechanical engineers, he did not like pins, slides and bearings to operate in the gritty, wind-swept conditions of railway track. Besides, he had long felt that steam engine practice should get nearer to the internal combustion practice of enclosure with pump lubrication. So he applied further thought to the gear shown in Fig 6 and came up with what was at first called the "⅜ valve gear," to develop which idea he brought C.S. Cocks from Doncaster.

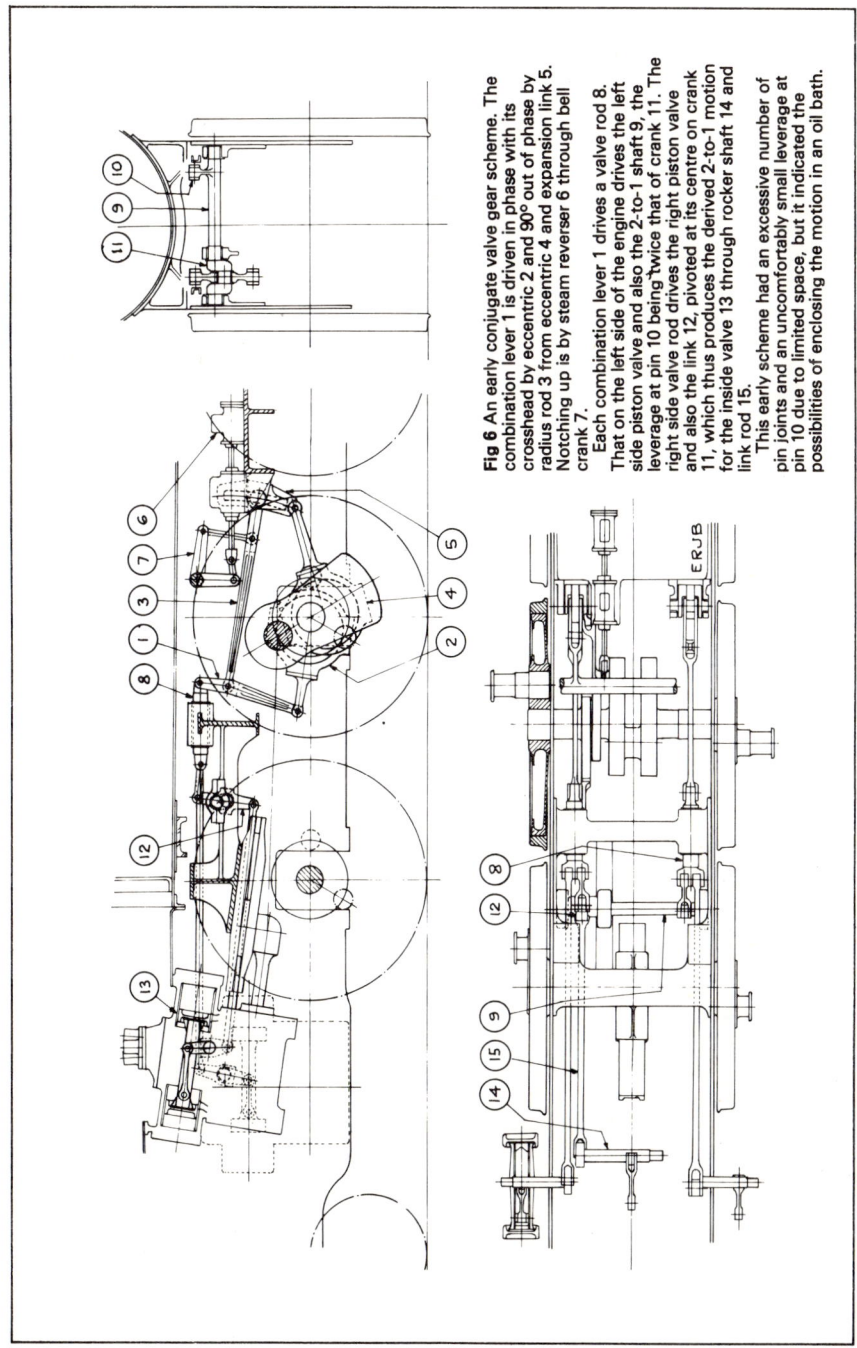

Fig 6 An early conjugate valve gear scheme. The combination lever 1 is driven in phase with its crosshead by eccentric 2 and 90° out of phase by radius rod 3 from eccentric 4 and expansion link 5. Notching up is by steam reverser 6 through bell crank 7.

Each combination lever 1 drives a valve rod 8. That on the left side of the engine drives the left side piston valve and also the 2-to-1 shaft 9, the leverage at pin 10 being twice that of crank 11. The right side valve rod drives the right piston valve and also the link 12, pivoted at its centre on crank 11, which thus produces the derived 2-to-1 motion for the inside valve 13 through rocker shaft 14 and link rod 15.

This early scheme had an excessive number of pin joints and an uncomfortably small leverage at pin 10 due to limited space, but it indicated the possibilities of enclosing the motion in an oil bath.

55

The concept, of three modified sets of gear contained, with the inside big-end, in an oil-bath was bold and technically quite feasible, but the motion from it had to be multiplied in the ratio 8 to 3 to provide the desired 6in valve travel. Hence the title "⅜ gear," but even that was flattering because the 8in arms operating the valves were driven by $2\frac{31}{32}$ in arms for the outside valves and, worse, a $2\frac{27}{32}$ in arm for the inside valve. This was due to the 1 in 7¾ inclination of the inside cylinder to clear the oil bath bottom plate over the leading coupled axle. Also, though most were in the oil-bath, there were more pin joints in this motion than in the four sets on a "Nelson," and a double chain drive from the centre axle was also needed. Interestingly, the multiplying lever gives better valve events than taking the full travel direct from the valve gear where this involves excessive angularity of the eccentric rod. A model of the new gear was built and the events were excellent. So with the advantages of oiling, and of the improved, glandless drive to the piston valves, and of the trail-blazing factor, Bulleid decided to proceed.

But like all designers he was beset with last-minute anxieties, and wondered if it would be better to use the improved Caprotti gear, which Gresley said was doing very well on the Great Central 4-6-0s. Col. Cantlie was both Managing Director of Caprotti Valve Gears Ltd and a Major, RE, at the War Office when in March 1940 Bulleid called without notice but with the relevant drawings and asked if they could do a Caprotti arrangement for a three-cylinder Pacific. "Oh yes . . . how soon?" "Well, I must know by to-morrow." Cantlie had his four draughtsmen working through the night and they produced a comparatively simple arrangement with one double and one single cam box and the necessary cylinder modifications. There was the usual outside drive to the two cam boxes and the only major problem, successfully overcome, was to keep the outside edges of the boxes

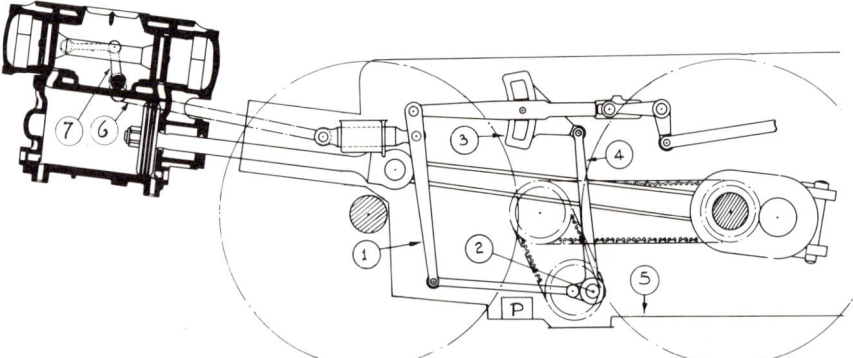

Fig 7 Bulleid's patented valve gear. The combination lever 1 is driven in phase with its piston from pin 2 on the chain-driven valve gear shaft. The expansion link 3 is driven 90° out of phase by eccentric rod 4 at right angles to its normal position in Walschaerts valve gear. The combined motion is applied to the valve through valve rod 6 and multiplying rocker shaft 7 operating in the exhaust cavity. 5 indicates the oil bath enclosure and P the oil circulating pump. The chain drive was adopted after first considering a bevel gear and cardan shaft drive from the rear coupled axle.

within the SR loading gauge. They took the scheme round to Waterloo next morning. It was turned down, for reasons not stated but probably a combination of slightly added weight, dislike by the railway of bought-in components, and Bulleid's confidence in his own enclosed valve-gear.

In use excessive play developed. This was very largely due to lubrication and reversing gear defects and had the result, approximately equal on all cylinders, of reducing effective valve travel at low speeds and increasing it at high speeds — a bonus aid to free running. The drawing office tried a larger version of the enclosed valve gear to give more travel and so reduce the rocker-arm magnification to 2 to 1, but they could not fit it in the confined space.

Reversible gear pumps in the oil bath distributed filtered oil to all the moving parts. The sump was filled through a filler pipe accessible between the driving and trailing coupled wheels about 15in above rail level. Sump capacity was about 40 gallons.

This admirable lubrication system attracted some weird criticisms, including ridicule poured on the idea of allowing a big-end to lash around in the oil. The term "oil bath" was not well chosen; it was merely an oil enclosure with a maximum depth of oil less than 2in. But there were design and operating errors: the whole casing was too rigid, and thick and thin sections were welded together without appropriate curves to provide elasticity, and the seals for the axle movement were inadequate. The cover and breather sealing was poor, allowing occasional ingress of sand and grit and water. Bad stabling caused water entry through condensation. There were techniques for creaming off the oil to the pump if water entered, devised by Ricardo, which could well have been applied. This oil-bath should certainly have been put right by Bulleid or by his successors if the complaints against it were justified. So should the minor defects in the mechanical lubricators.

Bulleid decided to do without reciprocating balance, and as a result the engine was virtually free from hammer-blow though stresses in the driving axle were increased. At a joint meeting of the Institutions of Civil and Mechanical Engineers in December 1941 Ellson showed diagrams of zero hammer-blow from "Merchant Navy" and Co-Co electric engines and Bulleid said he used 24in stroke compared with 26in or 28in as part compensation for having no reciprocating balance, and thereby saved 1377lb of dead weight per engine.

A steam reverser was prescribed by the unacceptably complex linkage needed to get round the wide firebox. Then Eastleigh drawing office adopted the unsatisfactory LSWR reverser instead of adapting the excellent James Stirling SE&CR (but Ashford) model. So the first ten engines had a dead slow reverser. Later engines had a faster version which, despite modifications and unless scrupulously maintained, teased drivers with creep, erratic setting, and in rare but unnerving cases a complete reversal of the engine while running at speed. As H.G. Ivatt once remarked "the engine doesn't like it." Nor does the valve gear.

The Bulleid-Firth-Brown wheel, in addition to its attractive appearance and ability to hide balance weights, was lighter, gave better tyre support, and succeeded in eliminating broken spokes and loose tyres. It allowed the improved lip fastening which became a BR standard.

The trailing truck was of delta type, pivoted to the main frame just behind the trailing coupled wheels, with weight bearers and lateral control springs behind the axle. It permitted an excellent, hopper-shaped ash-pan, gave drivers a first-class ride, and was adopted for the BR Pacifics.

The comparatively wide spacing of the coupled wheels, to conform with the weight-per-foot limitations of the track, allowed space for balanced clasp brakes with blocks on both sides of the wheels. These reduce axlebox stresses and proved satisfactory.

The frames were located on the centre-line of the axle boxes from *Cock o' the North* experience and on later engines the horn guides were welded in. This arrangement was later adopted by BR.

As for the axleboxes — "Bronze of course," Bulleid said, "they are the best and can be re-cycled." Moreover individual push-fits were used and often there was still no axlebox knock after 70,000 miles, compared with what rude Southern Railway engineers described as the "initial built-in knock" of the small tolerance specified by the LMS.

The objectives of the outer casing design were to facilitate automatic cleaning, to give a sort of sophisticated outline for modern Southern steam without exactly copying LNER and LMS streamliners, and to get more freedom in locating accessories and pipes without festooning the boiler. The casing succeeded in its aims, but introduced off-setting disadvantages: it irritatingly reduced accessibility to pipes and fittings and was itself awkward to remove, park, and refit. It impaired look-out and it collected oily accumulations which occasionally caught fire. Everybody surprisingly toed the line and called it "air-smoothed," not "streamlined," as requested.

The steam sanding was not satisfactory. Nor was the difficult access to the sand boxes high up under the casing.

Bulleid had a real desire, well publicised, to do all he could to ease the job of the footplate staff. In particular he provided the latest and best type of live steam injectors; steam-operated firehole door; complete protection against the weather; and electric lighting, including luminous gauge dials. These were all successful except that some found the cab "over-enclosed."

Drivers were helped a lot in preparing the engines by the enclosed lubricated motion, a benefit only slightly offset by having to attend to the generator. There was no economy to the railway, however, because the preparation time allowed depended solely on engine size after the 1931 agreement.

Disposal was helped a lot by the hopper-type ash pan and rocking grate, though the latter had design shortcomings. The large size of the smokebox and the clutter (when they were in your way) of pipes in it and the obstructed front access and tendency of fumes to hang about, were adverse factors.

Bulleid fancied the Continental method of numbering whereby a Pacific

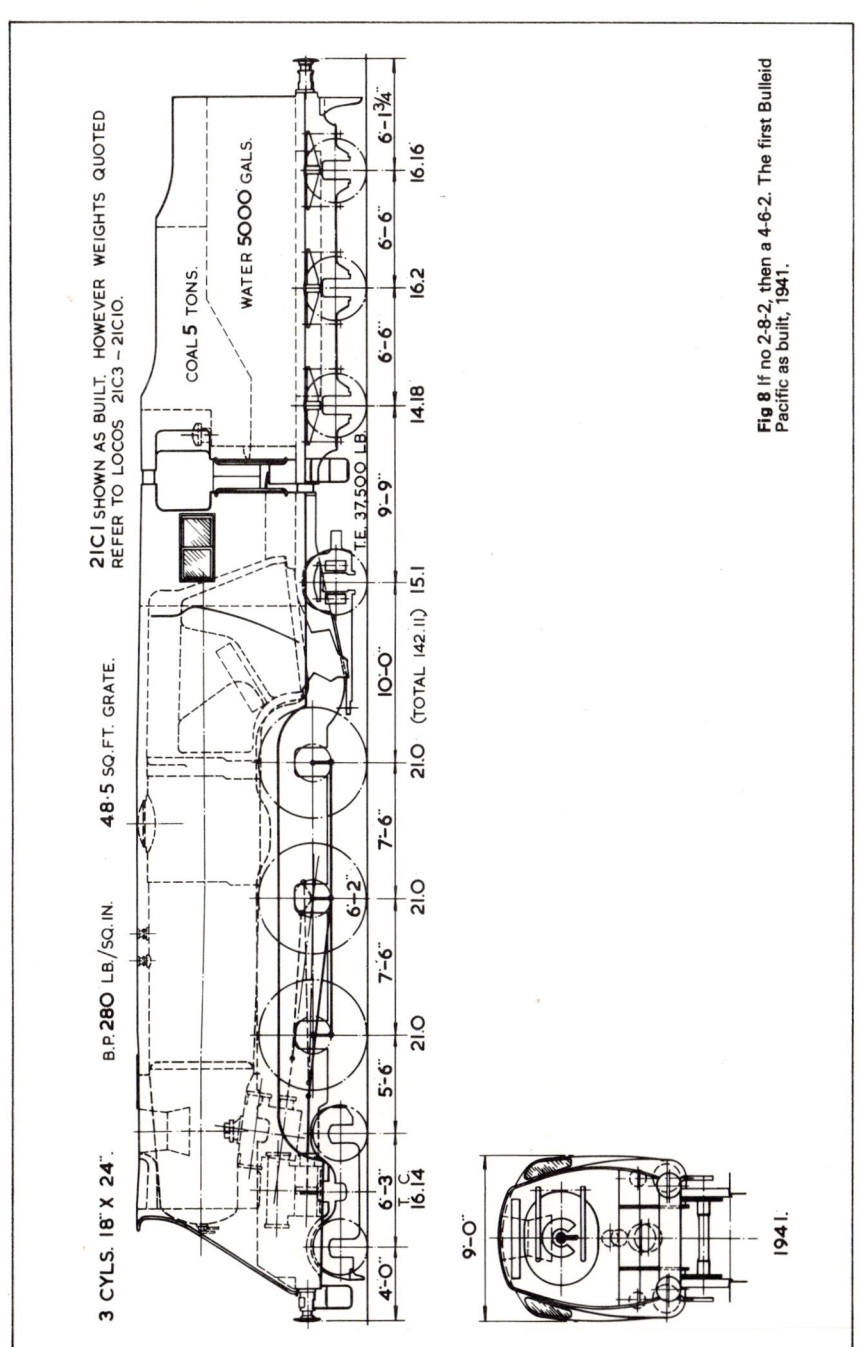

3 CYLS. 18" X 24". B.P. 280 LB./SQ.IN. 48·5 SQ.FT. GRATE.

21C1 SHOWN AS BUILT. HOWEVER WEIGHTS QUOTED
REFER TO LOCOS 21C3 – 21C10.

COAL 5 TONS.

WATER 5000 GALS.

T.E. 37,500 LB.

Fig 8 If no 2-8-2, then a 4-6-2. The first Bulleid Pacific as built, 1941.

59

is designated by its axles, 2C1, but he did not like the resulting ambiguity when the engine number follows, and so he placed the whole carrying wheel notation before the coupled axle letter and the engine number after. Hence the first Pacific became 21C1.

I have always thought it remarkable that there was never a serious accident due to running tender-first in cold weather with dusty coal on an ancient engine like a Midland Class 2F 0-6-0. Bulleid's tender was well-protected, rode well, and had a satisfactorily low tare weight, but lacked ingenuity and a good look-out. It carried 6 tons of coal and 5,000 gallons of water. Later tenders had 6,000 gallons capacity.

Two factors militate against the Drawing Office pulling off an accurate weight estimate: the length of time since they last did it and the degree of novelty. These factors were both in play for Bulleid's first Pacific, and the working order weight was 99 tons compared with the estimate of 92½, which was revised when the locomotive was nearly complete to 96. Most CMEs who did anything suffered a weight or cost panic at one time or another, usually with the added annoyance of hearing unflattering comments flying between Drawing Office and Works. Curative action ranged from Bulleid himself taking a draughtsman round the engine and marking with chalk where lightening holes could be made, to substitution of the heavy brass decorative plates by a lighter material — paint. These measures reduced the weight to within a ton or so of 94¾tons, with no axle carrying more than a shade over the agreed 21tons, though admittedly Bulleid took a broad view of the first weighings, choosing the lightest. Why be too fussy about the odd cwt or two? After all, when a pair of 6ft 2in wheels lose ½in by wear, that reduces the axle weight by 2½cwt. Besides, having in mind the sweet riding and absence of hammer-blow there could be no question of the engines being unacceptable to the track. The Civil Engineer did agree, but reluctantly. Further action to ensure the weight of subsequent engines coming at or below the promised 94¾tons included fabricated frame stretchers, lighter sheeting, and moving from the front section to the middle section of the boiler the bottom taper needed to clear the inside piston valve; this lightened both the boiler and its water content.

All the circumstances of size, novelty, war conditions, and the long gap since it had happened before, kindled strong Eastleigh Works and Drawing Office interest in their new engine. Many watched with pleasure its first steaming and its journey to Bournemouth on February 22 1941 hauling twenty carriages. The naming ceremony on March 10 was performed by the Minister of Transport (later Lord Brabazon) and the Chairman and most senior officers of the Southern were then hauled off to lunch with absurd ease by the smart, green-and-yellow, unconventional, sleek, No. 21C1 *Channel Packet*. All were suitably impressed and the General Manager sent the designer a congratulatory note.

Then of course came the teething troubles. They were rather above average for a major new engine, but distinctly below average per novelty.

SOUTHERN RAILWAY COMPANY

TELEPHONE WAT. 5100.

GENERAL MANAGER'S OFFICE,

WATERLOO STATION,

LONDON, S.E.1.

Monday
evening
—
March 10th 41

My dear Oliver,

Well done.

Yours ever,

Eustace Missenden

Fig 9 Missenden approves of the first Pacific, March 10th 1941.

Getting over them needed the concentrated attention of one senior man, Bulleid decided in October 1941 after a strong nudge from Missenden, and he gave the quite exacting job to L.J. Granshaw, who had recently been promoted to Assistant Works Manager, Brighton; it was completed by November 1942.

After the early teething troubles and a spell of freight working the new Pacifics, most in wartime black livery, were allocated to Salisbury and Exmouth Junction. By mid-1942 they were in passenger service and starting to delight their crews with their power, free steaming and free running, and to delight all those interested in sparkling steam engine performance with their flamboyant hill-climbing and attention to brisk timing. They were a notable morale booster in the drab days of the war and those who did not like their chimney-free, unadorned appearance could still relish their prowess. The only people not so pleased were the Shed maintenance staffs, because drivers' complaints were often hard to diagnose and still harder to get at. Few things are more exasperating to a maintenance man than to have his grumble "it's hard to get at" inaccurately countered by "it won't need any attention." But as always there was a credit side on the Sheds; many heavy and tedious jobs were reduced, more than a little help came from the drivers' uninhibited liking for the engines, and the engines themselves brought a certain prestige — you don't mind going to a bit more trouble for a star performer. Besides, most people in a steam Shed liked to have the *best* engine and here at last, on the good old Southern, was this very thing. You could claim without exaggeration, over a second pint, that it would show a clean pair of heels to any engine in the country *and* flatten the banks they were always going on about. "Just let them have a go," you might add — little knowing that one day they would.

Improvements inspire improvements. One letter received by the CME in

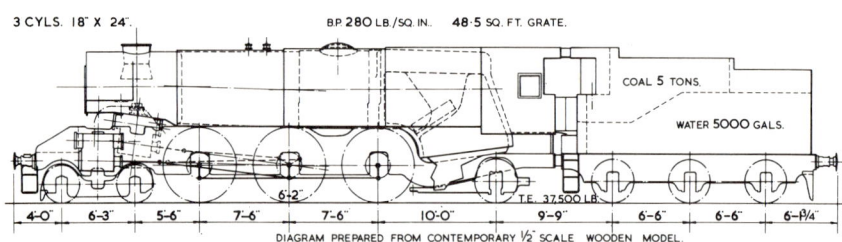

3 CYLS. 18" X 24".　　B.P. 280 LB./SQ. IN.　48·5 SQ. FT. GRATE.

COAL 5 TONS.

WATER 5000 GALS.

6-2"　　T.E. 37,500 LB.

4-0"　6-3"　5-6"　7-6"　7-6"　10-0"　9-9"　6-6"　6-6"　6-1¾"

DIAGRAM PREPARED FROM CONTEMPORARY ½" SCALE WOODEN MODEL.

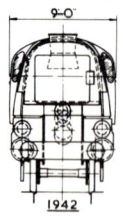

9-0"

1942

Fig 10 Q.l-itis. Austerity version of a Pacific done at a time of severe restraints in 1942.

1941 suggested making the pedal-operated firehole doors fully automatic, with an adjustable steam-operated timing device so that the doors would open of their own accord every so many seconds. It described a method and concluded: "Now sir, this is not to tell you how to do it. I can leave that to you. It is simply one method of improving the efficiency of the boiler and leaving the fireman free. With apologies for the liberty. Yours faithfully, An Old Railwayman." Not daunted by the absence of name and address Bulleid replied to this by having it published in the Southern Railway's excellent magazine and saying he liked the idea, but it had undesirable features and that he didn't understand why the writer of so helpful a letter should not have signed it.

The drivers' welcome to the "Merchant Navies," the growing acceptance of their modern appearance, and the conviction that remaining maintenance problems would be solved prompted Bulleid — as many other CMEs before him — to copy his design as closely as practicable when a follow-up was needed of a powerful, fast mixed traffic engine with exceptionally wide route availability. Accordingly, after considering and rejecting a 4-6-0, design work started in 1943 on the "lightweight" Pacifics, a term which emphasised an intention and recalled a failure. The objective of the "lightweight" design was to retain maximum possible power whilst strictly conforming to a total engine weight of 86tons and axle loads not greater than 19tons. Bulleid took four basic decisions:

(1) Not to alter the bogie, the coupled wheels, the axleboxes, or any motion details.
(2) To scale down the boiler and firebox whilst retaining the same boiler mountings.
(3) To save more weight by further application of welding and ingenuity.
(4) To reduce disposal time by grate and ashpan improvements.

Looking at these in a bit more detail, item 1 meant that alterations to wheels, frames, motion and cylinders were limited to decreasing the size of the trailing wheels, cylinders and piston valves. Item 2 resulted in another admirable boiler with the barrel length and diameters practically unaltered, superheater elements reduced by one row, but firebox shortened so that the grate area was reduced from 48½ to 38¼sq ft. The welding applications of item 3 included fabrication of all the frame stretchers and more welding of the firebox, including the light and ingenious U-shaped foundation ring which replaced the heavy conventional rectangular non-U section.

Rocking grates were provided for breaking up clinker and fused ash, and one section could be dropped to simplify cleaning. Also the hopper-type ashpan doors could be operated from the cab. There was anxiety as to whether the grate area had been reduced too much, and there was speculation and American influence in the decision to eliminate dampers. Bulleid always liked to get on engines and ask the crew what they thought about

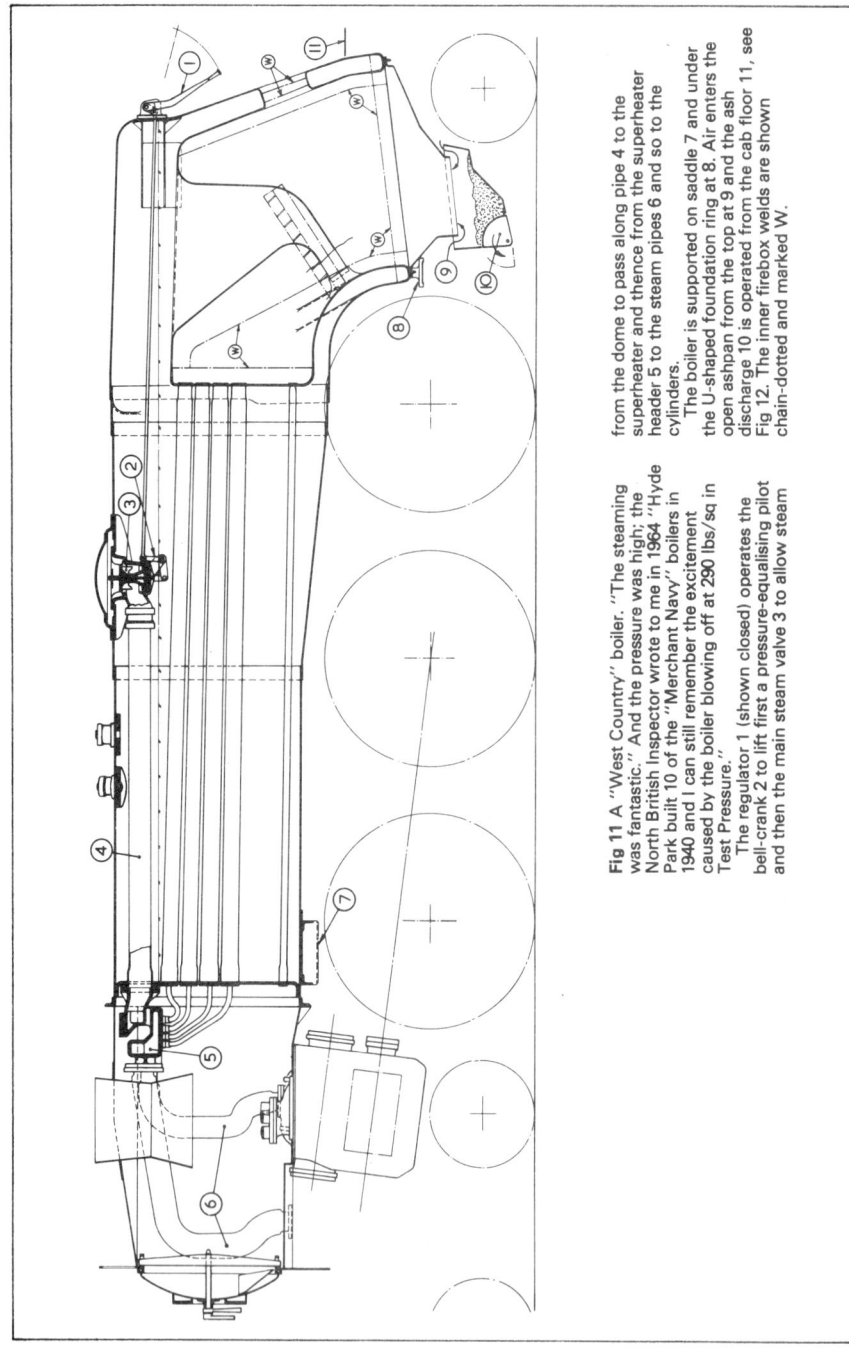

Fig 11 A "West Country" boiler. "The steaming was fantastic." And the pressure was high; the North British Inspector wrote to me in 1964 "Hyde Park built 10 of the "Merchant Navy" boilers in 1940 and I can still remember the excitement caused by the boiler blowing off at 290 lbs/sq in Test Pressure."

The regulator 1 (shown closed) operates the bell-crank 2 to lift first a pressure-equalising pilot and then the main steam valve 3 to allow steam from the dome to pass along pipe 4 to the superheater and thence from the superheater header 5 to the steam pipes 6 and so to the cylinders.

The boiler is supported on saddle 7 and under the U-shaped foundation ring at 8. Air enters the open ashpan from the top at 9 and the ash discharge 10 is operated from the cab floor 11, see Fig 12. The inner firebox welds are shown chain-dotted and marked W.

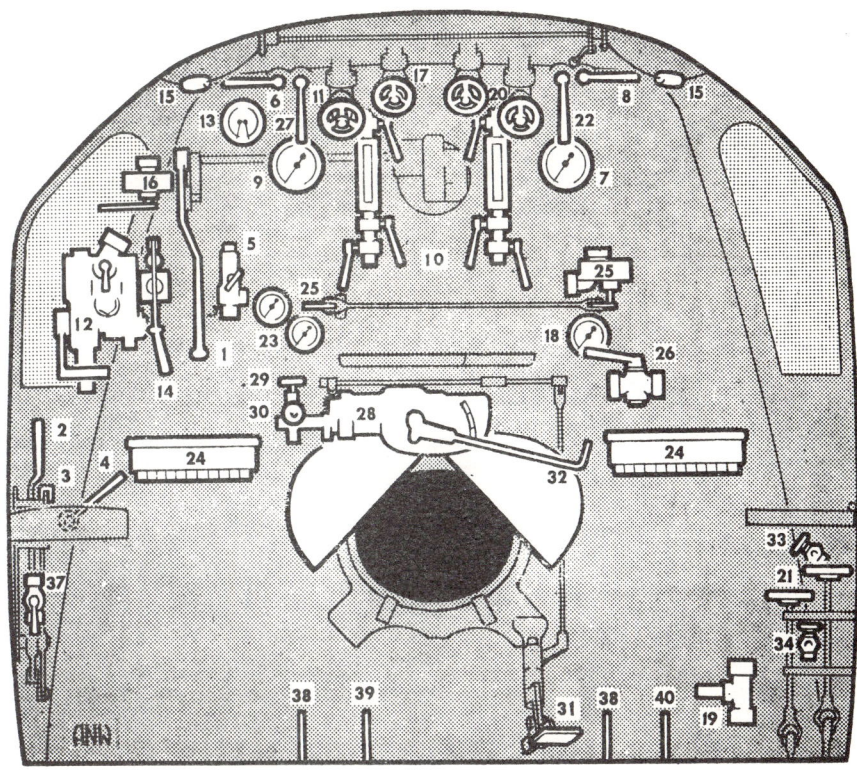

Fig 12 A "West Country" cab.

1 Regulator handle
2 Cylinder cock lever
3 Steam reverser setting indicator
4 Steam reverser control lever
5 Steam reverser lubricator
6 Steam reverser steam valve
7 Boiler pressure gauge
8 ditto isolating valve
9 Steam Chest pressure gauge
10 Water level gauges
11 Ejector steam valve
12 Ejector & vacuum brake control
13 Duplex vacuum gauge
14 Engine steam brake
15 Whistle
16 Blower
17 Train heating
18 ditto pressure gauge
19 ditto relief valve

20 Two steam valves for injectors
21 Injector steam & water controls
22 Steam to cylinder lubricating atomiser
23 Lubricating oil pressure gauges
24 Axlebox oilers
25 Steam sanding
26 Steam to electric generator
27 Steam for firehole door cylinder.
28 Firedoor cylinder
29 Firedoor cylinder inlet valve
30 Firedoor cylinder drain cock
31 Firedoor cylinder operating pedal
32 Firedoor hand lever
33 Water valve for hose
34 Tender spray valve
37 Windscreen water spray
38 Two rocking grate controls
39 Drop grate
40 Ash hopper doors

them. Once he put this question to a fireman who was losing a struggle to avoid blowing off on Waterloo station and got the testy reply "You'd have thought the b----- fool who designed them would have had the sense to fit dampers." "Dampers?" Bulleid countered, "dampers? I do not fit my engines with devices to prevent steaming." An ideal Bulleidism. Even so, their absence handicapped the less expert and was the automatic excuse for any blowing-off complaint, so they were later fitted.

The wide route availability also imposed a reduction of cab width to 8ft 6in, and the tender weight was down to 42½tons. When the first engine was weighed at Brighton Works, rather appropriately on VE day in May 1945, there was well-earned delight that the estimated weight was achieved and C.S. Cocks beamed with satisfaction. What turned out to be the inappropriate name of "lightweight" gave way to the apt and popular naming of these engines as the "West Country" class. This was thereafter commonly applied to all the light Pacifics, though a batch built for use in the south-east was named as the "Battle of Britain" class. They were built almost continuously from June 1945 till May 1950, totalling 110, and they displayed all the exuberance of their bigger sisters, if not more. A curious feature, perhaps due to the combination of narrower cab (to clear the SE&CR's Mountfield tunnel on the Hastings line) and reduced length (to suit 60ft turntables) was that it took a determined second glance to distinguish between a "Merchant Navy" and a "West Country." Sometimes it took a lot more than that to distinguish between their performance. So successful was this scaled-down Pacific that Bulleid could have kicked

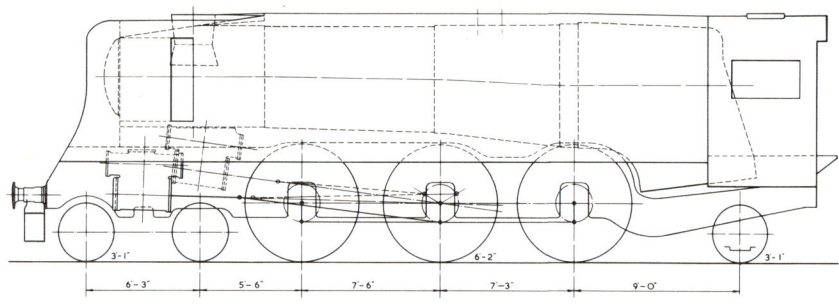

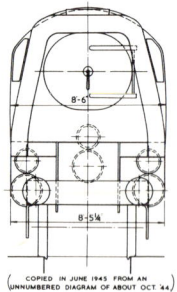

Fig 13 First diagram of a lightweight Pacific. Impressive front with Townend cowling and a vertical slot each side of the smokebox to emit air along boiler sides and so prevent downward drift of exhaust.

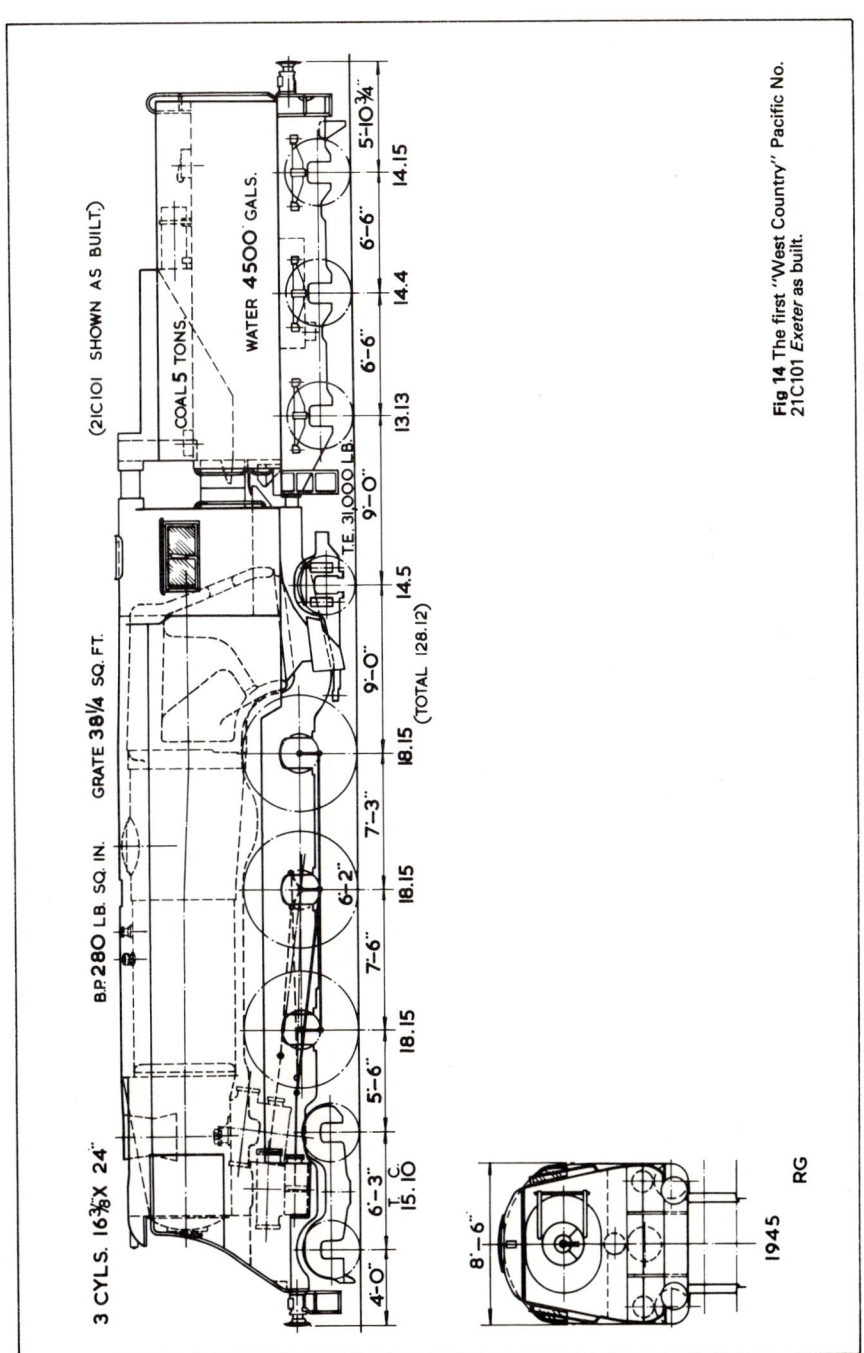

3 CYLS. 16⅜ X 24"   B.P. 280 LB. SQ. IN.   GRATE 38¼ SQ. FT.

(21C101 SHOWN AS BUILT.)

COAL 5 TONS.   WATER 4500 GALS.

4'-0"   6'-3"   5'-6"   7'-6"   6'-2"   7'-3"   9'-0"   9'-0"   13.13   6'-6"   6'-6"   5'-10¾"
15.10   18.15   18.15   18.15   14.5   14.4   14.15
T.C.   (TOTAL 128.12)   T.E. 31,000 LB.

8'-6"

1945   RG

Fig 14 The first "West Country" Pacific No. 21C101 *Exeter* as built.

67

himself (but didn't) for all the fuss they had been through with the weight of the original "Merchant Navies."

A feature of the "Black Staniers" was their ubiquity; Sir William himself used to enjoy recalling that "you see them all over the place, and the drivers like them." Precisely the same thing happened with the "West Country" Pacifics. With the weight right down to specification and the easy riding and freedom from hammer-blow the Civil Engineer had no fears in allowing them the freedom of the road far beyond the erstwhile sacred Pacific territories and they had nearly 90% route availability. The Southern Railway had classed track beyond Exeter (seen from Waterloo) as secondary, with generally shorter trains except in high holiday season but none the less with big demands of power for brisk running: this was exactly what the "West Country" Pacifics provided. Deep in the West Country, beyond Okehampton and Launceston to Padstow, beyond Barnstaple and the 1 in 36 Morthoe bank to Ilfracombe, over the delicate Meldon viaduct or through GWR territory to Plymouth where no *Great Bear* was allowed, the "West Country" Pacifics were all over the place doing their stuff, and everybody was delighted to see them. They also did their bit on the old Somerset & Dorset line to Bath from Bournemouth; and when they were on the Salisbury run and were unexpectedly given a "Merchant Navy" loading they seemed to think nothing of it.

"Things which never fail may be over-designed," Bulleid remarked philosophically when some frame cracks appeared on the "West Countries." Other tribulations included the unsatisfactory drop section of the rocking grates and the need for further deflector experiments to improve the look-out, impaired by the 8ft 6in cab width. Then Traffic said sorry, we don't want the engines on the restricted Hastings line after all, so 21C171 and later engines had 9ft cabs.

Most classes of steam engines were gone over from time to time and various improvements tried out, major and minor. Bulleid's engines had their share, two interesting major items being the mechanical stoker and the oil-firing experiments. Both were taken up in good time by Bulleid, who had warnings from his Government contacts and through the Railway Executive Committee about possible coming failures in the quantity and quality of coal supplies.

Several factors hinted at the desirability of a mechanical stoker on a "Merchant Navy." The grate area was only just short of the 50sq ft at which firing aid was considered justifiable; electric and diesel influences were beginning to make the manual firing job look disproportionately heavy; mechanising might permit more finesse in firing and thereby save coal; and, of growing importance, it might allow the use of lower-grade coal. Some of these factors had prompted the pulverised coal (please! not just "coal dust") experiments on the Great Central in 1922 which Bulleid had noted as a dead loss. This time he fitted 21C5 *Canadian Pacific* with an American Berkeley stoker. It had a crusher and a conveyor driven by a steam engine whose speed could be regulated up to a staggering 5tons per hour maximum feed to the steam discharge jets in the firebox. Though the Berkeley stoker followed its American habit of shoving unburnt coal straight through the chimney, it performed well and permitted the successful use of the lower grade coal emerging from increased mechanisation of the mines. To reduce spark-throwing the blast pipe nozzles were opened out to 2⅞in diameter and a thinner fire employed, after which came 18 months of practically faultless daily performance on the "Atlantic Coast Express." The experiment only failed when later supplies of the low grade fuel either contained lumps too big for the crusher or had excessive clinker and ash content.

During the Government-inspired 1946 panic to use oil for locomotive firing, the Southern Railway's quota included 20 "West Country" Pacifics. The first conversion, to 21C119, was not satisfactory, the equipment being more suited to a narrow firebox. The second conversion, however, to 21C136, made use of the Laidlaw-Drew "Swirlyflo" burner and was a complete success, delighting all firemen. With this triumph came the order to stop using oil and revert to coal *at once*.

Spark-throwing remained a problem with the hard-working Pacifics, all modifications tried having impaired the steaming. Then, years later, came the Giesl Oblong Ejector. Its arrangement of seven nozzles in line, with a long, narrow single oblong chimney, fixed in correct alignment and surrounded by a fine wire mesh spark-arrester, permitted greater exit velocity with reduced back-pressure. It gave better steaming, it arrested sparks, and its narrow exhaust band cleared the engine better. It fulfilled Bulleid's prophecy that a further development of the Lemaitre would be seen. Engine No. 34064 *Fighter Command* alone was fitted and proved the claims; but it was 1962 and curtains for expenditure on steam.

Experiments that should have been successfully completed were those

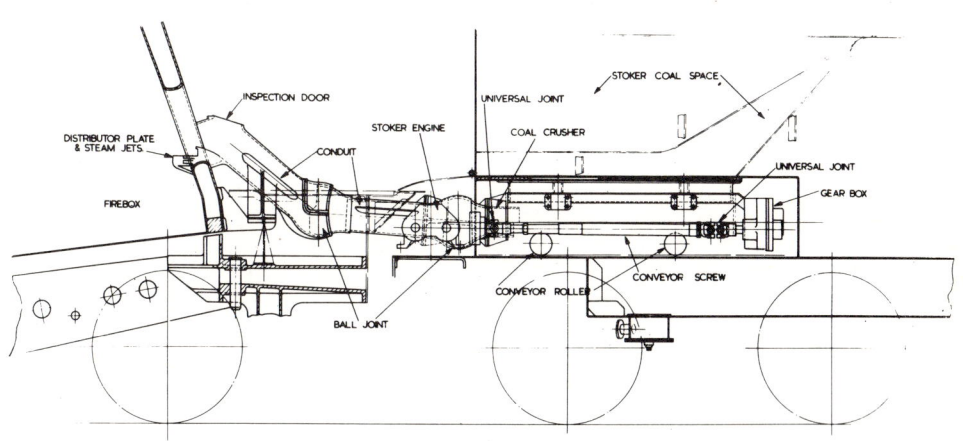

Fig 15 The American Berkeley stoker as fitted to No. 21C5.

aimed at reducing oil losses, increasing the accessibility of pipes and fittings under the cladding, improving the sanding and taming the steam reverser. Presumably they would have been if there had been major complaints.

And how about a control experiment? I once asked my father why he did not build one of the Pacifics with conventional valve gear. He said there was no point; the engines were perfectly good as they were, and besides it could not be done within the Engineer's weight limits. Even if it could, they would be rougher on the track and would not ride so well.

10

The 0-6-0

In 1941 there came from the Operating Dept. the well-known old cry of "More 0-6-0s — quick." Bulleid could see a lot of sense in supplying approximately what was asked for. The Maunsell Class Q 0-6-0s were good engines, had been improved by blast-pipe and chimney modifications, and could be further improved in motion and cylinder design. Moreover, if stringent weight-saving were applied a larger boiler could be fitted. Ellson was therefore consulted and he agreed to a maximum axle loading of 18 tons, adding the fervent hope that they might manage a ton or two less. Accordingly, with Government permission to build a batch of 40, Bulleid and Cocks together went over the possibilities and gave a remit to the Drawing Office of which the salient points were:

(1) Get in the largest possible boiler probably using "Nelson" class flanging blocks.
(2) Pay special attention to the cylinders, passages and motion to give a free-running engine suitable also for passenger duties.
(3) Aim at a weight of 51 tons, this being only 1½ tons more than the Q class; and make a virtue out of necessity by (a) extending weight-saving techniques, mainly by wider use of welding and (b) eliminating all non-essentials, remembering the shortage of materials and applying *austerity*.

The last of these points particularly struck home. When a new engine turns out overweight a black mark is always, and rightly, chalked up against the Drawing Office. But of course Drawing Offices were not born yesterday, and when it happens on one engine they close ranks to be darned sure it will not happen on the next. They had squirmed more than anybody when large holes had to be cut and metal chopped away from the Pacifics and fancy nameplates discarded; and though they knew perfectly well that 54 tons was the permitted maximum for this new Q1 class, they determined to hit the desirable 51 tons.

Design went along smoothly and is quite racily described by Bulleid in his talk to the Mutual Improvement Class at Feltham, see Appendix 2. The Stephenson's motion was designed to give 6⅞in travel with, after the usual tinkering on the motion model, very nearly equally good valve events in

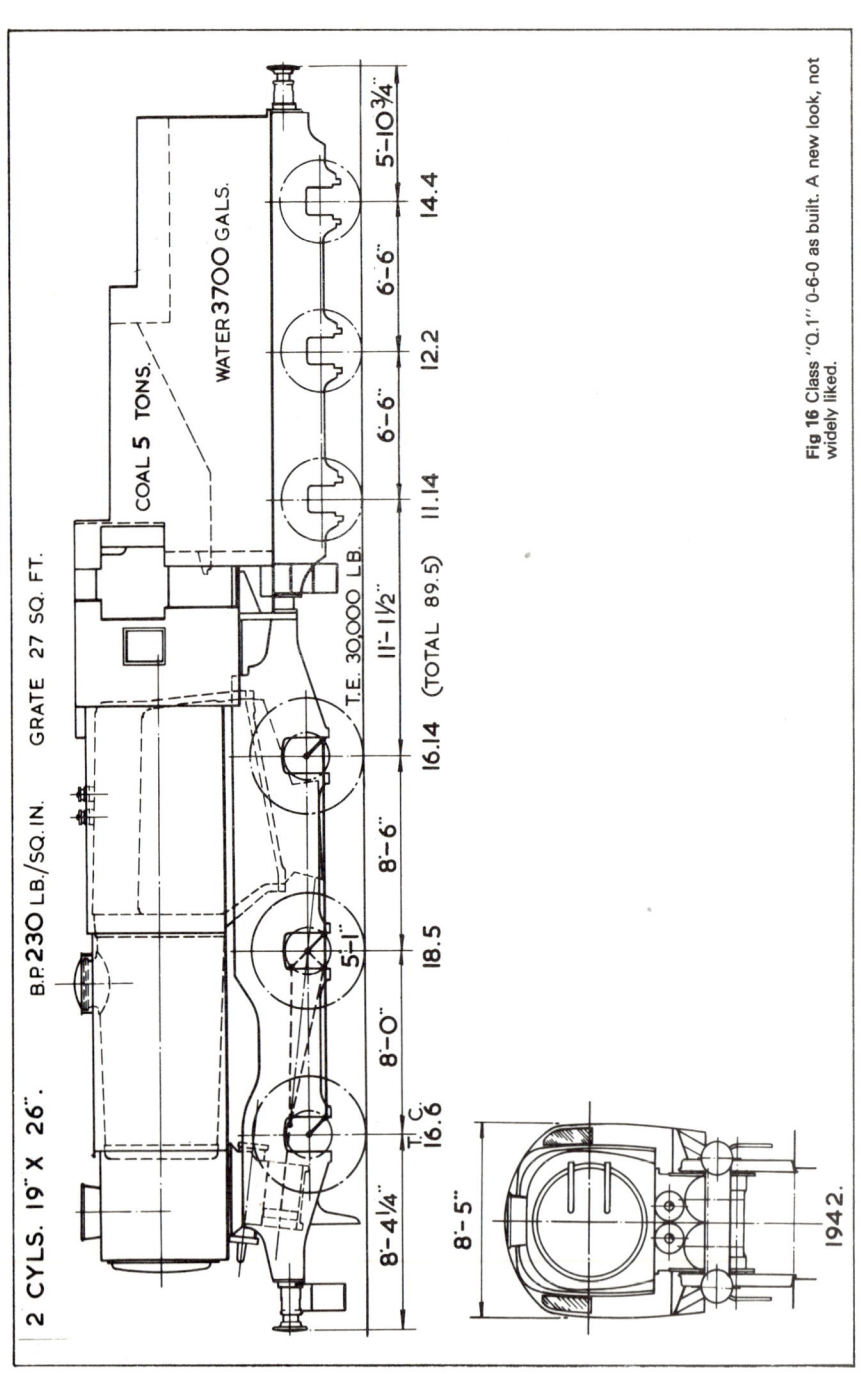

2 CYLS. 19" X 26".   B.P. 230 LB./SQ. IN.   GRATE 27 SQ. FT.

COAL 5 TONS.

WATER 3700 GALS.

T.E. 30000 LB.

8-4¼"   8'-0"   5-1"   8-6"   11-1½" (TOTAL 89.5)   6'-6"   6'-6"   5-10¾"
T.C. 16.6   18.5   16.14   11.14   12.2   14.4

8-5"

1942.

Fig 16 Class "Q.1" 0-6-0 as built. A new look, not widely liked.

72

forward as in reverse running. Bulleid got the Drawing Office to examine the possibility of enclosing it for oil-bath lubrication, but the available space was so small and so crowded that the idea was quite impracticable. Nothing was re-designed for re-design's sake. The steam reverser (lighter than manual and better for shunting) was the ex-LSWR Drummond design. The brake gear was straight from the Q class, which was a mistake as it was inadequate compared with the increased power of the engine. The boiler, designed for 220psi, looked so good to Bulleid that he arbitrarily increased the pressure to 230psi. Weight was saved and manufacture simplified by frame-supported sheeting over the fibreglass boiler lagging and by an unconventional flat-bottomed smokebox. The cab mated with a tender cab and slides were provided for enclosing the sides during the blackout. The engine part of the cab roof was shorter than usual and this was rather disarmingly explained by the draughtsman concerned; "I got to the edge of the paper."

With *austerity* writ large in everyone's mind, footplate and splashers became archaic anachronisms and were jettisoned enthusiastically. Traditionalists got rather misty-eyed when they recalled, for example, those french windows on the Aspinall Atlantics through which a driver, if sufficiently thin and intrepid, could venture to inspect funny noises coming from Joy's valve gear. "This sort of thing is no longer necessary," said Bulleid, firmly, digging out a good reason for what was convenient. No ideas were forthcoming for any off-setting, light-weight beauty treatment and so the chimney and dome were done as came naturally — which was not by any means fancy.

No one in the team had recently read I.K. Brunel's letter of March 6, 1838 to Thos. E. Harrison of South Shields which concludes:

"and lastly let me call your attention to the appearance — we have a splendid engine of Stephenson's it would be a beautyful ornament in the most elegant drawing room and we have another of Quaker-like simplicity carried even to shabbyness but very possibly as good an engine but the difference in the care bestowed by the engine man, the favour in which it is held by others and even oneself, not to mention the public — is striking — a *plain* young lady however amiable is apt to be neglected now your engine is capable of being made very handsome — and *it ought to be so.*"

Everyone concerned was highly delighted that their confident predictions proved right when, early in March 1942, the first Q1 class 0-6-0, No C1, weighed 51¼ tons. Their delight was sustained when the engine rode, steamed and pulled with much of the Bulleid panache established by the "Merchant Navies." Not only had they designed the most powerful 0-6-0 in the business, but they had achieved a better boiler capacity and a far better distribution of weight then ever before, shooting down the claim that there was no more scope left in 0-6-0 design. If, under wartime austerity conditions, you had to get maximum locomotive power from minimum materials, Q1 was undoubtedly the way to do it. An extra cause for satisfaction was that the weight on the leading axle was down to 16¼tons compared with 18 tons on the Q class.

Fed by Southern Railway publicity, the Press put over the *austerity* angle, which was also used on greetings cards for the New Year, 1943. Then it was less appropriately applied to, and stuck to, the war-horse 2-8-0s designed by R.A. Riddles for the War Department. They appeared in January 1943.

Users of the Q1s took readily to them on account of their steaming and performance, though they asked pithy questions such as "Are they safe when running tender-first at 70mph?" Bulleid said yes to this and then rode tender-first at 75mph to demonstrate, using engine No. C36, whose regulator and brake controls were duplicated at the fireman's side by a series of levers to assist reverse running. It also furnished an excellent advertisement for the tender cab, which removed the deathly chill of running tender-first in the winter.

Another worry was loss of water from the tender, very aggravating to a fireman. Ashford rather overdid weight saving on the tender, the thin bottom plate tending to buckle under the heavy hurly-burly of maximum daily use, causing cracks and then leaks. There was also poor performance from the displacement lubricators serving valves and pistons, so mechanical lubricators were later fitted. But the biggest worry was the brake power being so low on so powerful an engine; it was accentuated by comparative tests in 1943 between a Q1 and a 4-6-0 goods Class S15 over the long 1 in 250 downgrade from Basingstoke to Eastleigh. There were some dramatic moments of zero drama on these tests, with Bulleid and Attwell on the Q1 footplate coasting at 45mph and being pushed by a 900 ton train of non-fitted wagons. The handbrake was first applied, to be sure the loose-coupled train was bunched up against the engine and incidentally to avoid shaking up the guard too much. When the full brake application was made, nothing seemed to happen for several long seconds. It took nearly three miles to stop and they over-ran Wallers Ash home signal by just over a mile. In comparison, the S15 stopped within 1¾ miles. So the increasing of Q1 brake power soon got onto Durban's job list in the Drawing Office; but there were always more important jobs and no loud shouting from Traffic and so it never got done.

In practice the engines were used well within their capacity and always had bags of reserve power. They were rather given to rolling at high speeds and were formally limited to 55 mph, though often timed quite a bit faster, confidently echoing the 75 mph trial.

Non-users of the Q1s reacted very much as forecast by I.K. Brunel. Some were affronted. Some immediately said they were speechless. W.A. Stanier said "I don't believe it," but then realised he was looking at a real photograph and that it was uncommonly like the cheaper range (the austerity range) of gauge 0 tinplate clockwork models and said "Where's the key?" These were good-humoured comments compared with some made by less talented observers who said, in effect, "It's different — we loathe it." W.H. Hutchinson was giving one of them a hard professional look on Redhill station when a porter confided "That's a Japanese engine." Interestingly, painters and sculptors who produced similarly chunky departures from the traditional kept quiet, and defence came from sober appraisal by thoughtful editors and contributors in the *Railway Gazette* for April 17 1942 and *Modern Transport* for October 3. The travelling public came to recognise them as good time-keepers on their few passenger turns, and I expect most people got used to their appearance because all forty were handed over to the nation on January 1 1948, and no one ever attempted to pretty them up.

All good designers thrive on ratios and other comparisons, and one method favoured by Bulleid was to superimpose engine diagrams. Both the standard LMS 2-8-0 and the Riddles Austerity 2-8-0 were so superimposed on the Q1, which walked away with the honours for tractive-effort-per-lb *and* per-£, though it must be admitted that the comparison given in Appendix 2 is rather naughty in penalising the 2-8-0 for carrying more coal and a bit more water on the tender. The broad comparisons are given in the table below.

0-6-0-s & 2-8-0s Compared

	Maunsell 0-6-0 Q	Bulleid 0-6-0 Q1	LNER 0-6-0 J39	LMS 0-6-0 4F	Govt 2-8-0 Austerity	LMS 2-8-0 8F
Boiler pressure (psi)	200	230	180	175	225	225
Cylinder dia x stroke (ins)	19 x 26	19 x 26	20 x 26	20 x 26	19x 28	18½ x 28
Wheel diameter (ft-ins)	5-1	5-1	5-2	5-3	4-8½	4-8½
Combined heating surfaces (sq ft)	1432	1690	1670	1404	1991	1880
Superheater (sq ft)	185	218	272	246	311	230
Grate area (sq ft)	21.9	27	26	21.1	28.6	28.7
Tractive effort (lb)	26,160	30,000	25,664	24.555	34,215	32,438
Engine weight, Working order (tons)	49½	51¼	57¾	48¾	70¼	72
Ratios — Tractive effort / Engine Weight (lb per ton)	528	585	450	503	488	450
Tractive effort / Grate area (lb per sq ft)	1190	1100	990	1160	1195	1130

The first ratio gives a good measure of the Capital cost per lb. of tractive effort. The second indicates the demand made on the grate to support the tractive effort. Q1 comes out cheapest, and second-least demanding on its grate area.

It was H.G. Ivatt who first spotted the blindingly obvious fact that tender engines with tender cabs and intended to run tender-first should have at least the same vision cut-aways as is typical on the bunkers of tank engines. What makes it the more remarkable that Bulleid, Cocks and the Drawing Office never spotted this is that they got part way there by providing an opening for the fire irons through which they claimed rear vision was good. But in practice such an opening could only be kept clear of coal and other debris by removing the outer sheeting; and it is not surprising that the Running people found the lookout inadequate for high-speed tender-first running.

All 40 Q1 0-6-0s were built straight off at Brighton in one batch completed in 1942. None ever gave any serious trouble, nor received any notable modification, and most of them were good for another twenty years when scrapped in the 1960s.

11

Southern Railway to Southern Region

The Southern released its General Manager, Gilbert Szlumper, to the War Office at the outbreak of war. In consequence, Eustace Missenden was appointed acting General Manager in addition to being Traffic Manager, and John Elliot became Deputy General Manager. Both these appointments lasted till the end of the Southern Railway and both were advantageous to Bulleid. An excellent *rapport* and unity of purpose developed between them, and particularly between Bulleid and Missenden so that, for example, they spoke with one voice when convincing Government Departments that they had to build their new mixed-traffic Pacifics during 1940 — carefully remembering not to call them express passenger engines except in the seclusion of Waterloo. Equally, they worked extremely hard and successfuly during the darkest days of the war, helping the Government and the Services, undertaking the mammoth transportation tasks including the evacuation from Dunkirk and the D-day invasion, and keeping going throughout the blitz and the flying bombs in their very exposed "railway front line." There was a nice touch of defiance when they re-opened the LB&SC Brighton Works as a manufacturing unit in 1940.

During the intensive bombing from September 1940 to May 1941, 92 incidents affected the running lines in the 2¼ miles from Waterloo to Queens Road alone, and the New Cross area fared little better. George Ellson's men repaired them all with astonishing speed, many quite serious night incidents being made good in time to carry the morning traffic. Parallel prodigious efforts were made in the Works so that they could add a huge war effort to their usual repair and building programme. The major jobs included 172 launches and landing craft, 500 fitted-out bodies for mobile workshop lorries, 200 Horsa glider tail-planes, 80 bomb trolleys (the first one designed and manufactured in 60 hours), 1510 2-pounder gun barrels, 240 2-inch rocket-gun assemblies, pontoon bridges and many railway vehicles. The full illustrated list was given in a September 1944 report on the war work of the CME's Department, crediting E.A.W. Turbett the Asst. CME, F. Munns the Eastleigh Works Superintendent, and Works Managers M.S. Hatchell at Ashford and O.G. Hackett at Brighton and Lancing.

Early in 1942, after the Q1 had been designed and the "Merchant Navy" modifications completed, some Eastleigh draughtsmen began to feel that their work on locomotive design was not vital to the war effort, so they asked the Ministry of Labour to be transferred to direct war work, which was agreed. But Bulleid felt that the locomotive work, part of the huge SR transport contribution, was just as vital and he went to the Minister of Labour and had the decision reversed. He then transferred six Eastleigh and two Brighton draughtsmen to Waterloo, where their first jobs included preparations for the manufacture of Stanier 2-8-0s in the SR workshops. On several occasions, as when presenting gallantry awards at Deal in September 1942, Bulleid emphasised and got visiting Government Officials to endorse that "Transport was absolutely of first importance and everyone engaged on it was as much in the industrial front line as it was possible to be."

Throughout the war period the SR Works kept up their normal loco repair work and also completed 20 Pacifics, 40 Q1s and 130 2-8-0s for the LMS and LNER. They built 12,000 wagons. Bulleid himself solicited some of the war work and "foreign" railway work and he progressed it all and sought and obtained great enthusiasm for it in all the Works, founding lively Production Committees to give the shop floor a real voice. He was the instigator of Works Open days to provide cash for charities and to add interest and appreciation to the job. He was also at pains to ensure that the Southern's war effort was properly understood and acknowledged. After completing 64 2-8-0s, one was demonstrated to the Minister of War Transport, Lord Leathers, at Charing Cross before he was given a lunch with the Works and Stores Staffs concerned. Bulleid took the opportunity of emphasising the Works skills (and the SR engines rather than the 2-8-0s) by presenting the Minister with two small model locomotives — a "Merchant Navy" and a Q1. He stressed output again when he opened the National Savings Centre at Ashford Works in February 1944, saying "The Ministry of Labour requires more and more output. This means more and more wages which will help everyone to save more."

In addition to his two-monthly Works Managers meetings at HQ, Bulleid often visited all four Works in the same week, involving much driving, and much of it in black-out conditions as he seldom left a Works before late afternoon. The Good Cause and the great contribution they were making to it kept up his spirits. Once in 1942, making very good time along the Kingston by-pass in his 1929 fabric-bodied Crossley UR 5164, of which he was always very fond, he soliloquised and actually wrote down the result whilst held up soon after:

SOLILOQUY on KINGSTON BY-PASS.
Two letters on her plates only
What on the road is more lonely
Than my old, old Crossley?

The silent Rolls, the lordly Daimler,
The skittish Jaguar, the fleeting Rover
Now seem to ignore her.

Were she some ten years younger
She'd show them she'd been a runner.
None in her day could quite hold her.

Here is the open road and space
No need to spur her to show her pace
High speed alone is her solace.

Two letters only
What is less lonely
Than my old Crossley?

All this driving was too much of a strain and so the Southern provided a chauffeur. Cars were not easy to come by but Bulleid got hold of two almost identical Humber Snipes for himself and the General Manager. Characteristically he gave what he thought was the better of the two to the boss, but after a while a semi-serious rumour reached him that Missenden thought he had kept the best for himself. So what to do? Simple. He had them switched. As he later remarked, "Eustace Missenden was very pleased with himself and I got the better car." (This is not a genuine Bulleidism, being far more typical of H.G. Ivatt, but perhaps that only proves that in some ways they are all alike.) The Bulleid chauffeur from May 1945 till September 30 1949 was A.F. Hills, who drove him 59,700 miles in that time. He also travelled a lot by train, but oddly enough he could work better in a car where nothing seemed to distract him.

In 1943 it became clear that the design office and most of the CME's Headquarters department would best be centralised at Brighton, and with Marsh and Richardson established there Bulleid switched to a female secretary at Waterloo, Miss Anderson, who had so acted for Maunsell and knew the ropes. "Andy" had joined the Southern at Ashford in 1924 and always took meticulous notes to avoid forgetting anything. Often Bulleid spent the day at one of the Works or the Brighton Office and only returned to Waterloo around 5 o'clock, when Andy promptly rustled up the standing order of China tea and Jacobs water biscuits and then jotted down his new list of tasks. Occasionally, sipping tea, he would take time off from the immediate business to say "Good gracious, Miss Anderson, there's no need to write that down. I don't like all this note-taking, it weakens the memory."

The Southern's genial Chairman Robert Holland-Martin died in 1944 and was succeeded by Col. Eric Gore-Brown. Both were enthusiasts of the Bulleid Pacifics. So of course was Missenden, knighted in June 1944, just before D-Day, the culmination of the Southern's mighty transport task. Then started the wearing months of the flying bombs, causing their first damage to SR property on June 15. They were a constant aggressive menace, often uncomfortably close. Bulleid entirely ignored them despite being within range, though he had plenty of trips out of range as when the second batch of "Merchant Navies" started operating in the West and he gave a talk about them to the Mutual Improvement Class at Salisbury, taking with him the working model of the valve gear and a number of slides and greatly enjoying the resulting questions and discussion.

As the flying bomb and V2 menace faded, victory thoughts began to stir and with them the post-war Railway policies. The Southern decided to build passenger tanks, shunters for Southampton docks, and a further 50 light Pacifics by the end of 1947, which would bring the total to 70. The decision was taken by the General Manager on the recommendation of the Traffic Manager and then approved by the Board. The quantity of engines ordered had nothing to do with the CME, who was not responsible for operating them. So any criticisms that too many Pacifics were ordered should be levelled against Missenden and Elliot and the SR Board. Their convincing reply was that they wanted a decent collection of powerful modern engines. They were not in full agreement with the Midland/LMS policy of "exactly" matching engines against duties, partly because they could see that this system went haywire whenever a Shed was short of one of the more powerful

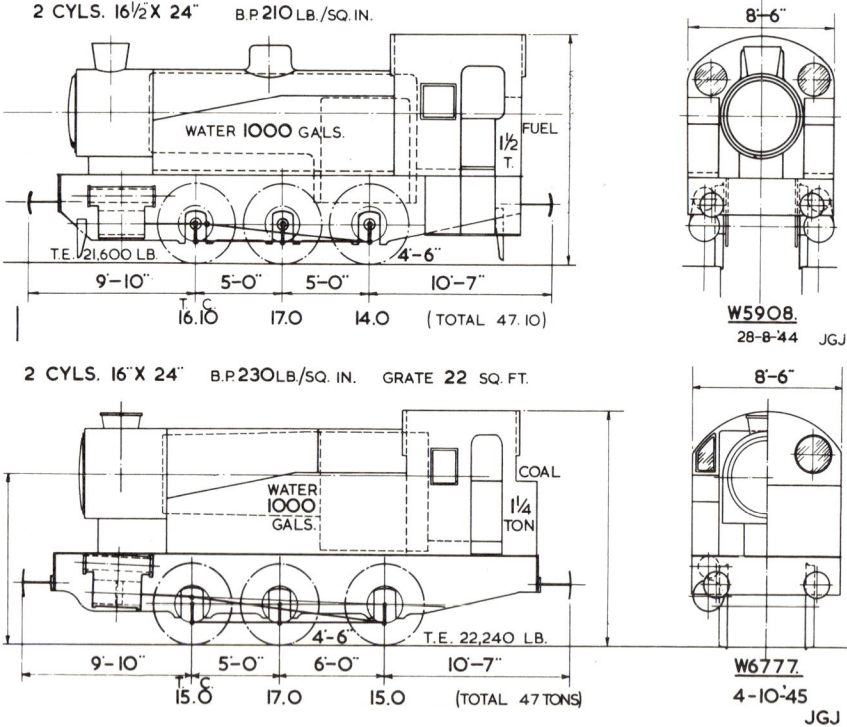

Fig 17 (top) First shot at a new tank engine for Southampton Docks, the building of ten being agreed in January 1945.

Fig 18 (above) Final shot at a Docks shunter in October 1945, simplified and lightened and tractive effort improved. But never built due to economical purchase of surplus 0-6-0s ex USA war effort.

80

engines, and partly because they were not impressed by LMS passenger train time-keeping. Both the senior executives concerned were promoted to high positions after Nationalisation.

More tangible post-war signs appeared in 1945. In January the first boat train left Victoria for Newhaven adequately hauled by Ivatt/Marsh Atlantic No. 2038 *Portland Bill* and including the almost forgotten comfort of a dining car. Ahead of their full scale return on the Dover run, trials were made with 450-ton trains hauled by "Merchant Navy" Pacifics — their prime duty — and the 90 minute timing was established. Then the first "West Country" Pacifics appeared, soon to demonstrate their ability to flatten Mortehoe bank. Everyone was pleased that orders were on the Works for a lot more Pacifics. Or perhaps not everyone: at the Southern Railway Annual General Meeting in March 1945 a shareholder told the Chairman "I hope no more streamline monstrosities will be seen on this line again." Col. Gore-Brown was affronted but calm as he replied that "they have been doing the most marvellous work and I will not promise you for one single instant that we shall not have some more of them." (After all, there were 70 more on order). The shareholder had one last shot: "All I can say is that you can get absolutely equal power without covering the engine with biscuit tins." At least he had the originality to avoid the conventional 'spam-can' or 'flannel-jacket' jibe.

The slight relaxation after VE day in May and VJ day in August 1945 permitted a bit more time for peripheral activities and in August Bulleid made another trip to G.L. Nicholson's cool little railway empire on the Isle of Wight, presenting various awards including a retirement gift to R. Sweetman, Loco Foreman at Ryde, who had worked there for 55 years. "He possesses one of the greatest attributes of a good foreman," said Bulleid, "that of persuading those under him, by his example, to work willingly, conscientiously and well."

Though the CME's department remained at Brighton, all the Chief Officers were back at Waterloo by the end of 1945. It looked a bit dingy, thought Bulleid, with every office uniformly dark green to waist height and pale green above, a scheme thought very modern in 1924. He had his painted white throughout, causing a minor sensation. "It will show any marks," said Miss Anderson. "Then they can be cleaned off," Bulleid briskly replied, characteristically countering any implied defect in the adopted plan.

The Chief Officers and the Board were engrossed in speeding-up post-war recovery and the fight against the looming threat of Nationalisation, both described by the Chairman at the March 1946 AGM. In May the Deputy Chairman, Henry Brooke, took charge of the anti-nationalisation plans and met his opposite numbers on the other railways. Unfortunately he found no will to fight in the LMS and LNER, whose falling coal and freight haulage receipts showed little hope of future profits. The only forward-looking inter-company plan was for a greatly improved North-South link through London on which Brooke again represented the Southern, but it proved an abortive concept. On its own, the profitable Southern was planning electrification of the Kent coast lines and the secondary routes to Brighton, new cross-Channel steamers, modernisation of Southampton docks, and of course the CME's new locomotives and carriages, including the latest electric and diesel-electric locomotives. These were specifically announced by Missenden in November 1946 as "the first steps to replace steam by electric or diesel-electric traction." Moreover, the Southern always seemed to have something to show: the 'Golden Arrow', personally hauled by 21C1 *Channel Packet,* made a very spirited reappearance in May 1946. In October No. 21C18 *British India Line* whisked the first post-war 400-ton all-Pullman 'Bournemouth Belle' to Southampton and Bournemouth in a minute or two under the 2hr 5min schedule.

But Missenden's diesel thoughts were very real, and were strengthening. In June he had sent out the Southern's "Delegation to North America" with the remit "to review and report on recent advances in railway practice in USA and Canada, with particular reference, as a result of their visit, to the possible use of diesel traction on the Southern Railway as an alternative — or partial alternative — to further electrification." The four young men of the delegation were:

J.L. Harrington for the General Manager
S.A. Fitch for the Superintendent of Operation
M.S. Hatchell for the Chief Mechanical Engineer
S.B. Warder for the Chief Electrical Engineer (C.M. Cock)

Their report dated September 20 1946 broadly recommended limiting future electrification to high-density traffic routes and operating all the others with diesel-electric locomotives and perhaps railcars.

Naturally a strong pro-diesel camp developed from this well-reasoned report, headed by Missenden, Elliot and Cock and only restrained by the fact that the most powerful diesel locomotive obtainable was of 1,600 hp against a requirement of 2,500. The facile idea of using two diesels with one driver made the capital cost fantastic in comparison with steam, though of course it was an excellent way to learn about diesels. In the anti-diesel camp Bulleid was rather a lone figure. Though he saw as clearly as anybody that it was only a matter of time before a diesel locomotive of 2,500 or 3,000 hp was developed, and that these powers were unattainable with steam under UK conditions, nevertheless he was horrified at the capital cost involved, at the rejecting of home-grown fuel, and at the suggestion that steam had no more to offer.

A steam stronghold needing a helping hand after the war was the Romney, Hythe & Dymchurch Railway, which fed useful quantities of passenger traffic to the Southern. Bulleid and MacLeod visited them in 1946 and undertook to repair two engines at Ashford and to build two "decent-sized" bogie tenders for them. Top SR brass later paid their small friend a good-will visit, during which Bulleid could not help enthusiastically advising that "What you really need is a couple of small 'Merchant Navies'." Missenden agreed on the spot. But it became obviously impolitic to add such a pair to the Southern's building programme, with nationalisation looming so large and so much in the thoughts of the Government.

The Minister of Transport visited various Railway Works including Brighton, and another activity was the setting up of a Committee "to investigate Railway operation, to ensure the utmost fluidity throughout the system and see that the capacity of rolling stock and Workshops is used to the best advantage." Bulleid and T.W. Royle, an LMS vice-president, were appointed to this Committee. What did it do? The only Bulleid job I could trace was his early 1947 visit to the LNER Shed at Haymarket, Edinburgh, where all the Scottish Pacifics and V2s lived. He looked through the Engine Repair Book with the Shed master, G.H.K. Lund, and expressed concern at the amount of attention demanded by inside big ends. That really deserves an exclamation mark!

The inevitability of nationalisation utterly exasperated Bulleid and he found welcome relief in his extra work as President of the Institution of Mechanical Engineers. He presented his Address in October 1946 and used the occasion to outline a CME's duties, to specify improvements achieved with the Pacifics, to list the famous desiderata* for a modern steam locomotive foreshadowing the "Leader," and to summarise and illustrate the Southern Railway's Workshops' war effort. Size for size, Bulleid's was probably the outstanding wartime production achievement by a railway.

Prominent among Bulleid's stalwart helpers were the Works Managers and Turbett, promoted from Works Manager Eastleigh to Assistant CME in May 1942. Turbett was very good with Labour and Administration and improving manufacturing facilities, but he lacked design experience and had no steadying influence on his Chief's designs. He contributed to the Southern's outstanding advances in welding techniques and applications, and when the scale of work suggested switching from traditional oxygen cylinders to a liquid oxygen plant he went with the Stores Superintendent A.B. MacLeod to see the set-up at Crewe and collect all the data from R.C. Bond.

*(1) To be able to run over the majority of the Company's lines.

(2) To be capable of working all classes of trains up to speeds of 90 mph.

(3) To have its whole weight available for braking and the highest possible percentage thereof for adhesion.

(4) To be equally suitable for running in both directions without turning, with unobstructed look-out.

(5) To be ready for service at short notice.

(6) To be almost continuously available.

(7) To be suitable for complete "common use."

(8) To run not less than 100,000 miles between general overhauls with little or no attention at the running sheds.

(9) To cause minimum wear and tear to the track.

(10) To use substantially less fuel and water per drawbar horsepower developed.

When things further hotted up in the post-war arena of 1946, Bulleid promoted Hatchell from Works Manager Ashford to be his Principal Assistant at Brighton. The CME's department at Waterloo then consisted only of his Presence, post-box, and *pied-à-terre* for Headquarters meetings. Its staff consisted of Miss Anderson, who soon shook it by leaving to get married. Brighton was the natural venue for Bulleid's farewell presentation to her, at which he dropped a rare clanger by praising her "loyal service with the Company for 22 years." "I still remember the gasp that went round the room as they worked out my age," she recollected in 1975.

CMEs often receive advice on how to do their work better, sometimes from most unexpected quarters such as Sir Sam Fay, sprightly at 89 and really a Southern man, having started his railway career as booking clerk at Kingston in 1872 before becoming General Manager of the Great Central in 1902. He wrote to the *Railway Gazette*, for all CMEs to read, about his Provisional Patent No. 24294/46 covering a six-wheeled locomotive, the front axle driven by an ex-aircraft surplus engine and the rear axle by an air turbine fed from a forward-facing duct. The procedure suggested was to get up speed with the aircraft engine and then the rush of the wind would take over and drive the turbine. The diagram showed quite clearly how it worked. Yet it never went beyond a Provisional. It reminded Bulleid about trying to explain the rollers at Bawtry.

Another *Railway Gazette* reader reported that many drivers had told him what excellent engines the "West Countries" were, their only disadvantage being the poor look-out, worsened by clinging exhaust steam. He therefore suggested changing to oil-firing and turning the engine round so its chimney was next to the tender, and then building a new front to the existing, reversed cab. Utter disaster would have followed this proposal because the Government soon countermanded their 1946 oil-burning directive — a great disappointment to Bulleid and perhaps to the cause of steam.

Early 1947 was a time of many trials: the worst winter weather in memory, chronic and growing shortages of fuel and basic materials, no easement of rationing, altogether a dispiriting check to post-war betterment. For Bulleid a grave addition to these anxieties was the fact that his only daughter was suffering unhappy matrimonial complexities; these caused worries at home and wounded pride, very hard to bear and uncomfortably expensive, and they ultimately clouded also the first year of his retirement.

There were compensations at work as the winter at last lifted. The Southern Railway in conjunction with the Air Ministry agreed names, starting with *Winston Churchill*, for a batch of "West Country" Pacifics to be used in the south-east over which occurred the main combat commemorated by the "Battle of Britain" class. The appearance of these new Pacifics was in remarkable contrast to the July 1947 decision by the LNER Loco and Traffic Committee to replace 32 Pacifics by diesel-electrics.

In June the 'Devon Belle' Pullman was inaugurated, a train of twelve Pullman cars including the observation car at the back, dividing at Exeter for Plymouth and Ilfracombe. Then the last of the traditional SR links with the Continent was restored when the 'Night Ferry' steamed out of Victoria on December 15 led by "Battle of Britain" 21C156 *Croydon* — piloting, oddly enough, a Wainwright/Maunsell Class L1 4-4-0.

It was Bulleid's idea to lay on a proper celebration for the Centenary of Ashford Works in October 1947, only a couple of months before national-isation, and several Southern directors turned up headed by the Deputy Chairman, Henry Brooke. There were also local VIPs and the opener was Lord de L'Isle and Dudley. Good speeches were made, Bulleid striking rather a practical note under the circumstances when he said they were proud of themselves at Ashford and were sure they would be there in 1,600 years' time — just as there were blacksmiths there 1,600 years ago — though they might not be serving a railway. The staff at Ashford Works, he added, who had not allowed production to be interrupted by the noisy exigencies of war, would not allow a change of ownership to perturb them.

Well, the change duly happened on January 1, 1948, and Bulleid was at least glad that Missenden was the Chairman and Riddles the Mechanical Engineer. But he stayed as engrossed as possible in his own work, mainly on the "Leader" and on the Carriage side, and was pleased also to spend three weeks in the Spring in Spain looking over the Rio Tinto mineral line to Huelva on whose engines he had been asked to report. Of course he shared

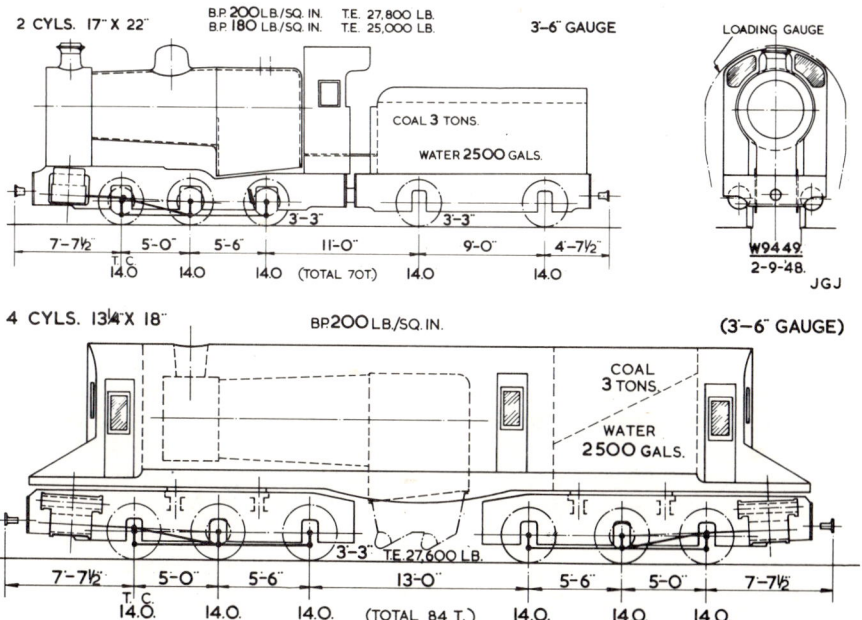

Fig 19 (top) A conventional powerful small-wheeled 0-6-0 for the heavily graded Rio Tinto line.

Fig 20 (above) a modern power-bogie steam locomotive proposal for Rio Tinto. But diesels took over.

in Southern delight at the sparkling performances of the Pacifics in the 1948 interchange trials, and was pleased that the first locomotive naming since nationalisation should be his "Battle of Britain" class No. 21C159, *Sir Archibald Sinclair*, who himself performed the ceremony. And of course he did everything possible by discussion and example to smooth the organisation changes and to ensure that his staff would perform well and happily under the new regime and even teach it things. But the thing was, he had joined the Southern Railway, not the Southern Region of British Railways, and he could already feel what he called non-progressive standardisation starting to interfere. E.S. Cox well described the Bulleid good manners and freedom from hypocrisy at their first meeting in early 1948 after Cox was appointed Executive Officer, Design, for BR:

"He assembled all his principal technical staff for lunch at the Old Ship Hotel at Brighton to meet me. His charm and tact eased a confrontation which could have been difficult and he offered then, and loyally upheld later, every assistance from his people in what we wanted to do. He did not disguise his attitude however, and expressed in an extremely gentlemanly way that he had cast his pearls before swine, and that if we found nothing to learn from his "Merchant Navy" and "Leader," so much the worse for us."

Then, none too soon, in July 1948, Sir James Milne asked him to help his Committee which was examining transport in Eire, and Bulleid was very glad of the chance. Sure enough, it led to the offer of a job as Consulting Engineer to CIE which he formally accepted in April 1949. Accordingly, on May 14, he wrote a characteristic letter to his Chief Regional Officer, John Elliot:

"I wish to retire from the service of British Railways on the 30th September next.
   I would like to say how much I have appreciated being in a position to help in the transfer of the Southern railway to the Railway Executive, and hope I have been of assistance in the difficult period of the change.
   I would also like to pay my tribute to the Chairman of the Railway Executive to whom the major credit must be given for the remarkable work of reorganisation he has carried through with such an absence of trouble. I am proud to have served under him first as General Manager of the Southern Railway and subsequently as Chairman and shall always remember the encouragement and support he unfailingly gave me.
   I wish to put on record too, my appreciation of the help and friendship all the officers of the Region and you in particular have shown me, and of the loyal support given me by my own staff of all grades."

There was a round of farewell parties including one with 66 Foremen and Assistants from the four Works. The Eastleigh Workshops staff gave him a nicely-inscribed gold watch which he particularly treasured. On his very last day with the Southern he was guest of honour at the Boilermakers centenary dinner at Brighton, being always a champion of this craft.

His colleagues, the successful, close-knit Southern team at Waterloo, joined for the occasion by Missenden from Marylebone and led by Elliot, all paid personal tributes: Robertson (Civil), Biddle (Docks & Marine), Cromwell (Labour), Smedley (Legal), Smart (Supt. of Operation), Chrimes (Running), Warder (Electrical), Graseman (Public Relations), MacLeod (Stores), Endicott (Estates), Stockdill (Accounts), Hammett (Commercial) — all had something to say. It was very nostalgic and the euphoria increased with the stream of tributes. They were decidedly genuine and everyone was further delighted by Bulleid's obvious pleasure at moving to a new CME arena where he could carry on without technical interference.

There were also many quiet, private tributes. Part of one which Bulleid found specially pleasing and amusing ran thus:

"Sir.   Wimbledon 26.12.1949

Some time ago I had an interview with you in your room at Waterloo to discuss the position of heaters in the cabs of electric trains. You very nicely fell in with our views and had the heaters put in a convenient place for us and we have had cause to bless you this winter. It is a pity for our sake that you did not stay with us a while longer to complete all the cabs, but it does not stop us from saying "thank you" and wishing you every success in Ireland. After the Interview at Waterloo I "cadged" a ride to Salisbury on one of your engines and enjoyed it very much. As usual, with anything new in the way of locomotion, there are faults found from some and praise from others. I can only speak from an 'armchair critic's' point of view, as I have never handled one, but there is nothing on the old Southern Region to touch the Merchant Navys or West Countrys for getting out of the way for us 'Electrics' to run.

Best wishes for good number of New Years in the Green Isle.

Yours faithfully,
H. Allpress. Motorman."

12

Electrics
and Diesels

As might be expected on a railway like the Southern, where the Electrical side was showing distinct signs of outpacing the Steam, there was some antagonism between the Chief Mechanical Engineer and the Chief Electrical Engineer, who pretended not to be able to understand why he should not design, build and maintain all the mechanical as well as all the electrical parts of the electrified stock. The simple answers were: (1) that in next to no time the railway would have two different sets of mechanical gear doing the same duties; and (2) that there would be an untenable divided responsibility for signing the annual certificate of maintenance for the Board of Trade.

These facts were clearly seen by General Managers, but still H. Jones kept fighting the losing battle against Maunsell and in 1938 A. Raworth started similar skirmishing against Bulleid. "But it wasn't nearly so bad," W. Marsh later recalled, largely due to Bulleid not taking it very seriously because of reassurances from both Missenden and Elliot that the CME would remain the overall mechanical boss.

This featherweight drama, which would have read so entertainingly in a gossip column in a railway magazine, must have alternately amused and annoyed and sometimes been fuelled by the departmental staffs concerned. Luckily it did not prevent the Electrical side starting the design of an electric goods locomotive in London Bridge drawing office in 1937, shortly before Bulleid arrived. It was a good initiative, but with no enthusiasm from Management because the electrified routes were essentially short runs operated by motorised passenger stock and with plenty of steam engines around for freight duties.

Then Bulleid came on the scene and by the end of 1938 he had persuaded Raworth to go for a considerably more ambitious mixed traffic locomotive, suggesting a top speed of 75 mph with about 1,500hp and weight around 100 tons. It would have been interesting to hear Bulleid's reactions if a colleague had tried bettering his steam locomotive specifications. Anyhow, Raworth was certainly not going to say these targets were beyond him, and in taking up the challenge with conviction he had no difficulty (with CME backing) in getting Board sanction for three such locomotives. In collaboration with English Electric he came up with a successful arrangement of six 245hp, 400volt motors supplied from two motor generators which took current at 660volts DC either from third rail or by pantograph from overhead wires, and which were fitted with 1-ton flywheels to maintain power over gaps in the third rail. This gave a further advantage over the conventional resistance controllers in that control was finer, with 26 notches, but had the disadvantage of extra weight and slightly reduced efficiency. The six traction motors gave the locomotive a 1-hour rating horsepower of 1470. Bulleid prescribed 3ft 7in BFB wheels and with a 65-tooth spur gear on each axle mating with 17 teeth on the motor shaft the tractive effort was 45,000lb. The energy stored in the six motors running at speed added to the difficulty of braking and so Bulleid provided clasp brakes with their extra advantage of being easier on the axle bearings. They were operated by 24 small brake cylinders powered by two Westinghouse compressors. Two exhausters were provided for the train brakes, and a 380kW electrode boiler for train heating.

Bulleid designed conventional body, cabs and framing for this locomotive, which he naturally numbered CC1, but he introduced a novel bogie, without bolsters or central spigot and support. Instead there were four segmental bearing pads taking the weight and the traction and braking thrusts, and centring springs.

The preliminary mechanical design work was done by Percy Bollen at Waterloo and sent to Ashford at the end of 1938 for completion. But early in 1939 Bulleid thought progress was too slow and sent Bollen temporarily to Ashford* to speed it up, remarking that he had seen the *Silver Link* designed and built in six months. The small Ashford drawing office completed the design by mid-1939 and Ashford Works completed CC1 in 1941. It was 56¾ft long and weighed 99¾tons. It promptly proved its capability of reaching 75 mph and of handling passenger and 1000 ton freight trains. And it is only fair to add that, when it needed its first general overhaul early in 1947, it had covered 270,000 miles.

CC2 was a replica of CC1, except that it was fitted with dual control in the vain hope of one-man operation. After nationalisation the pair became Nos. 20001 and 20002. The third of the trio sanctioned incorporated many improvements, including more space in the driving cabs and for auxiliaries, and more powerful motors. Its length was 58¼ft, weight 105tons, tractive effort unchanged at 45,000lb and it was completed early in 1949, No. 20003. It hit the news in quite a big way on May 15, 1949, being the first electric locomotive to haul the boat train for the Newhaven-Dieppe service, leaving Victoria at 9.35 am and reaching Newhaven 15min early with the 400ton train.

C.M. Cock succeeded Raworth in 1945 and kept up the battle of electrical versus mechanical one-upmanship and desire for partition. Several good cards were dealt him; close association with English Electric showed

* This temporary posting lasted till 1955 when Bollen went to Brighton on the British Rail Bo-Bo electrics, a lighter but more powerful development of the "Hornbys", as CC1 and CC2 were affectionately known on the Southern.

him the growing acceptance of diesel traction and he knew the same message was getting to Missenden from Trade sources and from the LMS. Then the Government's orders to use oil suggested using oil engines. Moreover there was the sort of joke, probably starting with Raworth, that diesels were really electric locomotives — after all, whether you carried your own diesel generator or picked up the juice from rail or wire, what the hell, both were just electric locomotives. Furthermore, neither needed the unwelcome attention of those CME steam types.

Sir Eustace Missenden rejected all thoughts of letting Cock go it alone, but he accepted the diesel idea and got Board sanction for three experimental main-line diesel-electrics with English Electric equipment, for express passenger services. It could not be said that Bulleid was wildly enthusiastic, but he was not a man to suppress competition, preferring to work in the open and beat them in reasonably fair contest. He had many calculations done at Brighton to demonstrate that a "Merchant Navy" could handle express passenger traffic better than any contemporary electrics or diesel-electrics, but when the decision to build the three diesel-electrics was taken he ensured thorough co-operation with the electrical side.

By July 1947 the main items of equipment were ordered and the project was announced. The locomotives would have 1,600 hp diesel engines with generators powering six axle-hung traction motors. The bodies and underframes to be mounted on two eight-wheel bogies each with three driven axles, 1-Co-Co-1 type. Each locomotive was to be 62ft long and weigh 120 tons, with a driver's cab at each end, and to be so designed that two coupled together could haul 500ton trains at express speeds under the control of one crew. Economies were expected in both fuel cost and engine availability, compared with steam engines. The first use of the new engines would be on the principal express services to Exeter and Plymouth. They would be capable of speeds up to 100 mph. Construction was to start shortly at Brighton Works and they were expected to be in service towards the end of 1948.

This announcement was made earlier than normal, and perhaps more optimistically, on account of nationalisation being only a few months distant. The same page of the SR Magazine announced Missenden's appointment as first Chairman of the Railway Executive of British Railways.

Again it was the small Ashford drawing office, seven strong including its Leading Draughtsman Percy Bollen, whose hard preliminary work, started in October 1946, permitted the timing and accuracy of this published statement of intent about the new diesel-electrics. Bulleid visited them regularly, thought them an excellent team, and saw no reason to hurry the job by expanding the office. Let George Ivatt get his two diesels out first, what did it matter? Anyway they made an obnoxious smell. Nor was C.M. Cock in any hurry, having thoughts of leaving the railway for a job with English Electric. And there was no pressure from above; Missenden had gone and Elliot was not going to get excited about the LMS building a couple of diesels, by the LNER saying they would order a fleet to replace some Pacifics or even by the GWR, who were now saying diesels were OK if hydraulic. Bulleid really only accepted diesels for shunting, so he was more wrapped-up in the design, also at Ashford, of a 500 hp 0-6-0 diesel-mechanical shunter. This was to be the next step forward from the 350hp trio bought by Maunsell and delivered in 1938. The new 0-6-0 was planned to have a top speed of 45 mph for occasional branch-line train services as well as shunting and minor freight duties. It had a prototype Davey Paxman engine and Sinclair-David Brown gear drive. Due to the repercussions of the fuel crisis of early 1947, which delayed bought-in items, this shunter was not completed by Ashford Works till 1949, as No. 11001. It did a good ten years' work but suffered from compromise; the gear ratio was just too high for shunting and just too low for train duties.

Meanwhile the little Ashford drawing office* pressed steadily on with the main-line diesel locomotive and carefully produced what turned out to be an excellent design. One speciality was the bogie, where the leading, non-driven axles were given a measure of articulation to guide the driving axles, for improved riding and reduced track wear. "Percy Bollen came in with this idea after a very long confab with OVB," George Baker recalled. "It was just a rough sketch and left plenty of problems to be solved, but it turned out in the end to be a very good idea." The bogies were bolsterless, like the electrics, and had similar bearing pads, wheels, and mounting of the motors and brakes. The long main frames were of deep I-section girders, boxed in to provide an additional water tank for the oil-fired train heating boiler. The overall length finally came out at 63¾ft and the weight 135tons. The body design was simple, but benefited in appearance from the curved sides as on Bulleid's post-war passenger stock.

Though design work was finished early in 1949 the first two engines, Nos. 10201 and 10202, did not emerge from Ashford Works till early 1951. The first made its bow, in good British Railways company, at the Festival of Britain South Bank Exhibition. One effect of the delay was that the 16-cylinder English Electric diesel engines had been uprated to 1,750hp compared with 1,600hp as ordered (and as supplied for Ivatt's pair on the LMS). The third Bulleid diesel-electric locomotive, No. 10203, assembled at Brighton Works, was rated at 2,000hp due to further hotting-up and some bearing size increases to suit.

Drivers liked their exceptionally good riding at all speeds and their ever-available power — though this took a bit of getting used to by steam drivers long accustomed to nursing boilers after a stretch of heavy working. For example, No. 10201 could apply its 1750hp throughout the steady 12-mile climb at 1 in 275 from Dover to Sandling Junction and easily gain a bit of time. Lifting the "Golden Arrow" from Victoria was just the same. You got a worry-free start. But not always. One cold winter's afternoon No.

* E.J. Larkin's October 1955 Productivity Report for British Railways singled out this small office as a valuable technical team.

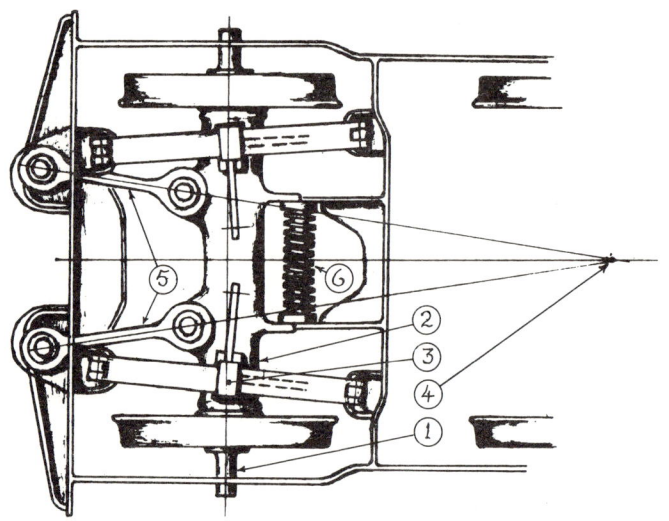

Fig 21 Leading truck of Bulleid's articulated bogie for 1Co-Co1 diesel locomotives Nos. 10201, 2, and 3. The bearings of the truck axle 1 are within the cannon box 2 which slides on bearing shoes under the buckles 3 of the laminated springs. The truck axle can move in an arc about the virtual centre 4 controlled by two links 5 from bogie frame to cannon box, ball-jointed at each end. The truck thus leads the bogie frame into a curve. Two side control springs 6 apply 2 ¼ tons centring force directly movement occurs, increasing to a maximum 3 tons on a curve of 5 ½ chains.

10202 was pulling the "Golden Arrow" briskly away from Victoria when the fireman came forward and said the train heating boiler was rapidly losing water. The driver had been puzzled by a show of steam at the front and realised that the front-end carriage heating cock must be partly open. So what to do? It chanced that J.G. Click was on the engine and that the previous week he had seen the "Golden Arrow" stopped by signals at Bickley Junction due to being early so that a Gillingham electric was crossing its path. Just the job! They were by then through Beckenham a minute or so early and approaching the two miles at 1 in 95, but No. 10202 was able to take this at full power. They were not far short of three minutes ahead of schedule when they were thankful to see adverse signals at the junction. So they pulled up smartly, closed the front heating cock, and were ready for off and still ahead of schedule when they got their signal.

Though these three diesels performed as promised, they made the usual obnoxious smell and all Southern passengers were pleased and all Southern steam enthusiasts delighted when they were packed off to the LMR.

When rapid dieselisation hit British Railways and R.C. Bond had the job of applying order and method, he decided to copy precisely the Bulleid bogie of these pioneer Southern diesels for the Type 4 English Electric locomotives, Classes 40 onwards, building nearly 400 between 1958 and 1963. These later engines developed up to 2,500hp and gave a tractive effort of 70,000lb. They also rode well.

32 *Above*: This shows the standard B-F-B wheel with cast steel centre, and the clasp brake arrangement; the lower shoes are in levers pivoted from above which carry the supporting pivots for the upper shoes and the brake gear linkage. Accordingly when the linkage is pulled to the right it applies all the brake shoes with equal force to each side of the wheel./*BR*

33 *Below*: The fabricated B-F-B wheel, fitted to No. 21C18 *British India Line*. Not so neat but cheaper, fabricated from four similar pressings and with the crank pin bosses and necessary infillings welded on, as can be seen only too clearly./*BR*

34 *Below*: No. 34030 *Watersmeet* crossing Meldon viaduct with the 8.30am Padstow to Waterloo "Atlantic Coast Express." No. 34064 *Fighter Command* is shunting hopper wagons into the Railway's vast Meldon granite quarry./*S.C. Nash*

35 *Bottom:* Erecting shop, Brighton, January 1942. "Q.1" boiler and smokebox being lowered onto frame and cylinders, all still looking fairly conventional./*BR*

36 *Above*: "Q.1" 0-6-0 No. C8 leaving Lancing Works in August 1942 with 40 "Covcars," tare weight 520 tons. This was used as a 1942 CME's Christmas card with left foreground replaced by the message: "May 'Austerity' bring you loads of Good Times this Christmas and the New Year."/*BR*

37 *Left*: No. 33009, as later fitted with mechanical lubricators driven from the leading coupling rod, on Shed at Guildford, November 1964./*I.S. Krause*

38 *Below*: No. 33026 delivering the goods to Reading, Western Region, in June 1949./*C.C.B. Herbert*

39 *Above*: The other "Austerity" — Riddles War Department 2-8-0 No. 90157 climbing casually, with smoke-free exhaust and resting fireman, on the 1 in 124 bank a couple of miles north of Oxenholme, oblivious of historical antecedents./*H.A.V.B.*

40 *Below*: War damage at Nine Elms in April 1941. No. 852 *Sir Walter Raleigh* was duly repaired but two of the Shed staff were killed./*BR*

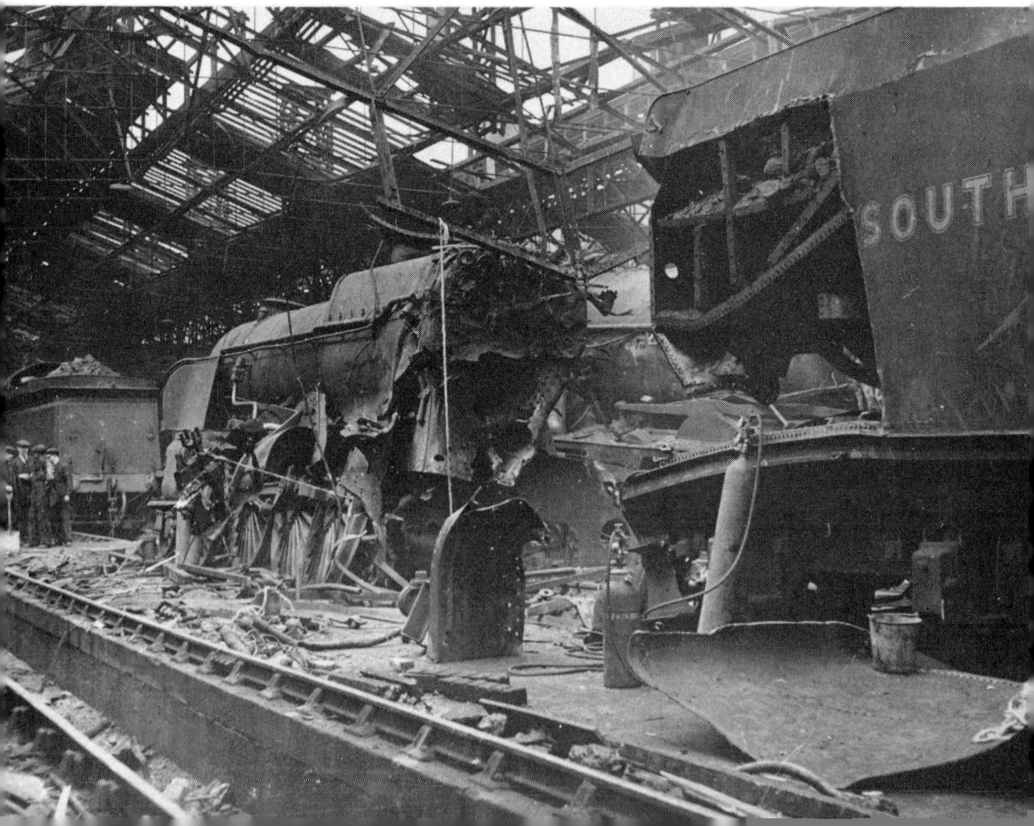

41 *Top*: At Ashford Works, January 1942, left to right: J. Finch, Assistant Works Manager, General Sir Brian Robertson, O.V.B., F. Munns, Works Manager Eastleigh./*BR*

42 *Above*: At Boxhurst, April 1942. From left to right, the author's wife, self, mother, brother, father with bored Yorkshire terrier, and sister. Deepdene, the Southern Rly H.Q. from 1939 till 1945, was a mere two miles away./*F. Vanderkelen*

43 *Left*: Upper pair Sir William Wood and Sir William Stanier; lower pair Noel-Baker (Parliamentary Secretary to the Minister of War Transport) and Holland-Martin; and Bulleid pondering on the 1935 design — at Eastleigh in January 1943 when the Southern Railway had completed the first two of these LMS class "8.F" 2-8-0s/*BR*

44 *Below left*: "King Arthur" class 4-6-0 No. 740 *Merlin*, one of twenty fitted in 1946 for oil firing. Some had been similarly fitted in LSWR days./*Frank E. Moss*

45 *Below*: Bulleid's "decent-sized" (15in gauge) bogie tender designed and built for the R.H.&D. at Ashford while they were overhauling *Green Goddess*. Both are here seen back at work in 1947./*J.C. Flemons*

46 *Bottom*: The up "Night Ferry" passing Bickley in March 1959 with No. 35028 *Clan Line*. The electric sets behind were in store for the Kent Coast Electrification in June 1959./*J.G.C.*

47 *Left*: On the down "Golden Arrow" approaching Brixton. This was Bulleid's favourite train. He associated it with trips to the Continent and with the original impetus for bigger engines on the Southern./*J.G.C.*

48 *Below*: SR Chief Officers at New Romney station on a visit to the R.H.&D. in 1947. Left to right: Driver Baker RHD, Missenden, Robertson, Goddard RHD, Bulleid, Richards, Capt. J.E.P. Howey RHD, Harrington barely visible behind, T. Holder RHD, MacLeod and Endicott./*Raphael, Hythe*

49 *Right*: Brighton Works' 1000th engine, No. 21C164 *Fighter Command*, in photographic grey including its wheels, just positioned by the restored LBSC *Boxhill*, in July 1947./*H.W. Attwell*

50 *Below right*: A visit to French locomotive engineers and builders in April 1949. Left to right: Corpet, Bulleid, SNCF Officer, Riddles, Legrand and de Caso at the gare de Lyon. Chapelon is represented by his 3-cylinder compound 4-8-4 carrying its indicator shelter; it achieved an IHP of 5,500./*S.N.C.F.*

51 *Above*: The electric CC1, Bulleid design but all electrics by Raworth. All axles carried equal weights, totalling 99¾ tons in working order. But why a pantograph? The SR only possessed a few hundred yards of overhead power at Norwood, Brighton and Balcombe./*BR*

52 *Below*: First Electric locomotive No. CC1, later No. 20,001, leaving Victoria with a Newhaven Boat train, 1952./*J.G.C.*

53 *Right*: The first SR Diesel express locomotive No. 10201 on a down West Country express at Milborne Port in 1951./*W. Vaughan-Jenkins*

54 *Below right*: Diesel 10202 at Victoria station in 1952 with plenty of smoke from the train-heating boiler but crew blissfully unaware that the front end carriage heating cock has been left open./*J.G.C.*

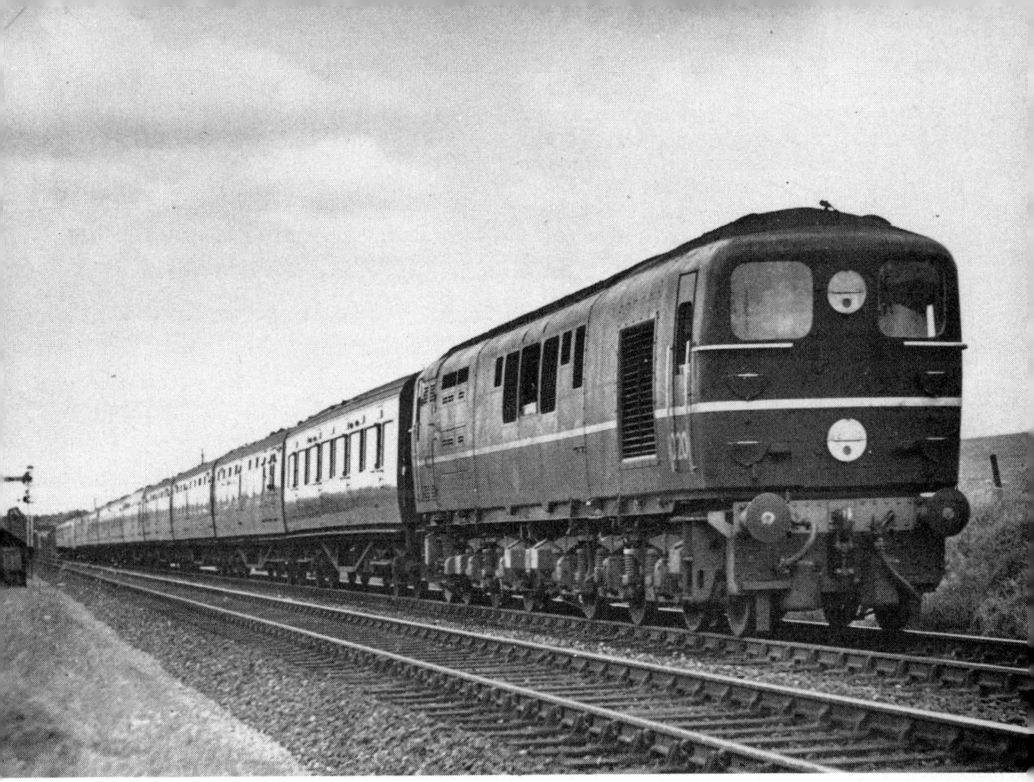

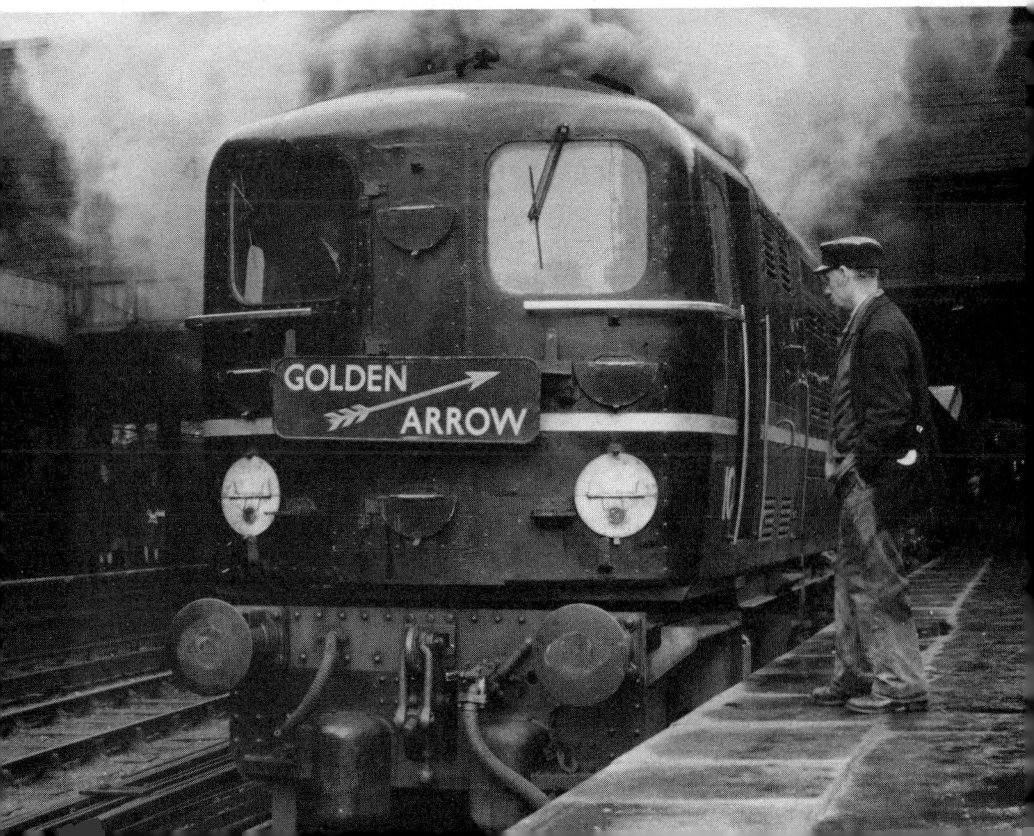
GOLDEN
ARROW

55 *Below*: New Southern Railway motor and
trailer cars for the Waterloo and City tube,
the green-and-silver scheme emphasising
the doors, seen above ground on trials in
October 1940./*BR*

56 *Bottom*: Nice place to linger over a cup of
coffee on the Bognor run./*BR*

57 *Top right*: Bulleid's tavern car, the White
Horse. Allegedly accurate reproduction

brickwork; and fundamentally standard
red-and-cream exterior finish./*BR*

58 *Centre right*: The double-decker.
Courteous station staff could offer
"Facing or back to the engine? Above or
below?"/*BR*

59 *Bottom right*: The double-decker on a trial
run at Haywards Heath in September
1949./*BR*

60 *Above*: No. 34002 *Salisbury* leaving Barnstaple with down A.C.E. while class "M.7" No. 30252 prepares to set back into the station with a train for the Torrington branch./*R.E. Toop*

61 *Below*: No. 34092 *City of Wells* with 450 tons and a well-lifted exhaust on the 2 o'clock Victoria to Dover at Bickley Junction./*J.G.C.*

62 *Above*: On the interchange trials. No. 34004 *Yeovil* with LNER dynamometer car on the 4pm Perth to Inverness at Dalnaspidal, approaching Druimuachdar summit, July 15th 1948./*C.C.B. Herbert*

63 *Below*: No. 35022 *Holland-Amerika Line* on test at Rugby in 1953. Its tyres were worn down to little over 6ft diameter./*J.G.C.*

64 *Above*: No. 34087 *145 Squadron* gaining time at St. Mary Cray with the down early morning boat train./*R. Russell*

65 *Below*: No. 35028 *Clan Line* on the down "Golden Arrow" and modified No. 34017 *Ilfracombe* on an up train from Deal, near Knockholt in August 1959./*D. Cross*

13

Carriages
and Wagons

Bulleid had always taken a powerful interest in "the carriage side," seeing it as the main testing link between the Company and the fare-paying customer. The Company's duty, through its CME, was to supply the best space, comfort and elegance that cash would allow. Space meant the interesting detail design quest for saving inches here and there, and comfort meant further ingenuity with new materials for better seating and less noise. It also meant riding quality; he had for years been a constant critic of the bad riding of multiple-unit electric stock, pointing out that with nose-supported motors it damaged the track and caused rail corrugation.

When he came to examine the Southern Railway bogies, he found them admirably simple and easy to make and maintain. Though he considered the laminated bearing springs too stiff and the auxiliary bolster springs inadequate he did not feel a re-design was justified, fending off any criticisms about their riding by criticising the track, as had been done by CMEs for so long that Civil Engineers had a stock set of replies sounding like an answering machine — lack of money, engines too heavy, wheelbases too rigid, or difficult terrain.

There was not quite the same scope with wagons on the Southern, though of course the predominantly passenger timetables encouraged Bulleid to air his long-held conviction that *all* goods vehicles should be fitted with continuous brakes, so that the trains could be run at or near passenger timings. He dismissed the counter-argument of excessive cost by claiming that such cost would stop users retaining wagons on their premises for long periods. He also advocated larger wagons, and was always striving to reduce tare weights, again seeing welding as a useful means to this end.

Then there was the interesting matter of the colour. All the railways had adopted their distinctive colours at the Grouping, and they were generally well liked. In particular the Southern had adopted green and used it everywhere and Bulleid agreed it was an excellent choice, specially for trains without engines. The only thing was, he didn't like the olive green chosen. Rather typically, he unearthed a technical disadvantage in the paint used in that its yellow pigment was less stable than the blue. Hence the colour gradually became more bluish, which had the twin disadvantages of looking sombre and accentuating rust staining. The brighter, bluer, and less conservative Malachite green favoured by Bulleid avoided these disadvantages, had a more modern look and would make his new designs that bit more distinctive; but how to sell the idea? Offering a choice of colours always causes dissension because each alternative gathers a few adherents so that the majority will not favour the ultimate choice. So he offered only one choice — malachite green — on a beautifully painted carriage brought to Waterloo for Board inspection. There was much discussion and many opinions were freely aired and debated. Bulleid always preached and practiced debate-without-vulgarity, and when he overheard one of the anti-malachites remark with emotion that "it ought to be spelled with an 's' instead of a 'c'" he wittily dismissed this as "rather a gutteral remark." When, some years later, I asked my father exactly how the colour was decided he wrote that "The Chairman and several directors liked the malachite but some of the older directors thought it was too light. Finally, to get a decision, I suggested we made it just a tone darker, and they all agreed. I have never known just what a 'tone' would be like." So he used the original malachite.

The first visible Bulleid contribution to Southern carriages was in the 1938 buffet car sets for the West Sussex traffic. The bar section had ten stools and the saloon section had four four-seater window tables, scalloped in front of each chair to win more space and faintly reminiscent of, though of course quite unconnected with, a story told to Bulleid by his mother of a certain fat man who had to have just such a table to get near enough to eat. Elegance was provided by bright and comfortable chair coverings, brass wall plaques, and royal blue Wilton carpet with gold diagonal bars. Bulleid took close interest in all details and there had been a moment of drama at Waterloo when all the sample carpets were delivered to his office and an immediate decision demanded by the already-late manufacturers. It was 11.40 am. "We'll have to see them on the actual job at Eastleigh," said Bulleid to Richardson, "help me to get them on the 11.45." Hence the emergence from the offices and rapid progress across the Waterloo fore-court of a crocodile led by Bulleid and Richardson with two messengers and other helpers each carrying an 8ft carpet roll. The public duly applauded their carpet decision and the general comfort, elegance and soothing unfolding of Sussex or Surrey scenery, by sitting over one modest snack all the way from Bognor Regis to Victoria, and perhaps liking it so much that they did the same thing again all the way back. This brought complaints from those who missed out and louder complaints from the catering people who lost turnover. These complaints did not fail to reach Missenden and Bulleid. The latter did not admit any error, but took very good note for the future.

By the end of 1938 Bulleid and Lynes had made distinctive improvements with curved carriage body sides and flush windows to win another few inches and seat six a side — "even six of my own ample proportions," the Chairman remarked at the 1939 Annual Meeting. They were also extending the application of welding, which was a space saver as well as a weight saver. It helped them to solve problems on the new stock for the Waterloo and City tube. This was built in 1939/40 by English Electric to Southern Railway design, made tricky by the small-bore tube, only 12ft 1¾in diameter. The 12 motor coaches carried 40 seated, 60 standing and the 16 trailers 52 seated, 80 standing. Two motor coaches could pull three trailers at peak traffic times, with combined tare weight only 115tons. They looked good and were highly popular, outshining their 42-year-old predecessors.

The war stopped carriage building, though the carriage drawing offices were kept very busy on war work. But some special wagons were needed and in 1944 ten four-wheel luggage vans were built, the bodies having a welded framework of 12 gauge steel sections, carrying plastic exterior panels for the roof, sides and ends. The plastic panels were reinforced with steel and cotton and weighed 11½oz per sq ft. To preserve the panels and the van contents from excessive shocks a spring cushioning arrangement acted between the body and the main frame. Tare was 20% less than previous vans of the same capacity. The first went on public display at Victoria station in March 1944.

Another 1944 requirement was for eleven four-wheel 20-ton well wagons. Here again Bulleid and Lynes determined to achieve a reduction in tare weight, and decided to go for lightweight steel castings for the main members which would be welded together. The main side frames were of box form, 32ft long. The wheel base was 26ft 2in, the loading space in the well 21ft long and height above rail only 1ft 5in. The tare weight came out at 12¾tons, saving about a ton compared with riveted conventional steel sections. The wagons were very popular with Traffic Department and with traders; the resulting continuous heavy use ultimately led to cracks in the castings at the ends of the wells, so they were reinforced by welding on flitch plates.

Bulleid did some pioneering work on wheel sets to reduce weight and to find a cheaper alternative to forgings. A number of steel pressings were welded together to form the wheel centre, after which the bore and the periphery were flame-cut to suit the axle and tyre, which were welded on. Despite its attractions for reducing weight and cost this method was not successfully developed. Then a number of Bulleid-Firth-Brown wheels were made for testing, but they were too strong transversely to pass the falling weight test. This was readily corrected by reducing the thickness of the webs, after which about 300 pairs of these wheels were used satisfactorily in motor bogies.

Often the layman asks why railway carriages and wagons have to be so heavy. The answer is that they are subject to buffing and other blows of considerable violence, so they require frames able to withstand shock loads, often obliquely applied, without deformation. Getting the same strength for less weight by stronger materials and better design is a target always in front of progressive CMEs, and Bulleid and Lynes together evolved the triangulated underframe which first appeared in prototype form in 1945, with final form follow-up in 1947 at Eastleigh. It allowed a saving of tare weight of about one ton on a standard wagon. It was later successfully exploited in Ireland by CIE. British Railways placed an order in March 1949 for 500 mineral wagons with triangulated underframes, but the order was amended to standard frames in February 1951 so as to standardise BR production and maintenance procedures.

This progressive designing during the war years was in addition to the massive help given by the drawing offices to the Works in the effective handling of "foreign" war-time orders. One record case was the Ministry of Supply order placed by Riddles in September 1941 for 1,000 open goods wagons for shipment in crates, unassembled, to Persia for routing overland supplies to Russia. The order was completed by Ashford Works in three months. Interestingly the Royal Engineers in the Middle East got them all assembled before the end of March and sent complimentary messages to Ashford for making the bits fit together so easily.

When there were signs of the end of the war, the Southern Railway felt free to ask its CME to build an Inspection Saloon, the duties of which would include taking directors and senior officials on periodic inspection tours of their extensive premises. The layout of the saloon, with central 2ft corridor, eleven bedrooms 9ft 5in by 3ft 5in with h and c, an attendants room, lavatory and shower, was not out of the way except perhaps the shower. But there were two important innovations, the plywood body and the radial-bearing bogie.

The design of this saloon was like an inverted ship's hull, the keep plate or ridge rail running along the centre of the roof like the keel of an upside-down ship. To this rail and to the underframe of the saloon were bolted preformed sections 9ft 5in wide made of $\frac{9}{16}$ in thick nine-ply birch, resin-bonded to the saloon framework which was made of similar plywood. Bulleid offered this design more as a demonstration that there were alternatives to steel and aluminium cladding than as a breakthrough, though it did offer an attractive quietness and solidity besides offering a sort of consolation to the many people who like things made of wood.

The bogie design was different in that the central spherical support of the carriage underframe on the bogie bolster was replaced by two radial bearing pads, one at the front and one at the back of the bogie, and 14ft 2in apart. These pads were sprung rather like small transverse bolsters, so they could accommodate both swing and fore-and-aft pitching of the bogies. The disadvantage of this arrangement is that, unless the pads are very well lubricated, the bogie is sluggish in rotating when it meets a curve and this causes wheel and rail wear and bad riding. For pad lubrication both oil baths and greased anti-friction inserts were tried, with sometimes excellent results. Sir Cyril Hurcomb made one or two trips in this saloon when he became the first Chairman of British Railways and he remarked to Bulleid that it was the most beautifully riding coach he had ever been in. Quite frankly this could not be called the opinion of an expert witness, but it pleased the designer, particularly because all present agreed with this high-level view. When the Inspection Saloon was coupled to a restaurant car it made an excellent mobile hotel for VIP inspection journeys and perhaps led to a mellow verdict. But not always. On one ghastly occasion after an overnight stop Bulleid joined his colleagues at breakfast late and in poor temper, very unusual for him in both respects. It had been his idea to install the shower, and though far from being an American-type shower addict he was jolly well going to use it. But the shower plumbing had not been properly cleaned out with the result that a shot of sooty oil mingled with the water. It must have reminded him of the Doncaster apprentices.

In the autumn of 1945 the Southern Railway was furbishing up its publicity and put a prototype improved post-war composite carriage (for steam train main-line services) on show at Charing Cross to seek users' opinions. In his memorandum on the subject dated September 27, Missenden first described the layout (three 3rd class compartments seating 24, four 1st class seating 24, two lavatories) and the dimensions (64ft 6in long compared with 59ft pre-war, with compartments 3in wider and tare weight unchanged at 34tons) and then listed the attractive improvements using, of course, text supplied by the CME:

"Seating comfort
Hammock sprung seating frames have been provided to support spring insert cushions, giving maximum luggage space under seats, reducing weight and helping cleaning.

Lighting, heating and ventilation
Diffused electric lighting is fitted in compartments and there are electrically-heated foot warming panels under the compartment floor rugs. (*Then followed a description of the air-extract system, the sliding top windows and the draught-preventing seals on compartment sliding doors*).

Decorations and appointments
Stainless steel is generally employed for all fittings, while compartments are decorated with polished veneers of Empire grown timbers. Mirrors in compartments have been canted out of the vertical plane to reduce reflection to the passengers when seated. Electrical indicators direct passengers to the first and third class sections and to the lavatories.

The exterior of the vehicle has been painted Southern Railway green without lining and with the usual lettering."

GENERAL MANAGER'S OFFICE   E.J. Missenden.
WATERLOO.
27th September, 1945.

The exhibition coach was visited by 25,000 people, of whom about 10% gave their view on various items. They voted three to one for compartments rather than open coaches, and other comments resulted in:

Individual bracket lights above all seats.
Heating in lavatories and corridors.
Improved lavatory ventilation.
Wider access to communication cord including lavatories.
Passenger-controlled heaters under first class seats.

Twenty-four of these composites were under construction in January 1947, bodies at Eastleigh, underframes and bogies at Lancing, half to be finished for the summer traffic and the rest by the year end. But they were delayed by the chaos which hit the country on January 30, with weather of exceptional severity and a fuel crisis taking terrible toll of all material supplies so that cancellations and postponements were the order of the day and the post-war recovery dragged on and on.

This did not hinder progress in the Drawing Office, however, and Eastleigh pressed on with the design of the new standard lightweight steel four-coach suburban sets, incorporating further detail improvements and welding applications and saving more weight. Then came the argument; should they be compartment type or open type? Open, said Bulleid and Missenden, so that in the rush hours people could move about better to equalise loading (or crowding, you could say). No, compartments, said Traffic Department, essentially conservative and perhaps not wanting it to be confused with a tube train and probably thinking of the 3-to-1 vote for the main line coaches. So Missenden had some of each type built and took a statistically significant sample of passengers' views. The result was a large majority in favour of the open type.

All this carriage building, placed under further pressure by the 1947 shortages and the need to replace the 83 carriages lost by enemy action during the war, bore heavily on the Works and Bulleid sought some relief by placing one order outside but this proved a failure when the prevailing shortages caused almost indefinite delays. Allocations became the order of the day, and there was a scene of tense drama when a senior Board of Trade official visited Eastleigh to find out why they were making such a ridiculous fuss about being held up for tin tacks; why couldn't they just send out for some? We have done that, they replied with great patience, and obtained nearly 6lb, but we are in immediate need of 10cwt.

When supplies improved productivity became the bottleneck. Bulleid and C.A. Shepherd, the Eastleigh Carriage Works Manager, had got the flow of work so well organised that although the output was already eight carriages per week they were sure it could be increased to ten. So they held a full discussion with the Works Committee, explained that material supplies and future work were assured, fixed an increase of around 20% in the piece-work earnings, and the same labour force succeeded in turning out ten per week. Bulleid was always very pleased with this effective co-operation, rewarding to all concerned, and particularly to the S.R. passengers.

Applications of low-temperature enclosed electric heating elements gathered momentum after the war and always attracted Bulleid, in both panel and textile applications. He tried this type of electrically-heated carpets in 1st class compartments on the Western section, but after some caught fire the experiment was given up.

When the Southern Region sanctioned the building of eight two-coach buffet/restaurant sets for completion in 1949 their intention was, as ever, to have something popular, efficient, profitable and newsworthy. Moreover, being still in the very early days of nationalisation, the only strings attached to the project by Marylebone were to stick to the standards being agreed upon and to paint the outside in the new red-and-cream main-line livery.

Neither Bulleid nor the Drawing Office were going to take any risks of being accused again by the Traffic and Catering people of encouraging lingerers with picture-window views and luxury seating. So they had the rather obvious idea of smaller and higher windows and hard, upright, 12-seater oak settees with matching tables. You find these features in certain quaint old pubs, not to mention less quaint new ones, so why not make that the excuse for putting them on the railway? They then looked up "tavern" in a well-known dictionary and were surprised and pleased to find that it simply meant "public house for supply of food and drink." Hence tavern car for public transportable house — more appropriate than "buffet" really. And yes! why not make the outside *look* like a tavern? With brickwork below and plaster above, and just a few old oak pillars showing, it would be essentially a red-and-cream colour scheme, as per standard. To complete this decor each car had its own inn sign, such as *The Green Man* or, Hitchcock touch, *The Three Plovers*.

Inside one found a half-timbered roof, square metal lanterns and "leaded" lights or panes in the windows, but a disconcertingly modern cocktail bar could be seen, just beyond. It was genuine 12-years-weathered oak in the ceiling, but the floor had red and black synthetic tiles and air conditioning was provided.

The idea was undoubtedly well carried out. The cars felt spacious, no one lingered long on the seats, and the staff found them easy to run and sales of liquor tavern-brisk. But inability to see out of the windows, particularly in the restaurant cars, brought many complaints, some presumably from ex-Bognor travellers. A tea-cup storm also blew in *The Times* for several days after the first Tavern Car was on show at Waterloo starting on May 25. Eleven people connected with art and design wrote in, calling it "the *reductio ad absurdum* of the mania for the fake antique." I think they were looking for industrial design commissions. There was a courteous counter from Marylebone, but then nine MPs wrote to say that Public Enterprise should set a new standard. They did not write anything about the current rail strikes and I think they were looking for votes. Then an American visitor wrote complaining, but I think he was grinding a small axe because he represented a Contemporary Art Institute. There was one straight grumble about the high windows; and one desperate request for pubs to be disguised as restaurant cars, so that people priced out of rail travel could enjoy a simulated experience. All this added up to a stronger reaction than was noted when the cars were first formally inspected by senior members of the Railway Executive, though admittedly their views and their remarks varied. Bulleid said they all liked it, and never even realised it was not to the standard colour scheme. Riddles said they did not approve of the departure from standard colours, nor the high windows, but did not like to grumble about them at the time. Elliot said most people liked them at first, but Press criticisms and the many complaints about the high windows made them think again. The catering people welcomed the improved sales and let others argue about windows and decor. The publicity was inexpensive and valuable. Even the brickwork was controversial. Shepherd and the Eastleigh Paint Shop Foreman visited Hampshire taverns to study ancient brickwork, but when Bulleid saw the result he simply said that the liquid refreshment must have affected their vision. So they persuaded him to come and see for himself, which he did, thereafter claiming it was an authentic reproduction but leaving many unconvinced.

While this prank was being plotted and played, a great deal of serious design work was in hand at Lancing on the perennial problem of over-crowding in suburban trains. Designers, usually keener on their technical job than the allied politics, sometimes let slip details of their current thoughts which are then publicised as decisions. This and the accompanying superficial comment, usually with a lacing of ridicule or a challenge to meet unheard-of targets, naturally cause distraction and irritation to the designers, and even more so to their bosses. So inevitably some secrecy descends — wisely, it has been proved time and time again — over the first faltering design thoughts in a new field.

The Press, seeing any attempt at secrecy as a personal challenge, and with an acquired knack of secrecy sensing, does sometimes come up with a constructive busting of the secret, and this was done on February 7, 1949 by the Brighton *Evening Argus*:

A full-scale plywood model of a type of carriage that may one day revolutionise railway travel is nearing completion at the Lancing carriage works.

It follows months of work by draughtsmen who have been experiment-ing with a design which may help railways to overcome the problem of rolling stock.

The "two-in-one" carriage is an idea which may take years to fulfil. It is in the infancy stage, according to railway officials, who are loth to talk about it.

In fact the model making at Lancing appears to be as secret as the latest development of atomic research. No one there will talk of the double-decker carriage.

Top officials say "Sorry. No statement. Not allowed to say anything," and lesser officials, with furtive, over-the-shoulder glances, say "We mustn't say anything — but we have seen it and it looks as if the idea is pretty good."

Despite the secrecy, the model *has* been built, and it looks as though the Railway executive are greatly interested in the possibilities of "up and down" railway travel.

In fact the double-decker came off the secret list that very month when the model was shown to the Press at Marylebone. It had originated as a 1948 idea, after nationalisation, between Missenden and Bulleid whose plan to design and build a prototype double-decker train was very welcome against the alternative of spending £10 million on platform extensions and rolling stock and power supplies for longer trains on the Dartford line, where congestion was really serious. It had the approval of Riddles and his staff as an important and valuable experiment. No originality for the idea was claimed by Bulleid or Lynes or the Drawing Office — ideas alone are all too easy — but they did rightly claim pioneering ingenuity in being the first to succeed in getting a double-deck arrangement within our pitifully restricted loading gauge, and doing so with the same length and tare weight as conventional carriages. The Dartford line loading gauge did allow them to increase the carriage height from the SR standard 12ft 4½in to 12ft 9in, and they managed to reduce the floor height above rail from 4ft 2½in to 3ft 8¼in. This gave them the only increased dimension, — the available internal height increased from 8ft 2in to 9ft ¾in.

The two four-coach sets made up a train of 1016 seats plus 88 tip-up seats, compared with 772 seats on a standard eight-coach train. The tare weight per passenger was down from 0.347 to 0.265 ton — the latter at last matching a small family saloon car carrying four passengers.

Wheels of standard design but 3ft 2in diameter were ordered to suit the reduced floor height, but when their delivery promise went awry Bulleid decided to risk using his fabricated wheel design. He wanted to include hollow axles to assist welding and save more weight, but he could not get anyone to manufacture the small quantity involved. As a further height-saver, bolsterless bogies were designed, the carriage body resting on eight bearing pads, four over each axle, to spread the load and aid lubrication.

Fig 22 G. N. Anderson's simple 1862 double-decker design for the Bombay, Baroda and Central India Railway, carrying 70 below and 50 above, and reported to be "most popular with the natives as well as economical for the company."

101

The pads were fixed directly to the bogie frame which had improved springing as some compensation for the lack of bolsters. The coach bodies were of lightweight steel, the fixed windows to the upper compartments were curved over into the roof, and there was electric heating and ventilating controlled by the guard.

A demonstration run was arranged for Press and VIPs including Herbert Morrison (then Lord President of the Council and interested as MP for East Lewisham), Alfred Barnes (then Minister of Transport) and O.V. Bulleid (then with CIE). Everything performed excellently, and Morrison, naturally enough not knowing who was in charge of what, said to Bulleid "This is wonderful. It is just what my electors want. How many can we have by Christmas?" The Press gave rather measured approbation. *Engineering* must have been chatting with someone from Traffic, because it concluded its review with a remark that, "the speed at which passengers can detrain and entrain will be watched with interest."

Thanks to the Southern's usual meticulous planning, the double-decker entered regular service the next day, making six return trips to Dartford daily. All the design features turned out on the whole satisfactory, except for the temporary wheels; tyre cracks were found after a few days and the train had to be withdrawn for some weeks till at last the standard wheel sets arrived. There were two factors contributing to this welded-wheel failure: imperfect welding technique in the new design and the greater stress imposed on the tyres by the rather sluggish rotation of the bogies on curves.

Though there were complaints about the hard seats and the ventilation, the double-decker carried its 1,104 seats more than 700,000 miles before it was withdrawn on October 1, 1971. It was replaced by an ordinary 10-coach, 960-seat train, mainly because it took too long for detraining and entraining.

14

Engineering Institutions

O.V.P. Bulleid joined "Stephenson's Lot," the Institution of Mechanical Engineers, as a Graduate in 1901. He made a shot-gun transfer to Associate Membership in 1910 and a leisurely transfer to Member in 1936 supported by Thom, Thompson, Gresley, Maunsell and Pendred of *The Engineer*. By this time his name had been discreetly corrected to O.V.S.B. Though always a vigorous supporter of the Annual Summer meetings, the first paper he presented was to the London Graduates section in 1945, "Locomotives I have known." He was elected to Council in 1938 and President in April 1946.

Despite massive support from staff and members, the President does carry key responsibility in his year of office and is kept pretty well at it with Council and other meetings, visits to the Branches and kindred Societies, and his Presidential address. He also had, since 1941, meetings of the "Three Presidents," the other two in Bulleid's year being Sir Wm. Halcrow, Civils and V.Z. de Ferranti, Electricals. Their business ranged across all Engineering interests and is now largely covered by the Council of Engineering Institutions.

The membership elects its President and Council and expects them to get on with the job of running and improving the Institution. In Bulleid's year the amalgamation with the Automobile Engineers was completed and Centenary preparations were vigorously advanced. Bulleid got on swimmingly with the Institution Staff, including the formidable Secretary, H.L. Guy — particularly after the incident of the gold watch. Due to a mishap never explained, but definitely not caused by rough riding, Guy dropped his gold watch down the lavatory pan of an LNER express to Kings Cross. Shrewdly guessing time and speed to the next landmark, he fixed the incident at 2 miles north of Biggleswade and reported it to Bulleid on arrival at Kings Cross. The LNER rose to the occasion, found the watch, had it repaired and handed it back to "another satisfied customer."

Bulleid presented his paper on "Merchant Navy" class locomotives in December 1945 and gave his Presidential Address in October 1946. It contained the first description of the "Leader" and also covered the duties of a CME, the Southern's maintenance, design and research work, the modern approach to labour and training, and the Southern's war effort. He repeated these papers at eleven Branch meetings. His persuasive powers reached a new peak when he coaxed short papers from Ivatt and Peppercorn, so as to provide one from each of the four Main Line CMEs for the Centenary meeting in June 1947.

The Mechanicals saluted Bulleid's wide-ranging achievements by electing him to Honorary Membership in 1951.

Smaller and technically closer-knit was the Institution of Locomotive Engineers, which Bulleid joined in January 1928 when Gresley was President, because they both thought their experimental work merited wider publicity. So Bulleid read a paper on the booster in 1928 and on poppet valves in 1929. Both were strong on data but weak on recommendations and a cynic would commend this against the minimal subsequent applications of both.

After becoming a vice-President in 1931 and serving on the Papers and the Finance Committees, Bulleid was elected President at the AGM in December 1939 — for the duration of the War, which Gresley hoped "did not mean in perpetuity." In lieu of a Presidential Address Bulleid gave a résumé of the activities of the Railway Executive Committee (see Appendix 3). When he handed over the Presidency to W.S. Graff-Baker in October 1944 the vote of thanks by W.H.W. Maass concluded: "The Council felt his willingness to serve for so long a period was magnanimous on his part, for the duties of the office were arduous and Mr Bulleid had discharged them admirably." Mr Bulleid in reply thanked the meeting for an unexpected recognition of what had been a very easy, pleasant and amusing five years' experience, adding that it was not true to say he had done a great deal of work; thanks to the Institution's very efficient Council and Secretary his own role had been to put in appearance as frequently as possible. He was a quite unrepentant steam engineer and had listened to rosy views of the marvels of other modes of traction — so rosy that they ignored the thorns.

In addition to attending most of the meetings Bulleid did his stuff behind the scenes, coping with wartime meeting problems, evacuation of HQ after bomb damage, and the occasional soothing of ruffled senior members. He also made many model contributions to the discussions at meetings, with constructive shots of praise or blame and often an apt supporting case from the past. Remember, these comments were made in a close technical circle and should not be taken too literally out of context: for example his "dislike of thousanths of an inch" was *not* in an instrument context. Again, there could be misprints, as when the famous Inchicore dimension "the black of my nail" $(=\frac{1}{32}$ nd when well manicured) had the "l" knocked out of it and so became a meaningless half-inch.

Fairburn's 1941 paper on diesel shunters collected a Bulleid rebuke for "almost contemptuous dismissal of anything in the way of a mechanical drive" and Holcroft on smoke deflectors got a rather melancholy "with the locomotive passing through a side wind there must of necessity be pressure on one side and vacuum on the other side of the boiler and therefore the problem may be almost insoluble." A livelier occasion came after the AGM and lunch at the Savoy Hotel in May 1941, when all present, including Maunsell, were considered sufficiently fortified to visit the Class Q1 0-6-0 brought specially to Charing Cross for the occasion. As later recorded, "such an opportunity at such a convenient spot was not to be missed."

Proving his perpetual interest, Bulleid's attendances kept up after his term of office. In November 1944 he was hot on the trail of his old friend D.W. Sanford of the Midland, who rashly still used U-tubes: "A debt of gratitude is due to Sir Nigel Gresley who, by fitting Cambridge gauges, demonstrated quite clearly that the U-tube as a means of measuring smokebox vacuum was grossly misleading. The Cambridge instruments showed quite clearly that between each impulse the pressure in the smokebox returned almost to atmospheric pressure." Then, warming up, he added: "I have an uneasy feeling that the paper is a masterly example of the adaptation of scientific formulae to accepted practice. Having been brought up in the school which holds that things are usually wrong and not right, I feel that the Paper is perhaps a little too complacent."

Sometimes he walked round the problem and viewed it from the other side. In a July 1942 discussion on Steam versus Diesel he drew the distinction between a locomotive's availability and its usefulness; and in January 1946, discussing E.S. Cox's paper on LMS engines, he said "I would like to quarrel with the author's statement that the average coal consumption of an engine is a better measure of the engine than the coal consumption obtained by scientific testing. My own view is that a locomotive is intended to burn coal, and the more coal an efficient engine burns the better; it means that the engine is doing more work. It is necessary to find means, by testing, so that an engine will burn coal in big quantities, produce plenty of steam, and use that steam efficiently; and then, I suggest, the management may usefully ask why a particular engine is burning so little coal and not, as is so frequently asked at present, why it is burning so much." Dealing with over-run of the Pacific inside valves in the discussion of B. Spencer's paper on LNER engines in March 1947 he said: "Over-running has always been talked about, but personally I always thought it a pity that we could not make all the valves over-run and get as fat cards on the two outside cylinders as on the inside."

For S.G. Smith's paper on Standardisation of BR Coaching Stock, in January 1951, R.A. Riddles in the Chair, Bulleid said: "I have come specially to this country to congratulate Mr Smith on his paper. He has suffered from me frequently and often. I have watched him at work and he is a first-rate fellow. Less than justice, however, has been done to the Chairman. What has been described is a wonderful example of standardisation and the author of it is sitting in the Chair. I can give the assurance that it requires someone with a good deal of drive to get carriage draughtsmen to agree on anything."

It was a pity Bulleid could not attend the 1951 annual luncheon on March 9. There were good speeches from old friends, including the new Chairman of the Railway Executive, John Elliott, who said: "There has been a darn sight too much talk about the Southern Railway. What is the matter with the London Midland Region? If you meet me at half past six to-night under the Doric Arch I will tell you! When I got to Marylebone the other day the first thing I called for was the new programme of locomotive construction. This is what I found: 2,400 Webb compounds, 1,600 Stroudley 0-6-0s, 1 Diesel-electric (not to be paid for till it has been tested for 56 years), 500 "Leader" class locomotives, capable of going from either end at the same time. (Prolonged laughter). Unfortunately I have had to cancel the order."

Bulleid continued to attend Council meetings till 1964 but his last major contribution was in September 1957, when Council was discussing a summer meeting in Belgium. Stanier proposed that either the West Country or Ireland would be preferable. Bulleid proposed Ireland, remarking that the Chairman and Board of CIE would ensure a successful visit and adding that there was a great deal to see, with Inchicore alone able to show some *modern* carriages and diesels, and the re-built 1847 Bury engine — and, oh yes, a modern steam engine on two power bogies and incidentally burning home-grown peat. Council decided to go.

Being an applier rather than an originator of welding techniques, it is not altogether surprising that Bulleid only joined the Institute of Welding when, as happens from time to time in the Learned Societies, his eminence fitted him for a stint as President in 1949. His Presidential Address illustrated the advantages and rewards stemming from bold applications of new welding techniques.

Past-Presidents often get asked for papers by kindred Societies, and the British Association asked Bulleid to perform at their Brighton meeting in September 1948. He included specific items like a brief description of the "Leader" and reducing wagon tare weights with triangulated underframes, and on railway traction in general he made three comments:

(1) It was not thought necessary to incur the cost of improving the permanent way to stand heavier engines, so all the tendency was to augment the power for a given weight.

(2) When times were more propitious we might expect to see the electrification of railways in all districts.

(3) Whilst Diesels were very good for shunting, their disadvantages elsewhere were high first cost, difficulty of full daily loading to absorb such cost, and use of a fuel that had to be imported.

The President of the Association of Railway Locomotive Engineers, R.E.L. Maunsell, was in the Chair at the October 1925 meeting when two new members were elected, O. Bulleid and D.C. Urie; and at the same meeting E.J.H. Lemon and O. Bulleid were appointed honorary auditors. G.H. Pearson was already a member and J. Clayton and Turbett were elected in 1927.

Bulleid took over as Secretary from Sir Henry Fowler in 1931 and generally wrote rather formal minutes. For example, minuting the February 28 1936 meeting, held unusually at the Great Northern Hotel, Kings Cross, he wrote: "Mr Gresley took members to see the arrival of the "Silver Jubilee" train and took them over the engine *Silver Link* and the train." But just occasionally he put in a good comment, as in June 1936: "Mr Pettigrew thanked the President and members for inviting the retired members to lunch, and was followed by Capt. Beames who spoke in his best 'Crewe' manner."

Automatically, by custom since 1923, Bulleid became a vice-President at the February 1938 meeting but continued as Secretary in the Fowler tradition. He was President in 1948. He always regarded the ARLE as mainly a social function, with bits of business done man-to-man outside the meeting, and therefore, quite honestly, just as easy to do without waiting for such meeting. But that did not prevent him from disapproving when Riddles wound it up, though of course he attended the final party in June 1949 at Gleneagles — fortified by cheerful telegrams from Granshaw about the "Leader" trials.

CMEs were also automatically commissioned by the War Office into the officers-only communications outfit called the Engineer and Railway Staff Corps, RE (TA). Major O.V.S. Bulleid (late Royal Engineers) was so gazetted Lt. Col. on December 28 1937; and in the same way resigned on September 30 1948, with permission to retain the rank of Lt.-Colonel.

Bulleid also enjoyed his membership of the Smeatonian Society; and was highly delighted when admitted to the Goldsmiths and to the Freedom of the City of London in 1946. He belonged to the Athenaeum and the Junior Carlton.

Due to his links with the Continent starting in 1908, the International Railway Congress Association was of particular interest to Bulleid, further boosted when he began translating for it in 1925. Though he took his translating very seriously, even ponderously, he freely admitted that to him the major attraction was not the monthly Bulletin with his translations, nor the papers presented at Congress held every few years in European capitals (which had sometimes been committee-edited into stupefying boredom), but in the peripheral contacts and discussions. Senior international people were there whose opinions counted, and there were elegant receptions. He was elected a member of the Permanent Commission of the IRCA in July 1939.

In LNER days he wrote several short reports for Gresley to publish in the IRCA Bulletin, but only one under his own name — for the November 1935 Bulletin, describing the "Silver Jubilee" train and engine. It was notable for strongly emphasising uphill locomotive performance, for publicising the average speed of 107 mph between Hitchin and Huntingdon on the test run, and for naming most of the contractors whose supplies adorned the train. It also had a good final paragraph: "The train has fulfilled all expectations."

For the Lucerne Congress in 1947 Bulleid helped to inspire a Question-naire on "Lightening Rolling Stock," and got Turbett to collate and report the replies. For the Rome Congress in 1950 he got Lynes and E. Pugson (representing H.G. Ivatt) to report on rolling stock improvements aimed at reduced maintenance.

Continental trips were also involved for meetings of the Railway "Engineers-in-Chief," on which he often accompanied Gresley. After a series of mishaps to their train from Calais on consecutive trips, one of the Frenchmen told Gresley he was a Jonah, and another suggested that, if he had to keep coming, he might perhaps travel via le Havre? It would be like a control experiment. Gresley's French was quite up to this jocularity and in support Bulleid was able to remind them of the time he was knocked unconscious, while sitting reading in one of their trains, by a water-column chain swinging through the window. He had in fact taken this incident very calmly, perhaps largely from being unconscious — much more so than the other occupant of the compartment, a Frenchman who was naturally alarmed and excited by the noise, the broken glass, the blood and the inert figure.

The prized compliment of Honorary Membership of the American Society of Mechanical Engineers was conferred on Bulleid in New York at their Annual Dinner and Honours night, November 30 1949. In reply he expressed the affectionate regard of the English Mechanicals for the ASME and the everlasting love of his wife's native land, Ireland, for the United States. Blurred by the emotion of the moment, this was transcribed as the speaker's native land, so in ASME records Bulleid is forever Irish. The following day he presented a paper in the Railroad Division on "Locomotive and Rolling-Stock Developments in Great Britain." He made the point of availability being more important than thermal efficiency and went on to urge basic re-design for improved availability, quoting some features of the Pacifics and the TIA water treatment. He also described features of his "Leader" class double-bogie engine, "now under-going experimental trials," and forecast further improvements including fan-controlled exhaust and return of exhaust steam to the boiler.

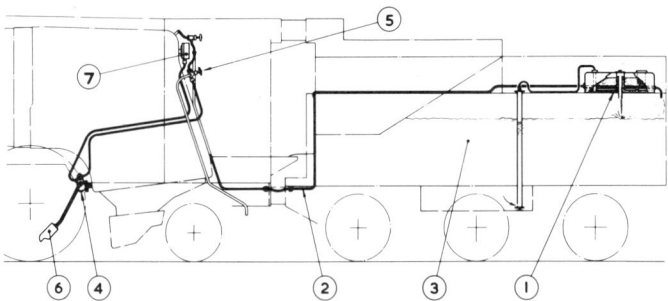

Fig 23 The T.I.A. (Traitement Integral Armand) process adds chemicals which keep the boiler feed water alkaline to prevent corrosion and which convert all deposit-forming salts to a removable sludge. The chemical fluid in tank 1 is kept molten by steam pipe 2 and is displaced into the tender tank 3 in proportion to the amount of water used. The steam-operated blow-down valve 4 is controlled by a 3-way cock 5 on the footplate, usually operated for about half a minute every 30 miles. The sludge is blown down via the baffle 6 and the operation is recorded on a weekly chart at 7.

15

Pacific Performance

By late 1941 reports of star performances by "Merchant Navies" were reaching the *Southern Railway Magazine*, then an austerity bi-monthly. On November 9 No 21C3 *Royal Mail* took a train of 527tons tare the 11¼miles from passing Surbiton to Woking stop in 12¼min and made such a good start from Woking that the 6¾ rising miles to milepost 31 took only 9¼min. In October 1942 the 17½miles from Salisbury to Semley summit were covered in 19¾min by No 21C9 *Shaw Savill* hauling 400tons gross. This prompted a reader to report a 1943 run:

> "On May 12 last I joined the 9 a.m. from Waterloo at Seaton Junction No 21C9 with 13 coaches (full) and a wagon, Driver Mitchell in charge. Leaving Seaton Junction at 12.50.0, we entered Honiton Tunnel at 1.0.40; on leaving the Tunnel speed was reduced to 10mph for a lengthy p.w. repair, and passing Honiton Station at 1.6.10 we stopped at Sidmouth Junction at 1.12.0. Leaving Sidmouth Junction at 1.14.2 we passed Whimple at 1.19.45, Exmouth Junction Box at 1.26.26 and stopped in Exeter Central at 1.28.50.
>
> The schedule is 40min and the time taken, 38min, which, allowing for the pwr check, gives a net time of about 35min; a very fine run indeed, and as for the climb up Honiton Bank — to lift some 450tons of train from a standstill, up nearly five miles at an average gradient of 1 in 80, in 10min 40sec is a truly amazing performance. Driver Mitchell's grin of satisfaction when No 21C9 came off at Exeter was well earned!

There was also a great deal of favourable publicity about the combining of the 10.50 and the 10.59am ex-Waterloo into one 16coach train, "Merchant Navy"-hauled, starting in May after successful tests with 20 coach trains.

It was about this time that the full significance of the power, the free running and the almost unbeatable boiler of the Pacifics became clear to a significant number of drivers, and then the Southern Steam Renaissance really got started, with scrupulous attention to permanent way slacks, storming up banks and flying down into the valleys, making up lost time often with the extra minute in hand. The Southern drivers saw their traditional wish becoming a reality.

Though war conditions limited opportunities, the *Railway Gazette* also found favourable "Merchant Navy" performances to report in 1943, with No 21C6 taking 17coaches = 570tons from Andover to Woking, 42miles, in 42min. Commenting on a run from Chard Junction to Hewish summit, 7miles of which two rise at 1 in 120, over which 61mph was maintained with a light train of 285tons, the *Railway Gazette* remarked that "despite their 6ft 2in wheels they have shown themselves capable of sustained speeds up to 90mph."

The "modernised," "air-smoothed" and "clean-swept" look of the Pacifics increasingly caught the public fancy, particularly in Southern England where their performances began to attract wider attention. As their popularity with drivers grew, jokes began to appear about how much better you could manage if only you had such an engine. Sometimes appearances alone were the wish, as with driver Fred in the March/April 1942 *Southern Railway Magazine*; he had demanded a bigger, streamlined engine and the fitters were discussing what to do:

Another bloke exclaimed with laughter
"Lets camouflage his old 'King Arthur';"
"By gum" said Foreman "That'll do it
Get out your tools and all go to it."
So when they knew Fred had gone home
They took off chimney, also dome
And with a hammer and a chisel
They even cut away the whistle.
The thing was then encased in boarding
Obtained from an adjacent hoarding.
Although of size it showed some lack, it
Did look like the "Channel Packet."
Fred, much to everyone's surprise
His engine failed to recognise
He murmured with uplifting stare
"The answer to the Driver's Prayer"
And to his mate said, with a snigger
"See what I'll do with something bigger."
Now, strange though it may seem to you
He worked his train to Waterloo
In record time, and back again
There never was a faster train.
And this is very strange, becos' it
Only goes to show — or does it?
          W.T.P.

But appearances alone certainly do not satisfy real drivers; handsome is as handsome *does*. With the second batch of "Merchant Navies" in 1944 and the first "West Countries" in 1945 drivers really were getting handsome doers, the light Pacifics in particular bringing new dimensions of power to

Fig 24 The camouflaging of Driver Fred's "King Arthur."

the Westward reaches. Despite the hindrance of its chaotic early months, the year 1947 undeniably found Southern Steam living it up with tremendous panache. The 60 Pacifics seemed to be fleeting everywhere, miraculously energetic, usually a bit ahead of schedule, looking out for lost time to recover, and brilliantly handsome in their post-war livery.

There were only two significant clouds on this happy horizon. One was that all this good work did seem to be costing a lot of coal, water and oil. The other was that maintenance, expected to be less than on conventional engines, was turning out to be rather more. But this caused scant loss of sleep to the drivers who kept proving by their 1947 exploits that the Southern had the best time-keeping tradition in the UK.

It was proposed by Riddles early in January 1948 and agreed by the Railway Executive on January 16, that comprehensive interchange trials should be made between the leading engines of the four Groups to compare performances and draw constructive conclusions. This now seems quite easy and obvious but it could have been a red-taped disaster. Instead Riddles gave an open remit to display the engines to their advantage, and got it done *quickly*, and thereby put on a superlative steam entertainment. No official briefing came to the Southern Region from Marylebone but it was assumed that economy in fuel allied to adequate timekeeping were the desirable criteria. Chrimes the Running Superintendent and Nicholson, DLS at Stewarts Lane, both thought that the LMS shape would appear in the BR standard engines whatever happened in the trials, and they knew in any case that they had not the faintest chance of winning the economy stakes. So they told their drivers, who did not need much telling, to show 'em what the Southern Pacifics could do. "Show them that you can get up those banks at a respectable speed and get the passengers home on time or early, Southern style" was the briefing message.

The Southern engines were at a decided disadvantage sartorially, because they were coupled to black LMS tenders to provide water-scoops. One also had its sleek outline impaired by the addition of an excrescence — the tablet exchange apparatus fitted to No. 34004 for working on the Highland line.

Three "Merchant Navies" were chosen to compete with the A4 Pacifics of the LNER, the "Kings" of the GWR and the "Duchess" Pacifics and rebuilt "Scots" of the LMS. The best performances came from three-year-old No. 35017 *Belgian Marine*, which lifted 535tons over Stoke summit at 47½mph after restarting at Grantham, covering the 5.4 miles in 9½min; and then on the London Midland Region knocked 6½min off the 27min schedule from Penrith start to passing Shap summit with 525tons. This was achieved on two consecutive trips.

In the mixed traffic class, the three "West Countries" chosen, Nos. 34004/5/6, were competing with 4-6-0s — LNER Class B1s, GWR "Halls" and "Black Staniers" of the LMS. The trains and schedules were naturally matched to these 4-6-0s, all equally powerful, and it was expected that a Pacific would liven things up, which is exactly what happened. They showed that they were needed on the Midland route from St. Pancras and the Great Central route from Marylebone to Manchester, to give passengers the sort of ride they might expect in the 1950s. The only recorded equivalent drawbar horsepower over 2,000, throughout all the interchange trials, was achieved by No 34006 *Bude* at Whetstone, accelerating at the foot of the 1 in 176 bank with a 375ton train on June 11. The same engine succeeded in knocking ten minutes off the scheduled time from Exeter to Bristol on the GWR line.

In July 1948, armed with short but encouraging experiences of the LMS line to Glasgow, driver Swain and fireman Hooker climbed onto No. 34004 *Yeovil* and set off for Perth. Their 450mile journey consisted of piloting duties and it is well said that when they piloted the down "Midday Scot" the ascent of Shap felt like an all-time record. There had been one faction at Perth resisting the driving of any trains by "foreign" drivers, but this was quickly forgotten in Scottish hospitality to the strangers and interest in their machine.

When Hooker went down to Perth shed on Sunday morning to look over his engine several fitters crowded around asking if they could see the motion. Permission was given by Inspector Knight and the sump cover removed, but the view was blocked by the inside big end being at the top. Needless to say *Yeovil* was closely hemmed in by other engines, typical Sunday shed fashion, but, nothing daunted, they fetched a shunter and shifted three engines and then came and moved *Yeovil* the necessary few feet to get the best view of "the works." Hooker later recalled that "I was really proud of her. Every detail was spotless and gleaming like chromium plate and looking a real picture." The Scottish fitters were highly impressed, as some even admitted.

The line to Inverness was gently rising for the first 35 miles, mostly single track, to Blair Atholl. There they picked up a banker for help up the 1 in 80 to Struan and further help up the longer 1 in 70 to Dalnaspidal, two miles short of Druimuachdar summit (1484ft). Put on its mettle by the sight of the bank, *Yeovil* made such a good start from Blair Atholl, with energetic help from behind, that they took the 1 in 80 at a speed not previously experienced by the banker, a Pickersgill 4-4-0, which arrived at Struan winded — less than 120psi on the gauge and no water in the glass. The Struan stop, lengthened by early arrival, enabled her to recover and give further help with the 380ton train to Dalnaspidal. Driver Swain steamed into Inverness about ten minutes early.

After three equally stimulating runs, there were feelings of regret as *Yeovil* threaded its way carefully out of the famous triangle of Inverness station for the last time. It swung south on the "direct" line at Millburn Junction and then opened out for the five miles at 1 in 60 easing to 1 in 70 before the favourable mile through Culloden station. Then, gaining speed every foot, it spanned the wide Strathnairn, the plumes of steam soaring to the sky and capping the majestic red sandstone viaduct. Then started the six miles at 1 in 60 through Daviot and, after an easier six miles to Tomatin, the final 3¼ miles to Slochd summit. There is no level at Slochd, and once again Hooker was worried to see his glass empty as the engine tipped from 1 in 60 rising to 1 in 70 falling in a few seconds. But the syphons gave added protection to the firebox crown and the only caution shown by *Yeovil* was a comparatively gentle descent, down the bank and curves to Carr Bridge and Aviemore. The southbound climb to Druimuachdar summit starts at Kingussie, with about 19miles, much of it between 1 in 100 and 1 in 80. Driver Swain made his last attack on this bank with 35% cut-off; and since, thanks to Hooker, a steam chest pressure of 235psi was maintained, they recorded an equivalent drawbar horsepower of 1950. It was a rather noisy ascent, but a delight to the passengers and the holiday enthusiasts and it helped to clip 20min off the schedule timings.

For the first stage of their long trek home, they were booked to take a train of 17 carriages, and an apologetic Running Foreman was explaining that due to holiday specials he could not find them a pilot for this over-load of five coaches. Then at the last moment a "Black Stanier" turned up, looking in such doubtful condition that driver Swain was put to it not to ask the question that sprung to his mind: "Do we have to pull the 17 *and that?*" In fact it did its share of the work but only as far as Motherwell, where they lost it and one carriage; and then the LMR pilotman expressed grave doubts about their ever re-starting with 16 on the severe curve and rising 1 in 120 out of Motherwell station. But they got away without trouble and lost no time over Beattock, hurrying back home.

Meanwhile good Pacific publicity continued at Waterloo for the naming ceremony of the 21st "Merchant Navy," No. 35021 *New Zealand Line.* The Chief Regional Officer, John Elliot, presided and said: "The "Merchant Navy" class locomotives designed by Mr Bulleid are now very well known. The engines are powerful and have improved the timekeeping: in fact, in some cases the time-keeping is better than pre-war."

When the formal report on the Interchange Trials came out it showed two things about the Southern Pacifics, both rather expected:

(1) They hogged the lists of most powerful performances:

Equivalent dbhp	Times achieved	Classes of engine involved
over 2000	1	"West Country"
1900-2000	5	"West Country" 3, "Merchant Navy" 2
1800-1900	5	"Duchess" 3, "Merchant Navy" 2

(2) They used nearly 15% more coal than the most economical Pacific, the LNER A4. This did not seem in any way to dull the praise and acclaim of those many passengers and enthusiasts who had noted the sparkling performances and compared notes. So some of the other contestants were sufficiently provoked to say "We could have done the same." But you see the thing was, they didn't.

Early in 1951 the Southern Region had all its 140 Pacifics in service but it was not until March 1952 that No. 35022 *Holland-Amerika Line* went along to take her turn at the Rugby Locomotive Testing station. Here she frankly behaved like a primadonna, refusing to act precisely as directed yet giving a memorable performance. They would set the cut-off at 15% and wham! a moment later it was at 20%. Power always seemed to *increase* at what were supposed to be fixed conditions. She also teased the Test Plant by shedding oil on the rollers, permitting her to race away with danger to side rods (and test Staff) and chaos to test data. These temperamental changes were duly reported as "not of such magnitude as would have affected the locomotive's ability to carry out its normal duties quite effectively, but were such as to make accurate measurement exceptionally difficult." They got a bit cross with No. 35022 at Rugby but she did not seem to care very much, having a great heart (boiler) and reckoning (rightly) that they could not do without it. In fact they never succeeded in reaching the maximum steaming rate, stopping a bit short with a 20min run at 42,000lb per hour rate, using South Kirby coal.

These tests, and the subsequent road trials between Skipton and Carlisle, simply proved that the engines had the best boilers in the business, bar none, and that the cut-off was liable to be later than the driver thought. But in the next two years some experiments on steaming were done which naturally turned out to be red-herrings — modifying the blastpipe and chimney, and removing the thermic syphons. The former impaired steaming and the latter merely reduced strength, safety and the stability of the brick arch.

Meanwhile the reputation of the Pacifics continued to grow, particularly of the lightweights, the "West Countries" and "Battle of Britains". Everyone had a favourite story of some fabulous recovery of lost time and numerous stirring exploits were authenticated and published. The appearance in 1951 of a rival mixed traffic Pacific, the BR standard "Britannia" of Class 7MT, seemed merely to enhance the prestige of the Southern lot. The "Britannias" were good engines and must have cost a lot less per lb of tractive effort, but when first used on the 8.20am Newport to Paddington they oscillated the leading carriage so badly that we were forced back down the train to do our urgent reading. This was in sharp contrast to the smooth haul of the "Castles" and in a testy moment I sent my father a Clerihew which I later heard him quoting:

Without wishing to be pedantic,
I could class *Britannia* as merely an enlarged Atlantic.
For something really tarific
See a Bulleid Pacific.

But in 1952 clouds already visible in 1947 were thickening. Worries about fuel consumption were deepened by the comparisons of the Interchange Trials, and worries about maintenance were growing for a variety of reasons. Minimal design effort had been directed at curing oil leakages and these were getting worse. The type of oil had been changed and this was held to be one cause of corrosion occurring within the oil bath; but the main cause for this and for lubrication failures was said to be a deterioration in general maintenance standards, more at some Sheds than others, due to the stringent economies forced on British Railways. And, worst of all, careless diagnosis and delayed attention could cause serious damage, which was disproportionately difficult and expensive to repair. Essential work inside the oil bath was greatly disliked, particularly by the younger fitters, despite special protective clothing. Then also there was the cold fact that valve events sometimes started to fall off after only 12,000miles, with maintenance needed at 36,000 compared with 48,000 for "Nelsons." All this was irksome to the Running Dept., specially as they had long enjoyed the exceptional freedom from wear characteristic of Maunsell's engines, where vast attention had been paid over the years to securing "long life" components. And of course they had been promised even less maintenance trouble on the Pacifics. So by the end of 1953 the oil bath and the enclosed motion were definitely and unanimously disliked by those in charge. There was also growing opposition to the air-smoothed casing: Shed fitters disliked it because it hindered both diagnosis and repair of trivial pipe leaks; many drivers preferred the better look-out with conventional cladding; its ease-of-cleaning became rather a poor joke as cleaning standards bit the dust; and seen from Marylebone its appearance would be preferable if it conformed with the shape of the new standard engines.

There was therefore very strong pressure on the CM&EE Department at Brighton to do something about it, and Jarvis was faced with three alternatives:

(1) Do nothing.
(2) Try to cure the faults without major modifications.
(3) Replace troublesome parts by standard parts.

Course 1 was not on and course 2 would indeed have taken a brave spirit because no one, then or previously, had any relevant constructive ideas. And frankly, how would it have been received at Marylebone? No prize for the answer. So Jarvis opted for course 3 and by the end of 1954 he had done all the preliminary thinking and outline design, building up a small independent section in the Brighton Drawing Office under M. Lockhart for this specific job.

Their report was issued by the CME&E, H.H. Swift, in January 1955. It sought permission to spend £760,000 by 1961 on modifying 140 Pacifics so as to save £2,051,400 by 1987, the estimated year for scrapping the class. Ignoring interest charges on the capital spent, the break-even dates were 1962 for the "Merchant Navies" and 1966 for the light Pacifics assuming all were modified by mid-1961. The case for modifying the "Merchant Navies" was slightly the stronger because they were proportionally heavier on maintenance and ran longer mileages: during the year 1952 the records showed that the "Merchant Navies" ran on average 50,000 miles and the Lightweights 43,000. Interestingly, despite the old grumble that the Southern Region was "lush with Pacifics," it was proposed to modify the whole lot; the report cannily added that "the increased availability of the modified locomotives will no doubt make possible a small reduction in the number of locomotives required on the region, provided that the workings remain the same as at present. The class and number of the locomotives will be decided when the modification to the "Merchant Navy" & "West Country" class locomotives has been completed."

The costings in the report were done by the Regional Accountant in accordance with the BR (ex-LMS) standard method. W. Marsh did not wholly agree with this method and submitted his own working, which was less favourable to the project, but the standard was accepted.

There was a slight moment of panic when it was found that the LMR "Coronation" Pacifics needed shopping at lower mileages than the "Merchant Navies", though I must say this fact had been previously pointed out in R.C. Bond's March 1953 paper to the Institution of Locomotive Engineers which gave the figures extracted in the Table opposite.

Given the decision to fit the engines with conventional valve gear and cladding, it is hard to fault the Jarvis plan; details are given in Appendix 4. Brighton drawing office approved, with the exception of the "too standard" front end of the engine, sloping from buffer beam to smokebox and nicknamed "the built-in snow-plough." The main anxiety was weight and in the event the modified "Merchant Navies" came out 2¾tons heavier and the others 3½tons heavier, details in App 4. These weights and the impaired balance would have been unacceptable when the originals were built, but in 1956 the only limitation was that the modified lightweights were banned from Meldon viaduct.

Average mileages between consecutive periodical repairs (intermediate or general) in the year 1951

Region	Class of Locomotive		Average mileage
LM	4-6-2	"Coronation"	73,188
	4-6-0	"Royal Scot" (taper boiler) and 5X conversions	70,495
E/NE	4-6-2	A1	93,363
	4-6-2	A2	85,671
	4-6-2	A3	83,574
	4-6-2	A4	86,614
	4-6-0	B1	78,396
Western	4-6-0	"King"	78,987
	4-6-0	"Castle"	87,424
	4-6-0	"Hall"	87,942
Southern	4-6-2	"Merchant Navy"	75,687
	4-6-2	"West Country" and "Battle of Britain"	74,650
	4-6-0	"Lord Nelson"	81,611
	4-6-0	"King Arthur"	70,995

Six engines were modified during 1956 and the second, No. 35020 *Bibby Line* went for road tests between Waterloo and Exeter where it behaved very predictably but not so very economically. It was decided to complete the modifications programme, and by mid-1961, when dismally tolled the knell of parting steam, all but 50 had been modified. The work was in fact running two years late and quite a lot of people were not sorry.

The Sheds reacted well to the modifications. Maintenance was both reduced and simplified. Preparation times were unaffected and disposal times were nearly halved thanks to the excellent rocking grate and better access to smokebox.

The drivers, rather characteristically, accepted them with grumbles. While conceding a better lookout they did not like the screw reverser and they missed the free running of the originals. They complained of less power, and here I must say, at the risk of being thought cynical, that I think Jarvis was a bit naive not to falsify the cut-off scale as H.G. Ivatt did with the Caprotti modifications to the "Black Staniers." After all, the original engines were known normally to run less notched-up than shown, so why not write that into the modifications? Drivers also complained of a rougher ride, which was true due to the new motion imbalance and to the coupled wheel springing being hardened; the latter prevented loss of weight from coupled to carrying wheels and thereby loss of adhesion.

The public and the enthusiasts seemed to be evenly divided. They made their opposing views very well known, technical opinions often taking second place to the emotional.

Bulleid unhesitatingly disliked the modifications, as would any designer. He grumbled a bit that no one had asked his views about it, but of course

117

he would have been astonished if they had, just as Maunsell would have been astonished to be consulted on the modifications to the "Nelsons". When some of the dust was dying down (and other dust rising) in 1960 he took C.P. Hopkins, General Manager of the Southern Region, an ex-LNER Traffic man, to a Smeatonian Society dinner and asked him for an appraisal. Hopkins wrote:

"You can take it that the modification is a complete success and has resulted — largely because of the basic excellencies of the locomotive as designed — in what is admitted in high quarters to be the most modern steam locomotive at large in British Railways. The foregoing statement is, I assure you, absolutely sincere.

As regards the effect of the modification, you may be interested in the enclosed copy of a memorandum that has been prepared at my request, extracting the leading figures from our files.

But, I repeat, there would have been no such success but for a magnificent basic design."

This was very fair comment, because the basic design fixes the boiler, wheel and cylinder sizes and stroke and these were never changed. His enclosed set of figures, reproduced in Appendix 4, also seem very fair, though these supporting figures are never wholly reliable, always tending to favour the action taken and the party line. Similarly there is always a tendency for a superseded design or machine to become a whipping boy, shouldering sundry blames and called on to support excuses. Morever we were then rapidly importing the American habit of denigrating anything recently discarded, after the style of commercial propagandists who want you to buy the latest model. Anything superseded is for the garbage bin, though of course a mere 50 years later it is desperately sought after for the museums. Some quite senior officials were tarred with this brush and, perhaps unwittingly, repeated grossly exaggerated stories of defects and lack of reliability in the unmodified engines.

But on balance the savings claimed were probably achieved though the improved availability was not exploited. The job cost a bit more than planned, and at the programmed completion date only 90 of 140 engines had been modified; the scrapping of them started in 1963, three years before the financial break-even date. So probably, if there had been a final reckoning, it would have been found that money was saved by modifying the "Merchant Navies", but that slightly more was lost on modifying the 60 light Pacifics.

So much for finance, fate once again fooling the accounting. But how about the engines? It was perfectly true, as Jarvis often said, that they remained "85% Bulleid." In fact he sometimes said "90%". But there was a loss of something well described by R.H.N. Hardy who drove them and ran them whilst Shedmaster at Stewarts Lane in the early 1950s:

"They were the unique product of a bold man's great brain, and in my judgment there was *nothing* in the country to touch them on their good days."

And R.A.S. Hennessey caught a little of their strong "presence" when he wrote in the *Leader* (Journal of the Bulleid Pacific Preservation Society) for January 1969 about "The peculiar — even mystic — appeal of these machines," adding:

"The steam engine was one of the highest expressions of art in the industrial age, not merely as a variable shape or form but as an aesthetic expression which impressed itself on many senses at once. It was the expression of its day as much as the sculpture and music. Much of the skill, technology and logic of the 1930s and 1940s were distilled and embodied in the Bulleid Pacifics."

This partly explains how they gave that star quality to Southern Steam. After modification they reverted to the LMS-cherished features which went to make the conventionally successful steam locomotive — the one which soon became a sitting target for annihilation by diesel.

To be constructive, however, it must be acknowledged that on available data modification was undoubtedly the correct decision and that it was exceptionally well done and reflected great credit on Jarvis and the Brighton drawing office. Bulleid took a strong dislike only to two details — the change to manganese steel axle-boxes and horn guides; and the elimination of the "hexagon-pentagon" securing cap for the coupling rods. The steel axleboxes certainly landed the engines with a new and unnecessary "play" of 0.03in before any wear increased it. As to the securing cap, my father kept up semi-serious attacks on the retrograde step of changing it and in 1970 I wrote asking him how it originated. He replied:

"The side rod cap fastening was due to R. Curl as all I had to do with it was to say a better design than a split ended taper pin was needed. Curl produced his design and the chief draughtsman had a model made in wood because he was sure I would not understand the drawing, much to Curl's amusement. It was not too easy to follow and we all thought Derby had not grasped its merits!"

The modified engines did suffer troubles with the replace fastenings, and with the screw reverser which had to withstand the racking forces of the motion. Regarding looks (as the mirror said to the model) the BFB wheels were not improved by the added balance weights for the heavier motion and the heavier, non-fluted side rods. But the total troubles on all these re-designed or "standard" details were undoubtedly below average and the modified engines, side-by-side with the dwindling number of originals, set about their duties with unabated vigour. I think many drivers hankered

119

after the "spirit" of the originals, but they achieved equal performances and maintained their timekeeping traditions with the modified engines.

Naturally they found great favour with R.G. Jarvis, and when I asked him for his pet recovery story he wrote:

"The following is the story of the remarkable "MN" performance on the "ACE" when there was a radio commentary.

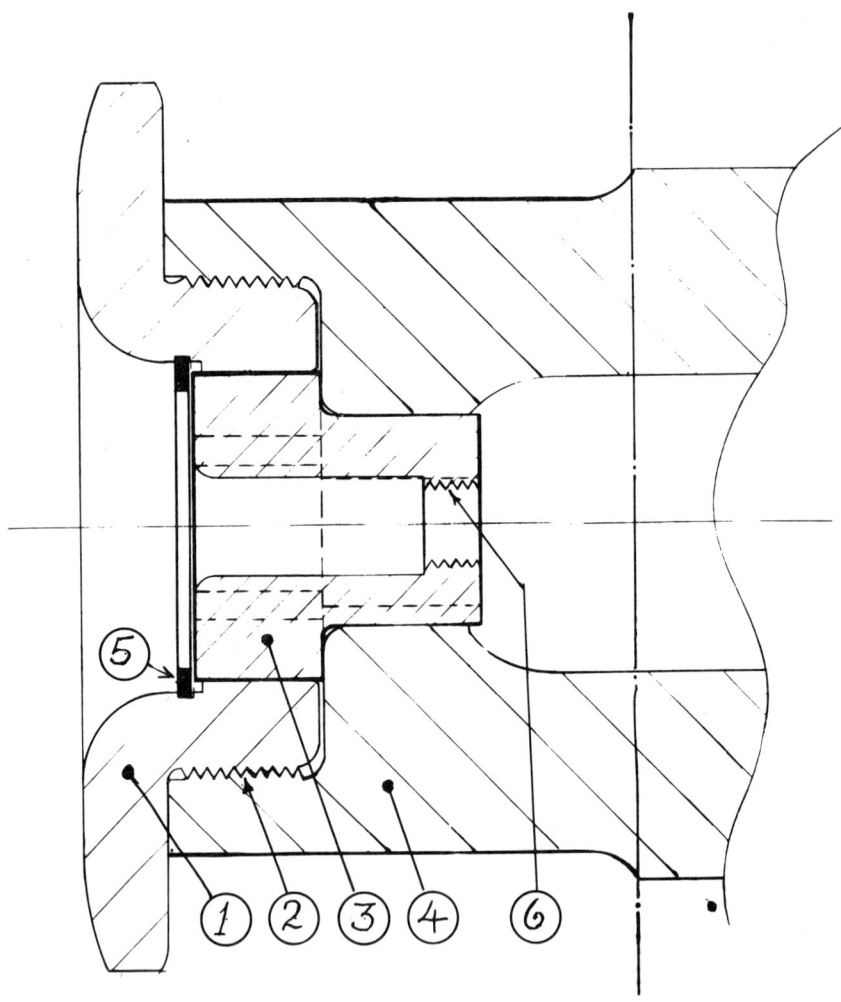

Fig 25 R. Curl's hexagon-pentagon cap for securing coupling rods. After fitting the coupling rod the securing cap 1 is screwed on by its 4½ inch diameter 8 tpi thread 2 and further tightened till the check 3 will slide into both the pentagonal slot in the crank pin 4 and the hexagonal slot in the cap 1. The check is then held in position by circlip 5. A thread 6 is provided for entry and withdrawal of the check. The pentagon/hexagon allows 30 positions per revolution of the cap so each represents an axial movement of 0".004 and thereby allows a fine fit.

120

"A modified "Merchant Navy" was hauling the "Atlantic Coast Express" in the normal way and there was a loss of 5min to Woking due to the rebuilding of a bridge somewhere in the outer London area. I expected this loss to be made up quite quickly, as it normally would have been, but it was soon evident that all was not well and at one stage the crew had to put the "pricker" into the firebox to try and liven the fire up a bit, the pressure being considerably reduced. No further time was lost to Salisbury and in fact running times were maintained by the engine. The commentator said that this was the kind of thing one had to expect from the old steam engine and it would soon be quite different with the new diesels and electrics.

"Of course I was disappointed that the 5min were not made up, but said to my wife 'You wait and see what happens between Salisbury and Exeter with the Exmouth Junction men.' We were doomed to disappointment, however, because at Salisbury the broadcast ended.

"I naturally made enquiries and it turned out that in the kerfuffle of getting everything set up for the broadcast at Waterloo, a handbrake was left on in the leading van. This so increased the work that the locomotive had to do, that the necessary steam production required a firing rate beyond the continuous capacity of the one fireman. Doubtless the engine crew knew that they had brakes dragging but decided to "have a go", hoping that the application would leak away after a time. However at Salisbury they had a cripple to take out of the train with wheels that had been red hot!

"At all events the locomotive was in good shape when the Exmouth men took over, but the start was 25min late. There was no report on the subsequent run to Exeter but arrival at the Central was not recorded as a late arrival, and therefore may be taken as being no more than two minutes in arrears. It seems probable that the locomotive, which had been castigated by the BBC, had gone on to pick up no less than 23min on the high speed schedule of the heavy "Atlantic Coast Express" over one of the most arduous main lines in this country."

In the Stephenson Locomotive Society Journal of July 1967 Norman Harvey reported the seventh authentic 100 mph run by a Bulleid Pacific:

"No. 35028 *Clan Line* was hauling an eleven-car load of 365tons full on an up Weymouth recovering a late start from Southampton. From passing Basingstoke to passing Fleet, a distance 11.3miles, the remarkable but not unprecedented time of 7min 13sec was noted. A maximum speed of 103mph is claimed before Fleet, and substantiated by the passing time of 2min 1sec from Winchfield to Fleet (3.3miles). This represents an average of virtually 99mph and is supported by a recorded speed of 98 through Winchfield and one of 100 at Fleet."

Sometimes, specially towards the end, the Running people did not know whether to cheer or groan at some Pacific performances. As S.C. Townroe feelingly recalls, "engines with sloppy valve gear could be badly out of beat, though this was only audible on starting and drivers did not worry too much. An engine might work for days with what turned out to be a valve uncoupled. You would expect a deterioration in smokebox vacuum to affect steaming, but not so. No wonder they were called *fantastic* in every way." Townroe also recalled one classic incident. "A 'Merchant Navy' with the up 'Atlantic Coast Express' arrived at Waterloo right time but somebody noticed the left front cylinder cover was missing. The driver said that 'he did recollect a bit of a bump' near Hook, but had not stopped because all seemed normal after it. The cylinder cover was found where he said, 42 miles behind."

These examples extol the reserve power of the boilers which gave all Bulleid Pacifics such good heart.

When, in mid-1964, D.W. Winkworth timed the up "Atlantic Coast Express" every day for a week on its fairly tough 80-minute schedule for the 83.7 miles to Waterloo from Salisbury with gross daily load of 390 tons, he found that the net times taken varied from 75½ to 78min. Driver Hoare of Salisbury had a modified "Merchant Navy" every day except the Thursday. On that day he did just as well, clocking a net time of 76½mins, with an unmodified "West Country," No. 34002 *Salisbury*. It goes to show.

16

The "Leader"

All engineers, over a quiet drink, will sympathize with Traffic Managers who have to state what engines they will require two years later. Travelling habits, progress of electrification, speeding-up plans, and withdrawals of existing engines due to age or other failings — all these affect the choice of what new steam engines the Southern Railway needed in 1944, to say nothing of personal preferences.

At a typical General Manager's meeting in December 1944 the CME and the Traffic Manager were asked to confer and report on the 1946 loco-motive building programme. They duly agreed on ten shunters for Southampton Docks and on 25 "West Country" Pacifics, but for the balance of 25 engines the CME first suggested building 25 more Q1 0-6-0s, for which material had been ordered and was still available. The engines had been shown to possess the necessary speed and punch, but the Traffic Manager wanted tanks and in a letter to the CME on December 15, 1944 he wrote:

"With regard to your suggestion that the material already available for the construction of Q1 engines should still be used for this type instead of for passenger tanks, an opportunity has been taken of inspecting locomotive No. C1 and the conclusion has been arrived at that the look-out facilities provided on this engine are not suitable for regular tender-first running. The rear lookout on the driver's side does not give a sufficiently wide range of vision, and the absence of a lookout on the fireman's side is a serious drawback, having regard to the fact that it is necessary for the fireman to assist in looking out for signals when not otherwise necessarily engaged and this is particularly important having regard to the fact that the normal position for signals is on the left-hand side. Unless, therefore, the observation conditions, tender-first, can be materially improved, I am afraid they will not be suitable to traffic requirements.

Another point I would like to raise is as to whether you are satisfied that these engines are suitable for maintaining necessary speeds running tender-first when light in coal and water."

H.N. Gresley could well have demolished this by a strong reply to the last paragraph only, but O.V. Bulleid agreed and on January 4, 1945 their recommendation to the General Manager was:

> "25 Passenger Tank Engines (to be built from material ordered for 25 Q1 class)
> 10 Shunters
> 25 4-6-2 "West Country" Passenger Tender Engines (utilising for the tenders the material ordered for 25 Q1 class)"

Missenden was far too shrewd a General Manager either to think the words "Passenger Tank Engines" would necessarily contain his CME or to offer a programme including 50 new passenger engines to the M & E Committee of the wartime Railway Executive. Accordingly he wrote a typical memo to the pair on January 30, 1945:

> "Further to our recent conversations, in order not to delay the supply of the information in respect of the anticipated building programme for 1946, I think we might, pending a decision being reached on the question of the passenger tank engines, indicate at the next M&E Committee that our building programme will be 25 mixed traffic, 25 freight and 10 shunting engines.
>
> Later on, when I have received your recommendation as to whether passenger tank engines are required or not (which I should like to have before the end of February), the programme can be adjusted as necessary."

This cannily left the Q1 material to be used as originally intended, always a better technique than admitting to a series of half-baked alternatives which one should keep to oneself.

Meanwhile, massive exploratory work was going on in the CME's department. It had started, naturally enough, with simple adaptations of

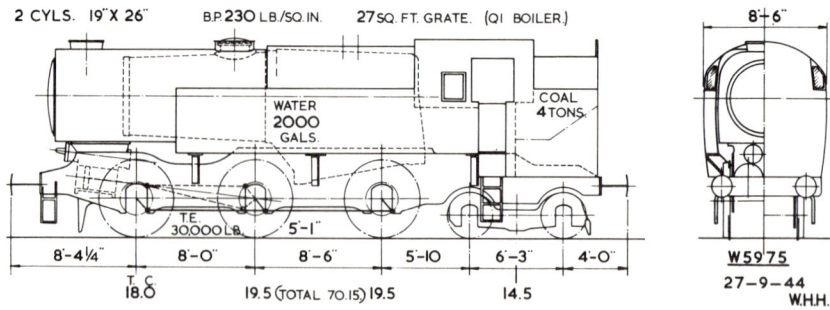

Fig 26 The first shot at a passenger tank, utilising "Q.1" material but probably the most unsatisfactory wheel arrangement in the history of steam engines.

124

66 *Above*: Smart getaway from Andover Junction on June 7th 1965 by No. 34032 *Camelford./D.T. Cobbe*

67 *Below*: Taking it easy with only nine on and a straggling exhaust — No. 34052 *Lord Dowding* in the New Forest./*I.S. Krause*

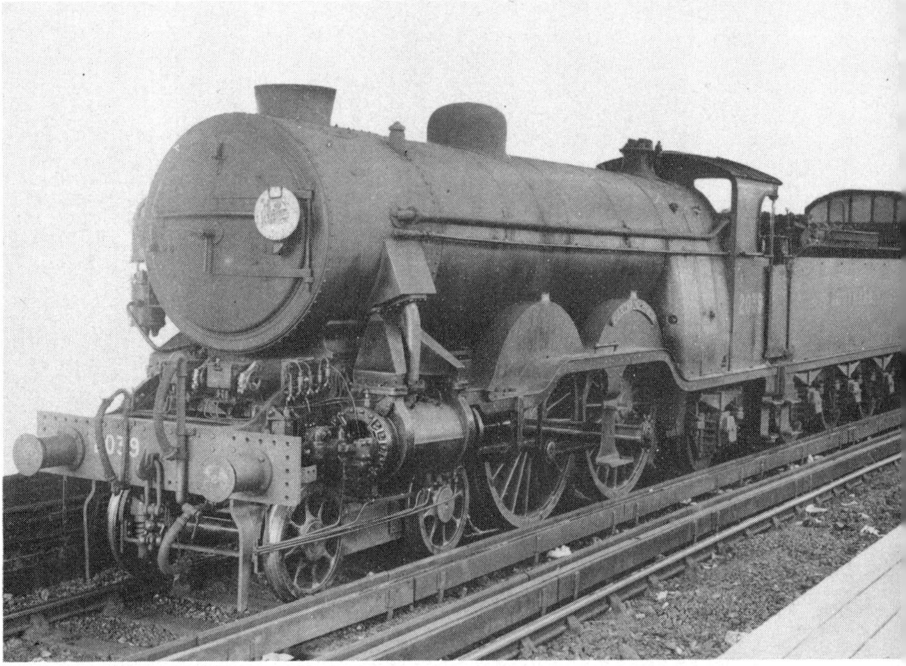

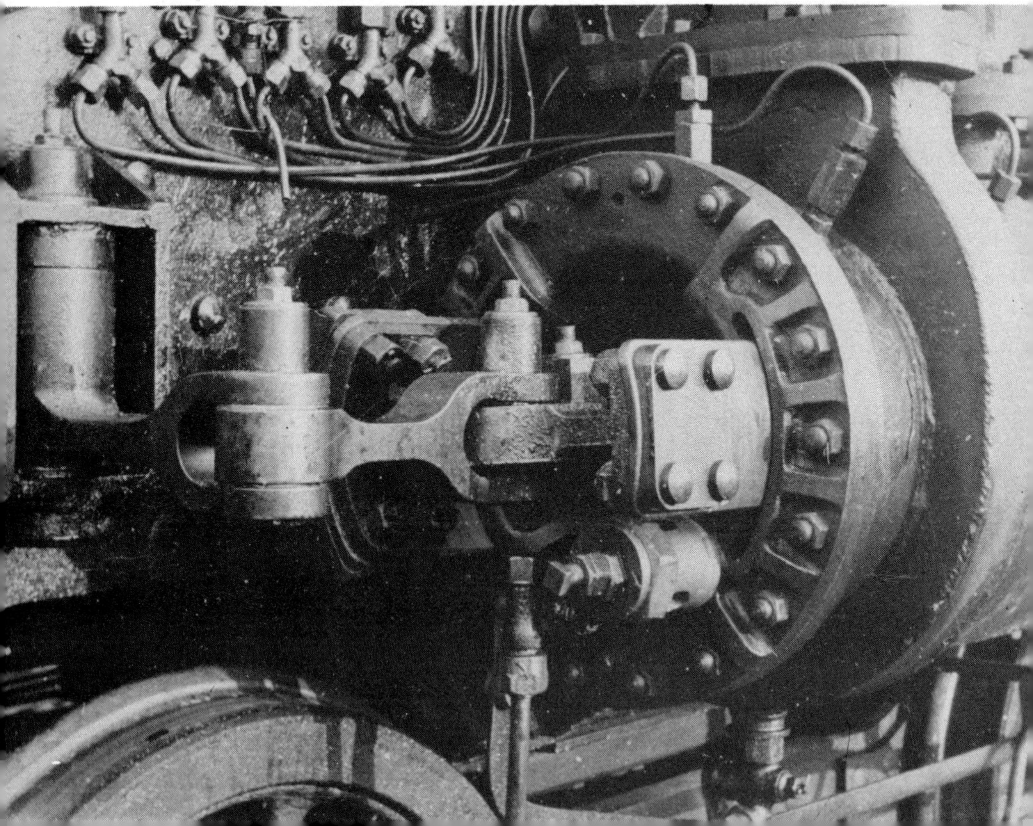

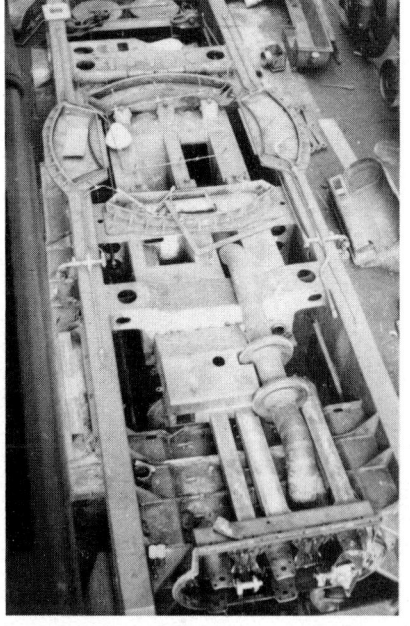

68 *Above left*: Marsh/Ivatt Atlantic No. 2039
fitted with sleeve valves, on a test train at
Brighton, September 1948./*BR*

69 *Left*: The lugs of the sleeve valve
emerging through slots in the cylinder
cover, were driven by a 1 to 1 lever from
the existing Stephenson's valve gear via a
link having a ball-and-socket joint to
permit the rotary oscillation of the sleeves
from an eccentric pin on a cross shaft
between the two cylinders chain driven
from the leading coupled axle./*R. Curl*

70 *Above*: A "Leader" power bogie showing
the cylinder block with sleeve valves
being tried in. The curved exhaust pipe
can be seen above./*BR*

71 *Right*: The power bogie, showing
cylinders and valves, exhaust pipe, four
bearing segments and, very top of
picture, the two brake cylinders./*A.P.
Hatz*

72 *Above*: The forged 3-throw unbalanced crank axle showing chain sprocket for driving the valve gear. One of the two axlebox cylindrical chambers for the spring pedestals can be seen, and the double sprocket for the chain replacing the coupling rods./*BR*

73 *Below*: "Leader" boiler under construction showing the firebox tubeplate, the syphons and the steel support for the firebrick sides of the firebox. Firehole door position shown dotted./*BR*

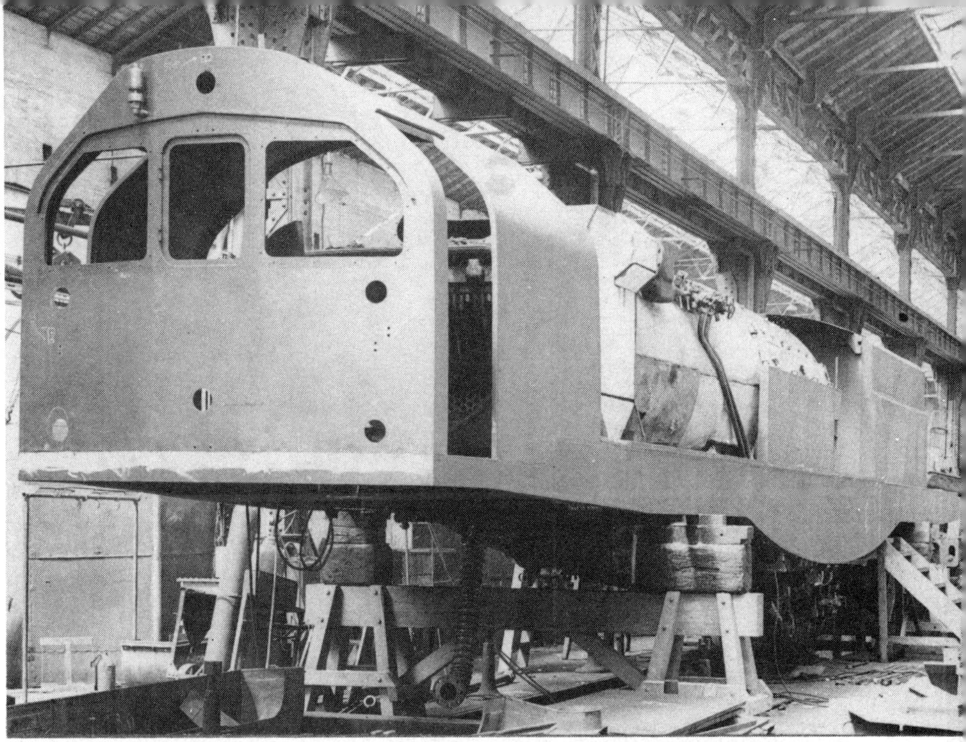

74 *Top*: Nearing completion in Brighton erecting shop. The steam manifold can be seen near the centre in the corridor space./*BR*

75 *Above*: The "Leader" ready to be lifted onto its power bogies, May 1949. The well-lagged steam and exhaust pipes can be seen, above the firing position./*BR*

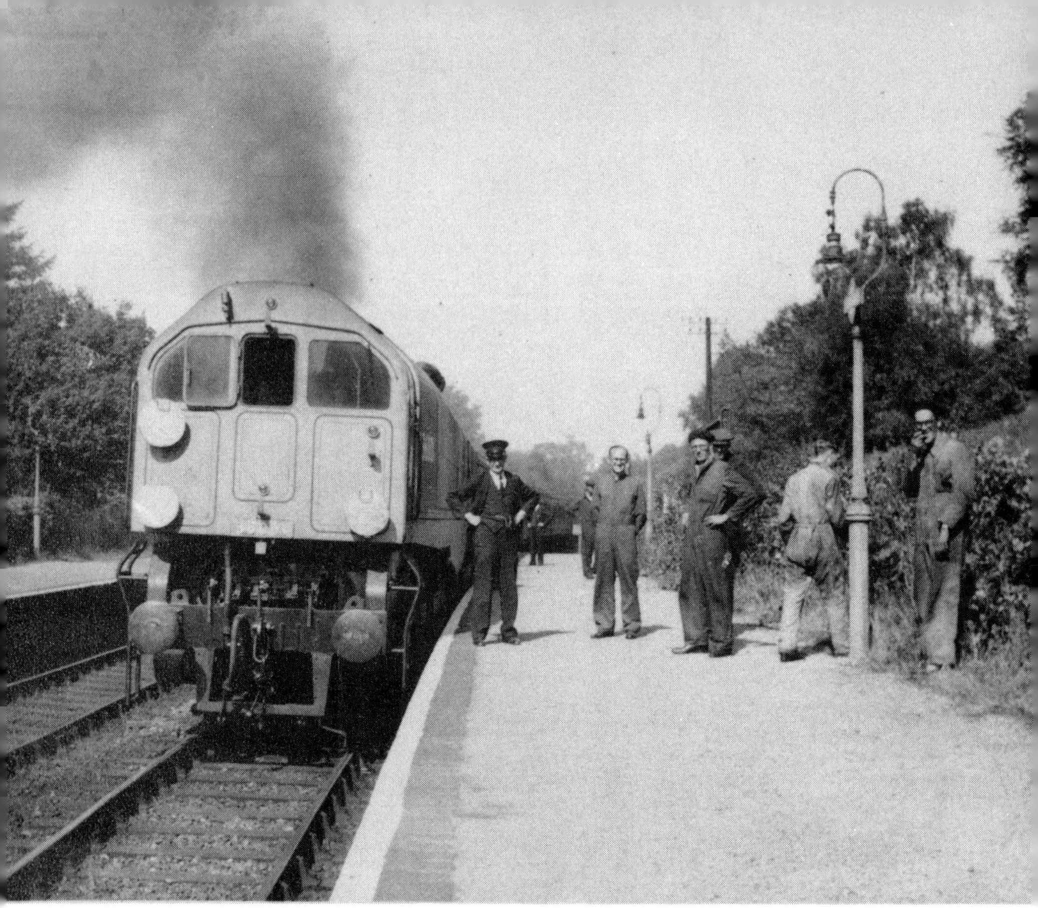

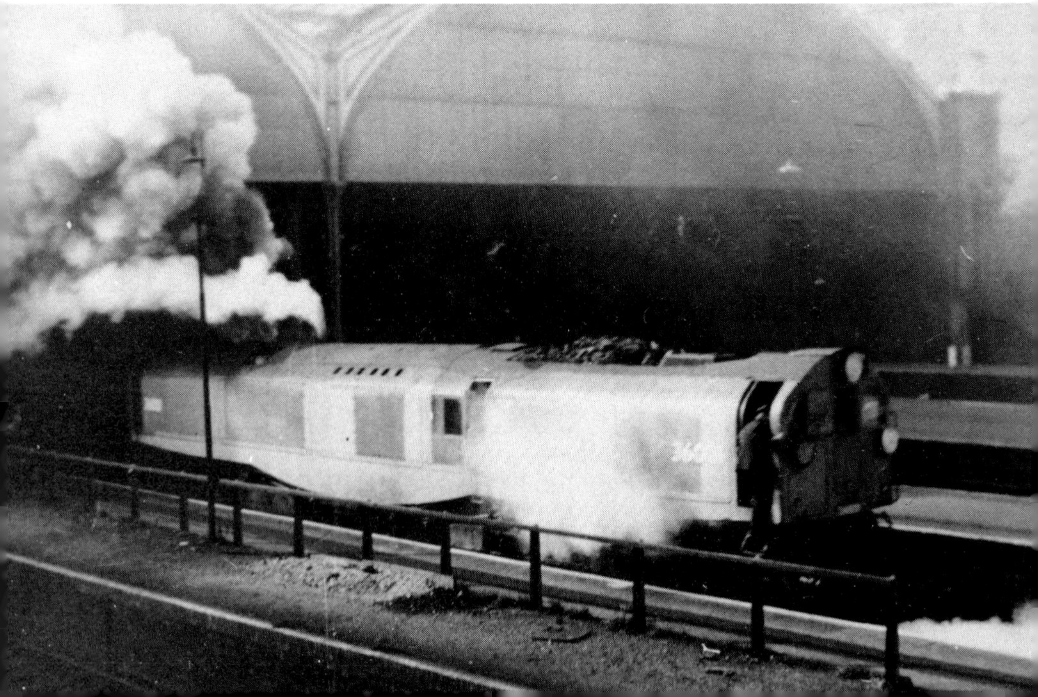

76 *Above left*: No. 36001 "Leader" class resting at Dormans station with test team including W.H. (Joe) Hutchinson (hatless) and Doug Smith./*H.W. Attwell*

77 *Left*: CME's office view of the "Leader" in Brighton station./*A.P. Hatz*

78 *Top*: The 4-wheel heating/luggage vans with Aluminium-faced plywood bodies. Their gradual withdrawal from service started in 1975 when higher speeds necessitated bogie vehicles./*J.G.C.*

79 *Right*: Bulleid's "Post Office bogie" with mail catching apparatus and triangulated underframe./*J.G.C.*

80 *Above*: Bulleid's light all-steel 12-ton wagon for C.I.E., 1957. Time has proved the value in service of the triangulated underframe./*J.G.C.*

A1
METROPOLITAN-VICKERS
ELECTRICAL COMPANY LTD
FIRST OF 94 DIESEL-ELECTRIC
LOCOMOTIVES FOR
IRISH TRANSPORT COMPANY

81 *Left*: Crash!! the 40mph collision staged by Bulleid at Thurles between old bogie carriage, left; and stationary, braked 12-wheeler, right. The Fischer automatic couplings locked and prevented telescoping. The impact shifted the bogie carriage body nearly two feet along its frame so it came to rest in line with its buffers as shown./*C.I.E.*

82 *Below left*: The first "A" class diesel landing on Irish soil, 1955./*O.V.B.*

83 *Right*: Momentary distraction from diesels, couplers and brakes on a Continental trip in 1954.

84 *Below*: Diesel No. A16 hauling a Wexford train of Bulleid lightweight carriages on the coast line at Killiney, overlooked by a short-term Bulleid home on the hillside above./*Deegan*

85 *Above*: An early steaming of C.I.E. 2-6-0 No. 356 at Inchicore with turf conveyor to load tender and Crosti type feed water heaters through which the flue gases were forced by a fan for ultimate discharge at the back of the tender. The exhaust steam was also led, via a jacket round part of the heaters, to the same exhaust point./*C.I.E.*

86 *Below*: Later turf burning trials on No. 356. The steam escapes, from left to right, are from: the induced draught turbine, loco boiler exhaust and turf smoke, safety valves and, at lower level, sundry leaks. Access ladders are well in evidence and of

the legend on the tender, "Experimental Turf Burning Locomotive" humorists have blanked out "Experi" and "Turf."/*J.G.C.*

87 *Above right*: The Turf Burner boiler from the firing side, before adding superheaters. Note the numerous longitudinal and transverse stay heads, and the U-shaped balance pipes between the three boiler sections./*J.G.C.*

88 *Right*: A complete engine being lowered into its power bogie in the erecting shop, Inchicore./*J.G.C.*

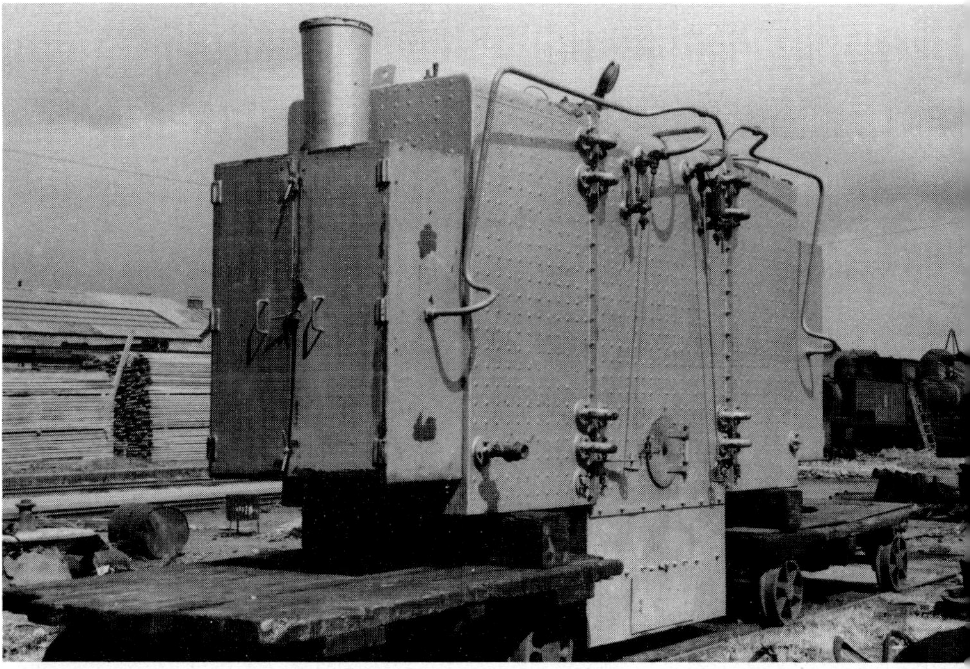

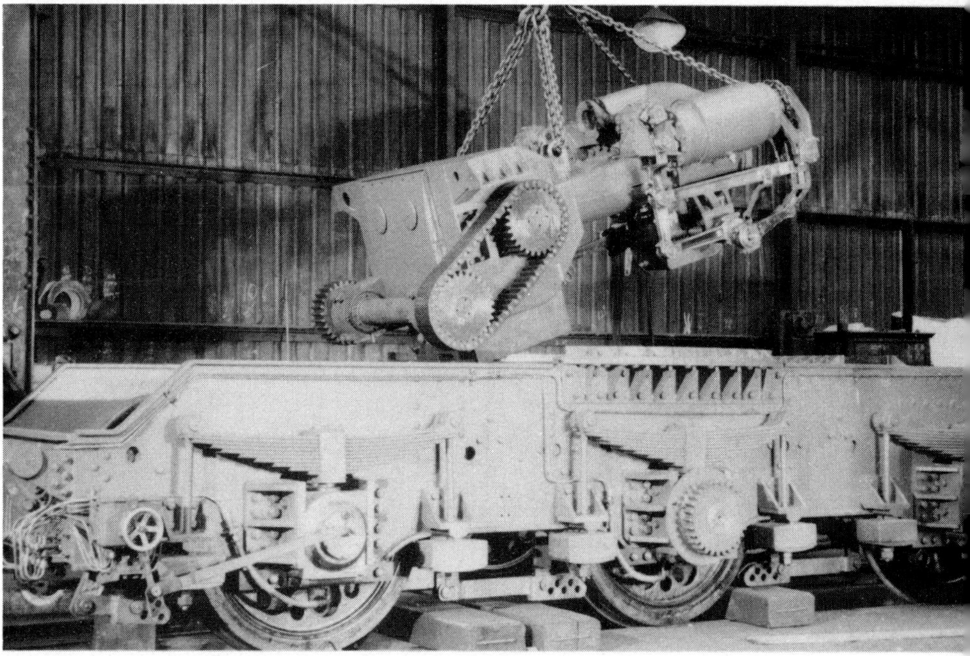

89 *Above*: The Turf Burner under construction. Note exhaust ducting ready to be assembled at the side of the smokebox./*J.G.C.*

90 *Below*: CC1 on steaming test (can be done stationary on a fan-draught engine) at Inchicore. The three exhausts are, right to left: the turbine; the safety valves; and the turbine and boiler feed pump at No. 1 end. A test assistant is looking at the turf fuel level./*J.G.C.*

91 *Left*: On the Turf Burner, speeding to Currah. You can see at a glance that it's in Ireland with the 5ft 3in gauge and therefore, as they might say, the central 6ft way being only 5ft 6in./*J.G.C.*

92 *Above*: On the Turf Burner at Inchicore, August 8th 1957. A Bulleid/Armand discussion temporarily interrupted by the photographer./*J.G.C.*

93 *Below*: The Turf Burner at Island Bridge Junction on return from Cork trip in October 1957. One of the 4-wheel heating vans is next to the engine./*J.G.C.*

94 *Above*: Starting trials with 11-carriage train by Inchicore Running Shed and some energetic steaming by the Turf Burner. *"Peat* to be used, not *Turf,"* instructed Bulleid at a late stage of the CC1 trials. Too late! It was, and is, irretrievably known as the Turf Burner./*J.G.C.*

95 *Below*: Where the testimonials started — Salisbury Running Shed, with No. 34056 *Croydon*. Spot the three undesirables: dirty outside motion, the "horrid" balance weight on driven wheel, and intruding oil engine at extreme right. Connoisseurs will spot the Salisbury breakdown crane behind *Croydon*./*George Harrison*

96 *Top*: The Giesl oblong ejector fitted to No. 34064, consisting of 7 nozzles in line and 6 blower jets between them. In use the spark arrester screens close around the assembly. It gave reduced back pressure, excellent spark arresting and better lifting of the faster and narrower exhaust emitted./*J.G.C.*

97 *Above left*: Another mock-up at Eastleigh, in 1963. The original caption read "No. 34023 re-named for photo." I got a copy endorsed "Please return. Should not be seen outside the family. OVB."/*J.G.C.*

98 *Above right*: The candid camera shot, November 1964. "He had his camera too near my knees," complained OVB later, but it was generally considered a very good likeness of the quizzical mood./*Rex Wailes*

99 *Top*: Winston Churchill's funeral train passing Staines on January 30th 1965 in charge of No. 34051 *Winston Churchill*. "Thank goodness they hadn't altered it," commented Bulleid, who had a great admiration for Churchill and did not want him to be insulted./*J.G.C.*

100 *Above*: No. 34051 *Winston Churchill* on happier duty with S.L.S. Special at Whitchurch heading for Exeter, May 1965./*G.M. Cashmore* the Q1s to tank engines — first an 0-6-2 and then an 0-6-4 as shown in Diagram W 5975 dated September 1944. C.S. Cocks liked these conventional tanks which used the Q1 parts and, being about twice as powerful as the Class M7 0-4-4 tanks, would surely find great favour in the Running Dept. Conversely, Bulleid found them stodgy and boring. Early in 1944 he had first seriously raised the possibility of a compact locomotive on two power bogies, and he raised it again now. Cocks again dissuaded him, though with difficulty, on the grounds of excessive novelty. So instead they explored electrical as well as mechanical methods of duplicating controls of regulator and brake on a Q1 so that the driver could operate from the fireman's side when running in reverse, and made some high-speed runs between Ashford and Maidstone with No. C36 coupled to a "West Country" tender to satisfy themselves on riding and safety. The result was a "double-fronted" version of Q1 as shown in diagram W6393 dated March 1945. It was not liked by the Running Department — and incidentally the drawing office failed to design a dual-control drive to their satisfaction.

Next to be tried were 2-6-2 and 2-6-4 tanks, followed by a 4-6-4 drawn in August 1945, diagram W6653, all using the successful Q1 boiler. Though quite an impressive-looking engine, and oddly enough seeming to suit better the austerity shapes of the Q1 cladding, dome and chimney, the 4-6-4 immediately rings two warning bells in the engineer's mind; what a waste of adhesion with all those carrying wheels; and how about the riding at high speed? So it comes as no surprise that diagram W6656, also dated August 1945, shows a twin-bogie tank engine with all twelve wheels driven. Each

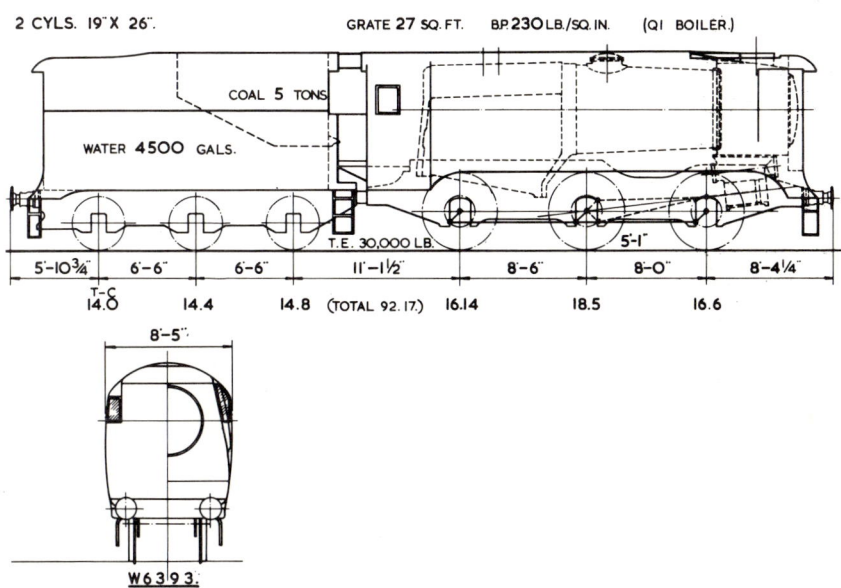

Fig 27 A disguised, double-ended version of "Q.1" Connoisseurs will note it faces right, LNER style.

125

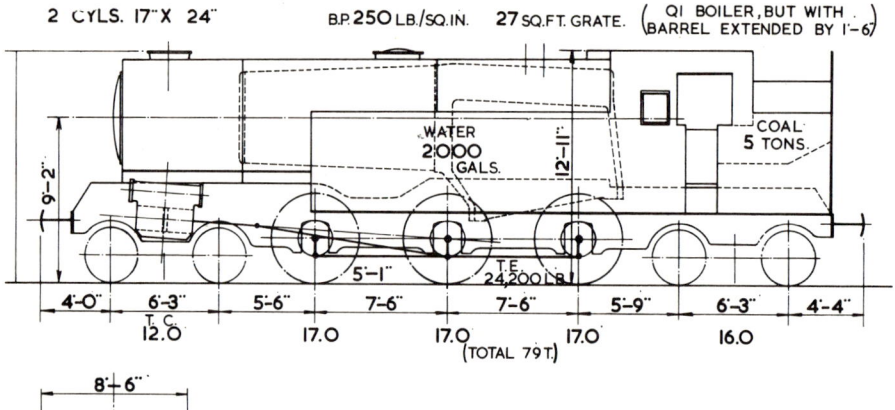

2 CYLS. 17"X 24"   B.P. 250 LB./SQ. IN.   27 SQ.FT. GRATE.   (QI BOILER, BUT WITH BARREL EXTENDED BY 1'-6")

9'-2"

WATER 2000 GALS.   12'-1"   COAL 5 TONS.

5'-1"   T.E. 24,200 LB.

| 4'-0" | 6'-3" | 5'-6" | 7'-6" | 7'-6" | 5'-9" | 6'-3" | 4'-4" |

T.C. 12.0   17.0   17.0   17.0   16.0

(TOTAL 79 T.)

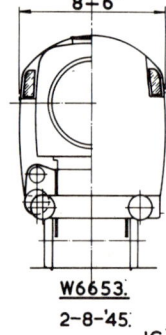

8'-6"

W6653.

2-8-'45.   J.G.J.

Fig 28 A "Q.1" based 4-6-4 tank. Glaring waste of adhesion.

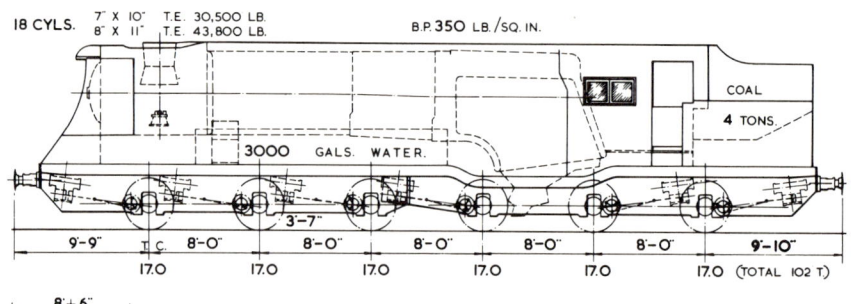

18 CYLS.   7" X 10" T.E. 30,500 LB.   B.P. 350 LB./SQ. IN.
8" X 11" T.E. 43,800 LB.

COAL   4 TONS.

3000 GALS. WATER.

3'-7"

| 9'-9" | 8'-0" | 8'-0" | 8'-0" | 8'-0" | 9'-10" |

T.C. 17.0   17.0   17.0   17.0   17.0   17.0 (TOTAL 102 T.)

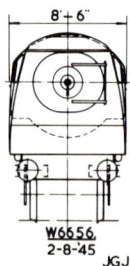

8'-6"

W6656.

2-8-'45   J.G.J

Fig 29 Same day thoughts on total adhesion, but many unanswered questions such as, how would the rear power bogie clear the ash pan?

126

axle has a separate gear drive from its own three-cylinder "high-speed" engine with cylinders 11in diameter by 10in stroke fed by a Pacific type boiler at 350psi. You can see at a glance that fitting in some of the 18 cylinders would present horrific problems, but the purpose of these exploratory engine diagrams was to work out feasibility, not to state it. Nor was any particular novelty claimed for this diagram; Gresley had toyed with a multi-cylinder geared locomotive in 1928, but the great art of engineering advance is periodically to review discarded ideas in case they suddenly become feasible in the light of later technological advances. There was enough feasibility surrounding diagram W6656 for W.H. Hutchinson to take the hint and save, as a likely source of useful ideas, the engine from the Sentinel railcar of the Dyke branch — a popular performer only withdrawn from service because it could not keep time when extra vehicles were attached. Bulleid added the thought that the reduced size and increased efficiency of a sleeve-valve engine might be needed, so he started Hutchinson on design work for an experimental sleeve-valve application.

By October the multi-engined locomotive idea was discarded as impracticable and attention turned again, with regrets, to the 4-6-4 arrangement. One interesting version retained the 350psi boiler and had two cylinders 16 by 24, giving a tractive effort of 30,000lb with standard 5ft 1in

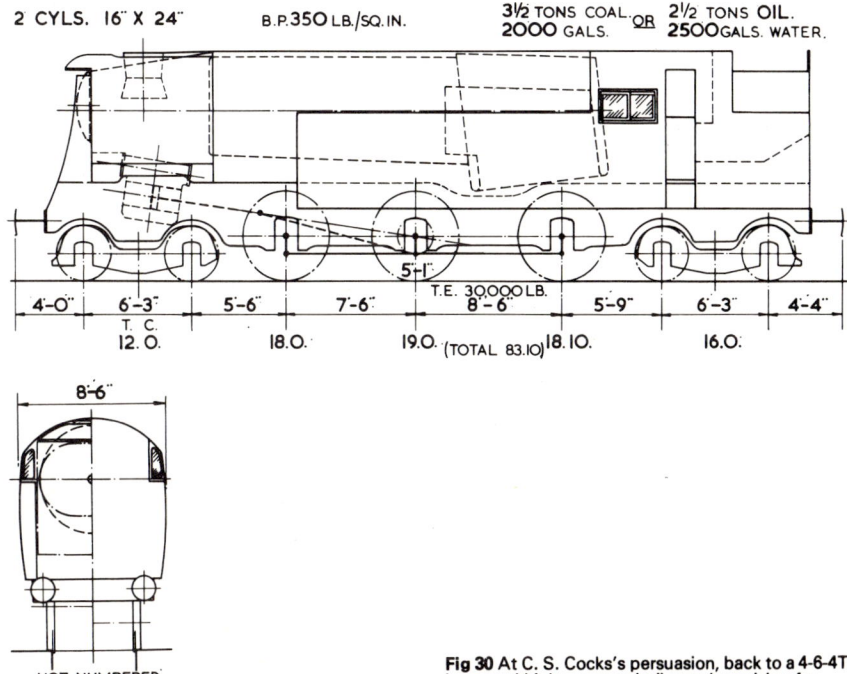

Fig 30 At C. S. Cocks's persuasion, back to a 4-6-4T but novel high pressure boiler and provision for coal or oil.

127

wheels. This diagram allowed for either 3½tons of coal or 2½tons of oil to be carried, the latter from rumours of the Government's intention to support oil-firing and from appraisal of likely advantages in a double-ended, centre-fired locomotive.

Soon after this, in December 1945, came diagram W6916. It was the last of the 4-6-4s, but of particular interest in being double-ended, having inside cylinders and enclosed inside motion, being oil-fired, and carrying a new design of boiler. About that time C.S. Cocks and W.H. Hutchinson did preliminary schemes for an all-welded water-tube boiler, with vertical tubes at each side of the fire area welded into two headers behind the main barrel, and this was considered sufficiently promising, particularly with oil-firing, to be indicated on diagram W6916.

It can therefore be seen that the design situation in early 1946 was decidedly fluid, but under growing pressure due to the year which had now elapsed since the Missenden memo. J.G. Jones was one of the expert diagram draughtsmen, able quickly to incorporate the newest idea and shrewdly to estimate the resulting axle loads — an essential for the preliminary submission to the Civil Engineer. Every draughtsman, and particularly those who have risen to section leader or higher, will sympathise with both parties when Bulleid came in at ten o'clock wanting a new

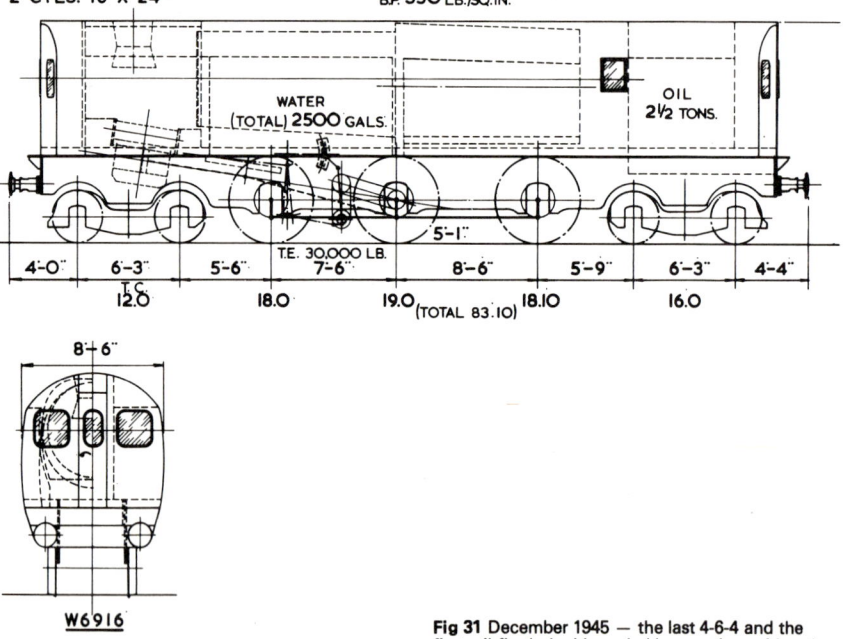

Fig 31 December 1945 — the last 4-6-4 and the first, oil-fired, double ended locomotive, with rather inaccessible cab at each end.

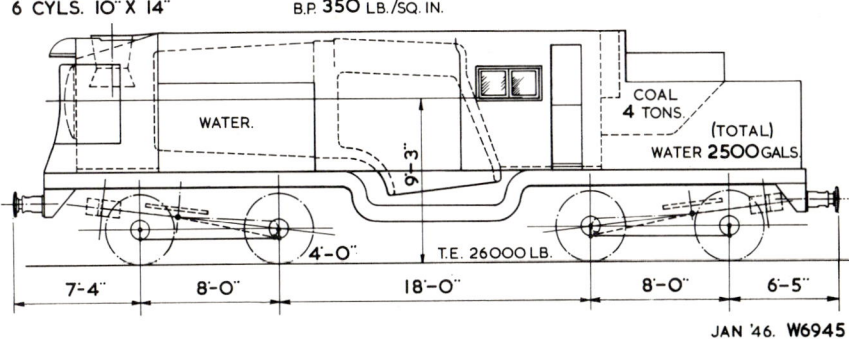

6 CYLS. 10" X 14"   B.P. 350 LB./SQ. IN.

WATER.

COAL 4 TONS. (TOTAL)
WATER 2500 GALS.

9'-3"

4'-0"   T.E. 26000 LB.

7'-4"   8'-0"   18'-0"   8'-0"   6'-5"

JAN '46. W6945

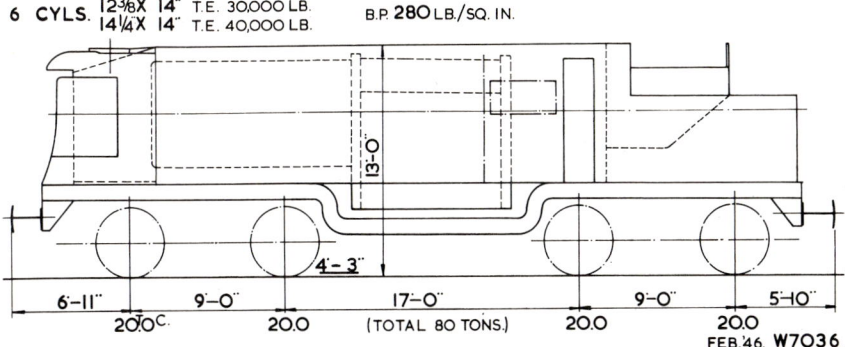

6 CYLS. 12⅜X 14" T.E. 30,000 LB.
        14¼X 14" T.E. 40,000 LB.   B.P. 280 LB./SQ. IN.

13'-0

4'-3"

6'-11"   9'-0"   17'-0"   9'-0"   5'-10"
20.0 C.   20.0   (TOTAL 80 TONS.)   20.0   20.0

FEB.'46. W7036

Fig 32 (top) The first of the "well-wagon" jobs, a serious look at a boiler on two power bogies.

Fig 33 (above) Another look at a B-B type, but with a water-tube boiler, the tubes forming the firebox sides and with two drums above. Welding problems in this design caused it to be abandoned.

diagram from J.G. Jones "in time to catch the 12.08 to London."

Behind the scenes the Traffic people were coming round to demanding a more powerful tank engine than a simple Class M7 replacement. Behind Government scenes the coal/oil story seemed to vary each day. The new boiler design was promising but not yet convincing. And through it all the one feature Bulleid felt to be really desirable was still wanting — the locomotive on two power bogies. But this idea was still being adamantly resisted by Cocks. At last Bulleid, not a man to be deterred, took advantage of his absence to start the drawing office on what was first called the "boiler on a well-wagon," diagram W6945, in January 1946. It shows two rather optimistically placed three-cylinder engines, an impractically shortened "West Country" boiler and what you might call an old-fashioned smokebox. Bulleid wrote on his copy, wisely and cautiously: "Return to Brighton drawing office to file at present."

By the end of February another version of the 0-4-4-0 arrangement was tried, with the water-tube boiler, diagram W7036, but the weight was found to be at least 80tons giving an unacceptable 20tons per axle. None the less, confidence in feasibility was strengthening. Bulleid felt that he would certainly arrive at a suitable boiler, that he could correct the weight problem by providing two six-wheel bogies, and that he could solve the problems of making these into self-contained power bogies. In one attempt to cram three cylinders and three piston valves into the confined space within a bogie having six 4ft 3in wheels, the crosshead guides were placed below the centre lines of the cylinders. Some of the components involved were actually manufactured to check feasibility, but I admit I was not surprised to hear H.G. Ivatt cry out in anguish when told about it. One had visions of a wide drawer openable from one side only. Even so, Bulleid was satisfied he could get results either from that or from something better, and he accordingly endorsed the type CC locomotive as their next steam locomotive project.

The crucial point in this technical saga came with the diagram W7169 in April 1946, when at last it seemed clear that they had a feasible proposition which would be acceptable to the Civil Engineer. Bulleid therefore got the Traffic Manager to make a formal statement of the requirement of the "proposed tank engine" which he did as follows:

"Routes and weights to be hauled:
Plymouth to Tavistock or Okehampton: 256 tons.
Okehampton Halwill Jct. and Bude: 256 tons.
Barnstaple and Ilfracombe: 325 tons.
Exeter and Exmouth: 384 tons.
Bournemouth and Swanage: 320 tons.

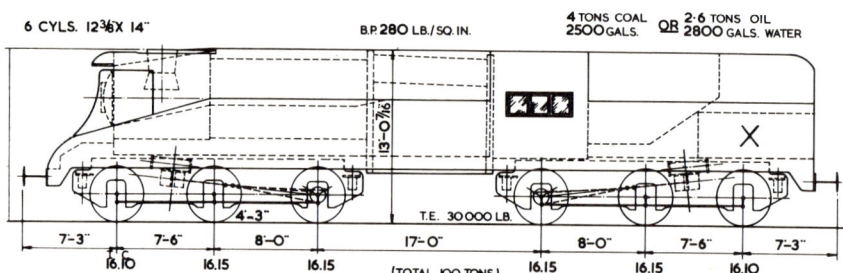

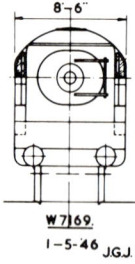

Fig 34 Diagram W7169 of April 1946, the first feasible locomotive on two power bogies. X indicates space for possible Holcroft/Anderson pressure condensing apparatus.

130

Brookwood (or similar outlying stabling grounds) to Waterloo: 450 tons.
Speed of trains: 50-60 miles per hour.
Distances to be run between taking water and coal: 60 miles for water
and 120 miles for coal.''

This data was received early in July, by which time there had been further
improvements to the layout of diagram W7169 and Bulleid's confidence in
the tank engine with two power bogies was fully established. He therefore
wrote to Missenden on July 11 quoting the Traffic Manager's requirement,
and continuing:

"In order to meet these requirements within the limits imposed by the
Chief Civil Engineer as regards permanent way and bridges, I propose a
locomotive in accordance with the enclosed diagram.

"The engine will have a maximum speed of 90mph will be able to work
goods trains which are normally taken by the Q1 and passenger trains
equal to the "West Country" engines, and will carry at least sufficient
water and coal to run 80 miles between taking water and 150 miles
without taking coal.

"The engine weights are so distributed as to enable it to run over the
whole of the Company's lines with the following exceptions:

Wenford Bridge line, Hayling Island Branch, Bere Alston and Callington
Line, Rye Harbour Branch, Newhaven Swing Bridge, Dover Prince of
Wales Pier, Axminster and Lyme Regis Branch, Isle of Wight Lines,
none of which is important.

"It is estimated that, if a batch of 25 engines of this class were built,

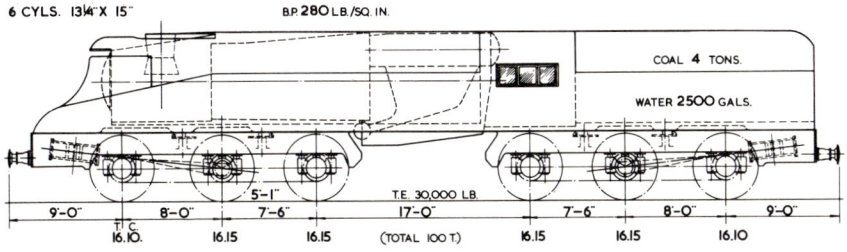

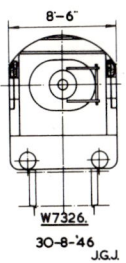

Fig 35 Diagram W7326 to which the first five
"Leader" class engines were ordered. It shows the
"Leader" type boiler and sleeve-valve engines.

131

cost per engine would be £17,000. If one prototype was built, the cost would obviously be greater, dependent upon the development work found to be necessary during construction and might reach £25,000.

"With reference to the conversation at the Progress Meeting on the 28th June 1946, I hope it will be possible to hold the proposed meeting soon as I am anxious to put in hand without delay the construction of the prototype in order to complete it by June, 1947

(sgd) O.V. Bulleid."

The meeting was in fact held on Sept 4, and for it Bulleid provided the latest diagram, W7326, and the following descriptive Memorandum:

MEMORANDUM

3rd September, 1946

LEADING CLASS. SHUNTING LOCOMOTIVE
C.C. TYPE

The principal features of the engine are as follows:

This design of engine makes full and complete use of the total weight for adhesive purposes and braking.

The type of bogie is similar to that introduced on the electric locomotive, the riding of which has been found to be satisfactory. The springs and gear will be above the axleboxes and under continuous lubrication.

The whole of the moving parts will be enclosed, and fitted with automatic lubrication, so that it will not be necessary for the driver to lubricate any part of the machine.

Each engine will have three "simple" cylinders driving the intermediate axle. The load is transmitted to the leading and trailing axles by chain drive in an oiltight casing. Roller bearing boxes will be fitted to all axles and will receive force feed lubrication. The axleboxes will be contained in the oilbath. Each axlebox guide is fitted with a "Silentbloc" bearing.

The leading engine will exhaust to the atmosphere, by way of the blast pipe in the smokebox, so as to provide the necessary draught in the boiler, but exhaust from the trailing engine will be used to heat the water in the tank, the hot water being pumped to the boiler by suitable hot water pumps.

The boiler is a new design which will obviate the maintenance inherent in the normal type of locomotive boiler. The engine will also be fitted with feed water treatment incorporated in the tender.

The controls of the engine will be such that both men will be able to carry out their duties seated and will be duplicated where necessary, so that they can drive in either direction.

The weight of water and fuel indicated should be ample for the normal requirements of the Southern Railway, especially as by condensing steam from one engine, the water consumption should be appreciably reduced.

The engine is fitted with 5ft 1in wheels, and this, in conjunction with the short stroke, will allow the engine to run at speeds up to 90mph. without exceeding the normal piston speed.

The engine will not be air-smoothed in any sense of the word, but the front end will be based on that successfully introduced on "West Country" class engines, in order to ensure that the steam, when the engine is working lightly, is carried clear of the cab.

This was duly reported in Minute 79 of the Rolling Stock (Repair and Renewals) Progress Committee held at Waterloo on September 4, 1946:

"RENEWALS OF ENGINES

It was noted that the CME had now produced a design of the proposed Passenger Tank engine, which was under consideration by the Traffic Manager.

The Chairman emphasised the necessity for an early decision being arrived at and the Traffic Manager was requested to submit his recommendation, together with justification for the 25 Passenger Tank engines, as quickly as possible so that authority could be given for five of the engines to be built in order that they may be available by the summer of 1947."

But, why no decision at the meeting? Because G.L.Nicholson, deputising for T.E. Chrimes, the Motive Power Superintendent, made a desperate plea, which was not well-received by the CME, not to commit Traffic to more than five of these new engines. "They contain so many novel features," said Nicholson, "that they are certain to have some initial troubles." Notice was duly taken of this, and Missenden certainly saw the point, and discussions and persuasions behind the scenes followed fast. The very next day Missenden wrote to Bulleid:

"PROPOSED TANK ENGINE

With reference to Minute 79 of the Meeting of Progress Committee held yesterday, the Traffic Manager informs me that he has had a further discussion with you upon this matter and he now recommends we proceed with the building of five engines to Diagram W7326.

I shall be glad if you will proceed accordingly."

On September 11 Order No. 3382 was thereupon issued to O.G. Hackett at Brighton, with copies all round, to "Build five tank engines to Diagram W7326," quoting the G.M.'s letter, the H.O. reference no., and the originating Board Minute of April 17, 1940.

And on October 3 the Traffic Manager followed up with his formal justification as follows:

SOUTHERN RAILWAY

From: TRAFFIC MANAGER.   A.
To: GENERAL MANAGER.   E.G.Pad.523/1.A.

3rd October, 1946

PROPOSED TANK ENGINE

In reply to your letter of the 5th September and referring to minute No.79 of the Progress Committee Meeting held on the 4th September. The case justifying the construction of 25 new passenger tank engines is given below.

At the present time and, indeed, for the past 45 years, the most powerful passenger tank engines on the Western Section have been those of the M7 class, 104 of which are still in existence.

These engines were built between the years 1897-1911 and although the last 49 embody slight improvements, the whole class was based on a design prepared in 1897 and now, therefore, nearly 50 years old.

They were originally built for L&SWR surburban passenger traffic and were, in due course, rendered redundant by electrification. They are now being used as general utility locomotives, 25% working empty trains between Clapham Junction or other stock berthing points and Waterloo, and the balance on local and branch line services on the Western Section. They are completely out of date and inefficient by modern standards, and their continued existence prevents any improvement on the services they operate.

In the report to yourself dated 1st December, 1944, upon our locomotive position in 1950, prepared by the Deputy General Manager and other chief officers, the whole of these 104 engines were condemned, and this recommendation was confirmed in the corresponding report upon the 1955 locomotive position submitted on the 3rd September, 1946.

The report dealing with the Engine Building Programme during the years 1947-1955 recommends the building of 60 new tank engines, diesel or steam, in addition to the 25 tanks already proposed, and I now recommend that the latter be constructed.

It is understood that the five engines to be built will be a guide as to the building of the subsequent 20.

Signed R.M.T. RICHARDS

Richards issued this just in time for the Rolling Stock Progress Committee meeting that same day and it was minuted with two comments:

"Mr Bulleid also said that only one of the new Passenger Tanks would be completed in June, 1947, and that the remaining four would follow as soon as possible thereafter.

"The Traffic Manager intimated that from an operating point of view it would be better if the five engines were constructed for coal burning in order to ensure greater mobility, particularly in regard to Depot allocation, and the Chairman requested the Chief Mechanical Engineer to proceed accordingly."

The reason for the coal-burning note was that the Southern were doing their share of conversions to oil firing at Government instruction, and Richards naturally did not want a further complication added. The reason for the reiterated June 1947 completion date, known to be impracticable with detail design hardly started and material deliveries in excess of six months, was the current knowledge that nationalisation was likely in 1948 and important projects should be completed under Southern Railway colours. The reason for Bulleid being particularly pleased at getting formal sanction for the five new engines was that it enabled him to announce them in his Presidential Address to the Institution of Mechanical Engineers on October 16 — casually inferring that anything diesels could do, steam could do better.

The evolution of the new boiler to its final syphons-and-drums form, and the first appearance of the sleeve-valve engines are seen on W7326. It is also named; Bulleid sketched name suggestions for "Leaders" on an old envelope thus:

MISSENDEN
Sir Eustace
General Manager Southern Rly. Co.

And

CHURCHILL
Winston P.C. O.M.
Prime Minister of Britain 1939-45

The drawing office used the first one first.

With design enthusiasm now running high, and not feeling unduly bound by W7326, Bulleid saw clearly the last defect in his new engine — the same old mediocre driving position. What did diesels and electrics do? Put the driver at the front. Well, so could steam. And at last, on diagram W7457 dated October 8, 1946, can be seen the boiler moved 6in to one side to provide a corridor, and duplicate controls for a cab at each end. This completed the "Leader" specification in the much-quoted form presented to the Mechanicals eight days later (see footnote, page 83). A second

135

version of diagram W7457 showed a corridor vestibule connection at each end of the engine.

From the "first final diagram" (as Inchicore might have expressed it) to the completed "Leader" took a long, brave step. There were problems galore to be solved, but there was also, with the job now definitely authorised, tremendous enthusiasm throughout the drawing office and not least from its boss, C.S. Cocks. The idea of the interchangeable power bogie was kept in mind throughout the design, though it was realised that a fleet of around 30 locomotives would be necessary to justify the technique of holding spare bogies to keep them in service when their bogies needed overhaul. Welding would also be exploited to the full — the Southern was then right in front of all the other railways in designing for welding and in workshops applications of welding. It was equally guilty, I must admit, in removing another subtlety of language by using the terms 'welded' and 'fabricated' as indiscriminate synonyms.

This is how "Leader" design progressed.

The 36 5¼in and 283 1⅝ in tubes were welded in the tubeplates of the all-welded boiler. The firebox contained four syphons, welded to the bottom of the barrel and to the underside of the firebox drum, which was welded to the back of the barrel. Total evaporative heating surface was 2,387 sq ft with 454sq ft superheater area and 43sq ft grate area. The firebox was a simple air-tight casing lined with fire bricks. The blast pipe had five jets each 2½in diameter with chimney 2ft 1in, widening to 2ft 5in at the top. TIA water treatment was fitted. Flexible steam pipes allowed the power bogies enough flexibility to take curves of 5½ chains.

The boiler posed no severe design or manufacturing problems and steamed very well, but the firebrick linings gave a lot of trouble.

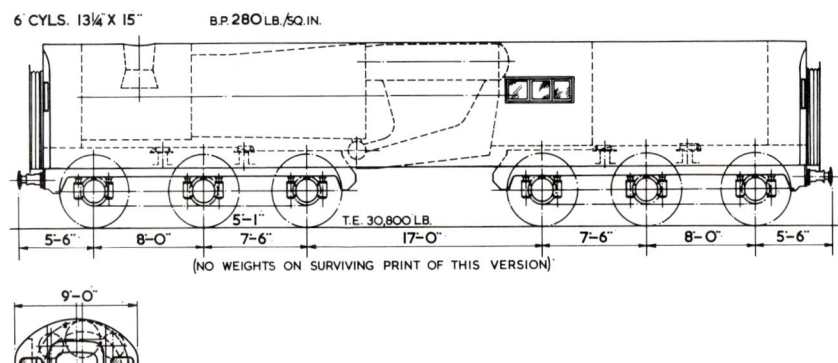

6˙CYLS. 13¼˝X 15˝   B.P. 280 LB./SQ.IN.

5-1˝   T.E. 30,800 LB.

5-6˝   8-0˝   7-6˝   17-0˝   7-6˝   8-0˝   5-6˝

(NO WEIGHTS ON SURVIVING PRINT OF THIS VERSION)

9-0˝

6˝

W7457.
APPROX. 9-'46.

Fig 36 Improved version with cab at each end, of which several variants were drawn.

136

Cleaning out a smokebox becomes even more undesirable when it opens on to an enclosed driver's cab, so thoughts reverted to Webb's 1870 experiment of periodically discharging ash through a duct in the bottom of the smokebox, fitted with a rudimentary cover operable from the cab to preserve smokebox vacuum. To update this legendary experiment a Class U1 2-6-0, No.31896, was fitted with a 6in square duct, permanently open, which got rid of most of the ash and did not seriously affect steaming,

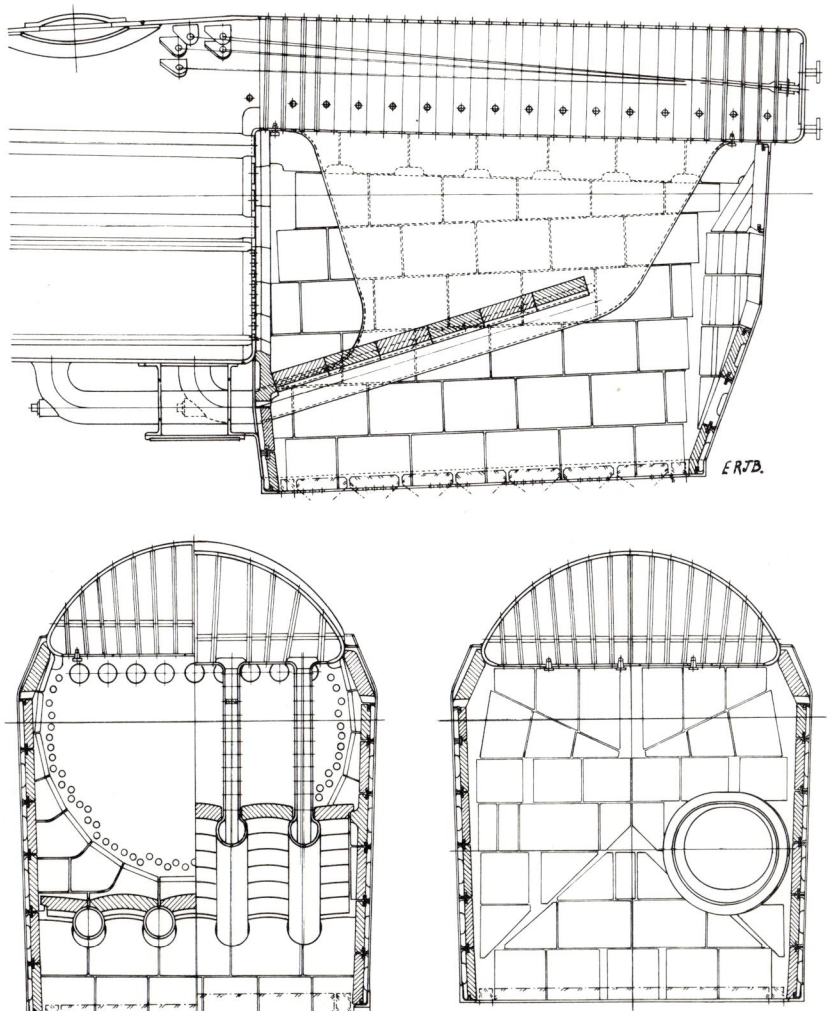

Fig 37 The "Leader" firebox as originally built. Top is a sectional elevation at the centre. Lower left is a pair of cross-sections looking forward, the right side taken at the back of the brick arch and the left side at the front. Lower right is a cross-section looking backward.

though No.31896 was in excellent condition from very recent shopping. Accordingly a similar duct was provided for the "Leader," but it was later found to impair steaming and was removed.

To assist mainframe design, a full-size wooden mock-up was made, which consisted of two fish-bellied side girders suitably cross-connected to carry the decking above and the bearing pads for the bogies below. Pre-fabricated tanks, coal bunker and cab sides were welded together to form the right side of the locomotive, the left side being the corridor. This design left two undesirable features, the uneven lateral trim of the locomotive and the excessively hot firing position.

A pre-fabricated cylinder block, buffer beams, cross-stays and the four bearing segments were welded to the hollow side-frames of the bogies, which also contained cylindrical pedestals to the springs over each roller-bearing axlebox. Chains were used instead of coupling rods, but provision was made for changing to rods. This power-bogie design was at fault only in specifying plain instead of self-aligning axlebox roller-bearings, resulting in fatigue failures of axles.

Bulleid saw two great attractions in sleeve-valves; by eliminating piston valves they made it much easier to fit the engine into the tight space of the bogie; and they permitted shorter steam passages and reduced clearance volumes, thus promoting thermal efficiency. By March 1947 Hutchinson had produced a sleeve-valve arrangement which Bulleid liked. He called in Sir Harry Ricardo, who also approved, except that he prescribed the addition of a rotary movement to the sleeves to improve lubrication and reduce wear. Next they looked round for a guinea-pig engine and first

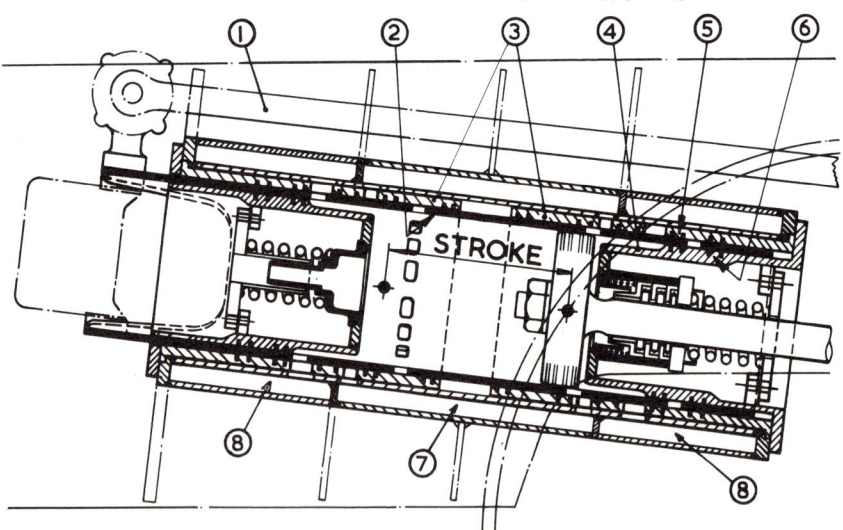

Fig 38 The "Leader" cylinder and sleeve valve arrangement. The valve rod 1 applies reciprocating motion to the sleeve valve 2 (shown black) which slides in the two liners 3. 4 is the inner cylinder cover with relief valve and 5, 6 are internal and external rings numbering 28 per cylinder. Live steam is in jacket 7 and exhaust in jackets 8.

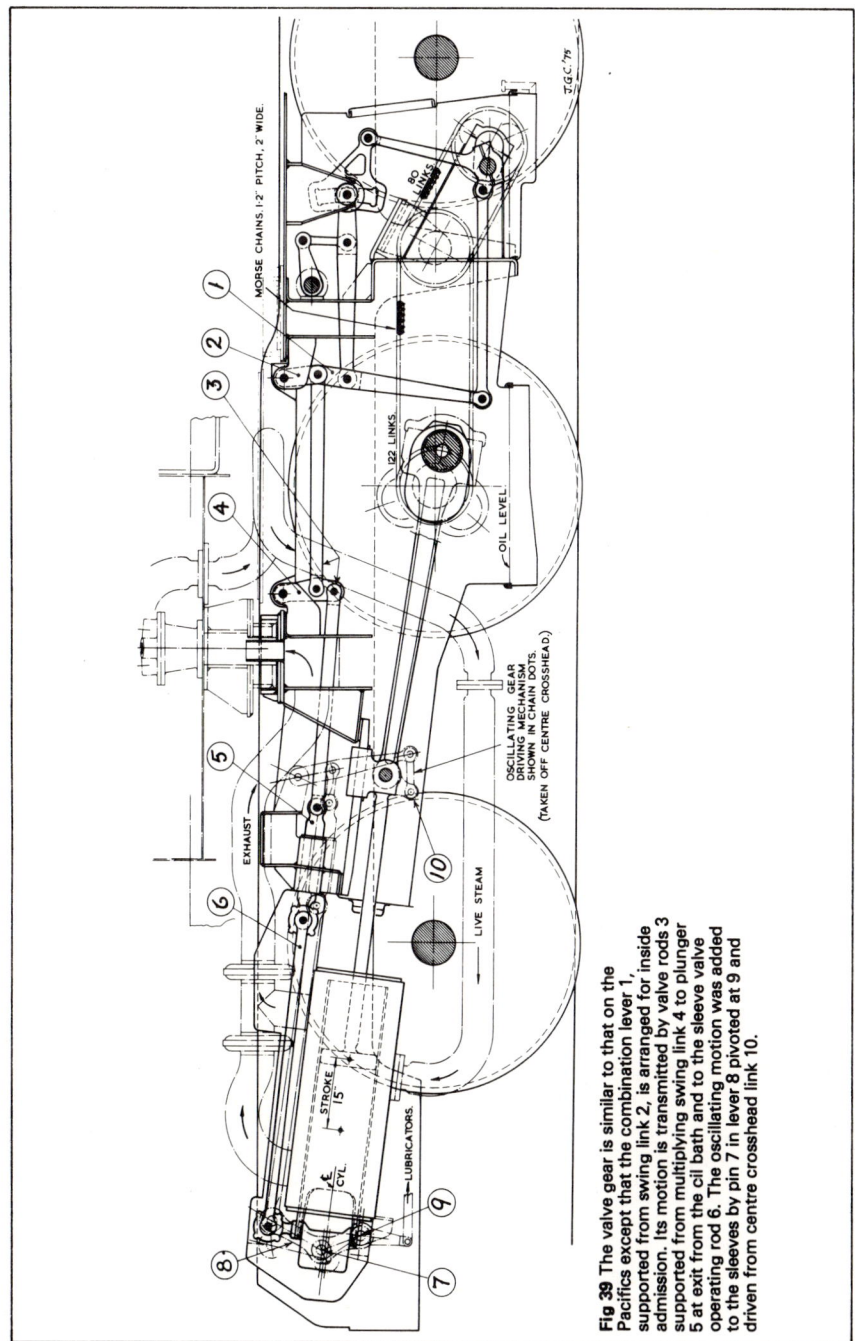

Fig 39 The valve gear is similar to that on the Pacifics except that the combination lever 1, supported from swing link 2, is arranged for inside admission. Its motion is transmitted by valve rods 3 supported from multiplying swing link 4 to plunger 5 at exit from the oil bath and to the sleeve valve operating rod 6. The oscillating motion was added to the sleeves by pin 7 in lever 8 pivoted at 9 and driven from centre crosshead link 10.

MORSE CHAINS, 1·2" PITCH, 2" WIDE.

122 LINKS

OIL LEVEL

OSCILLATING GEAR DRIVING MECHANISM SHOWN IN CHAIN DOTS. (TAKEN OFF CENTRE CROSSHEAD.)

LIVE STEAM

EXHAUST

LUBRICATORS.

STROKE 15"

CYL.

T.G.C. '75

139

selected a "King Arthur," but adding sleeves with the existing pistons increased the width over the cylinders enough to foul the loading gauge. So then an Ivatt/Marsh Atlantic, No 32039 *Hartland Point*, was selected; it was due for scrapping and so the sleeves were added at the expense of a corresponding reduction in piston diameter and tractive effort. Provision was naturally made for fitting rings, but first Shop tests made with no rings prompted a yard trial on December 3, 1947, to which Bulleid rather rashly invited H.G. Ivatt. The engine ran all right but was completely enveloped in clouds of steam, which naturally amused the visitor more than the designer. So rings were fitted and then many successful tests and runs were made and a maximum speed of 80mph was credibly reported. This fully supported Bulleid's earlier decision to go for sleeve valves despite the combined rotary and reciprocating motion needed — a headaching complication in the confined space of a bogie. For reassurance a quarter-scale model was built: it showed the "figure-of-eight" sleeve motion correctly produced from the adapted Bulleid valve gear and gave good valve events. (It was later handed over to British Railways Archives).

Each engine had three steam-jacketed cylinders 12¼in diameter by 15in stroke driving the middle axle. With boiler pressure 280psi and standard 5ft 1in wheels the tractive effort per bogie at the normal fix of 85% boiler pressure was 13,150lb. So the tractive effort of the locomotive was 26,300 lb compared with, for example, the 24,600lb of an LMS three-cylinder 2-6-4T with 5ft 9in wheels — or the 30,000lb of a Q1.

Flood lubrication was established before the locomotive moved off by a gear pump driven from a steam turbine. It supplied the completely-enclosed big ends and valve gear and also the axle bearings and springs. Pressure lubrication for the pistons and sleeve valves was from three mechanical lubricators per bogie. A comparatively thin special oil was used with a filter to trap abrasive particles.

Clasp brakes were fitted, worked by two vacuum cylinders per bogie. Driver's controls were duplicated in each cab with a device for making those in the unoccupied cab inoperable. There was no sanding, due to total adhesion.

Unlike the days of the "Merchant Navy" and Q1, Bulleid seldom visited the drawing boards during the "Leader" design, working almost entirely from his own or C.S. Cocks's office.

The ordering of material started in December 1946 and manufacture started in July 1947. The project got a decided fillip when 31 more "Leader" class engines were sanctioned in November, but this was largely a pre-nationalisation gesture and material for them was never ordered. The first set of main frames was set up in Brighton erecting shop in May 1948, and though building could then be said to have started there was still a lot of design to finish. Naturally there were enquiries from many sides and many levels as to when the first wonder engine would be ready, and Bulleid gave urbane or calculated replies in the usual code: that he hoped it would be in traffic "in a month or two", or, for variety, "in a matter of weeks."

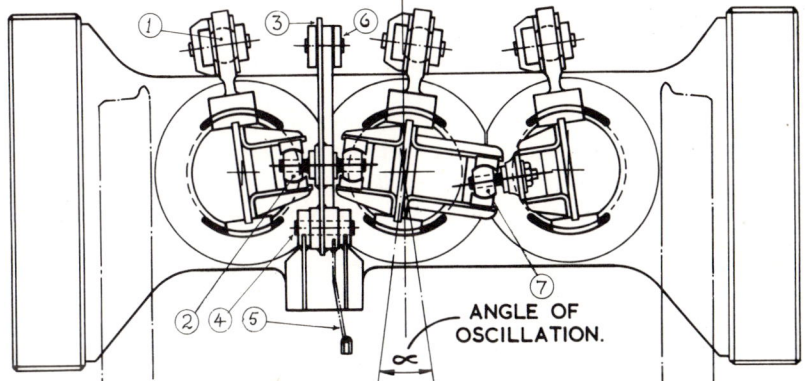

Fig 40 External view of "Leader" cylinders with valve oscillating gear. The reciprocating motion comes from the valve rod 1 with ball-and-socket joint to allow the oscillating motion from the arc described by ball joints 2 attached to lever 3 pivoted at 4 and driven by a rod 6 linked to the centre crosshead. An extension on the centre sleeve provides the same oscillation via ball joint 7 to the third sleeve. Extension lever 5 drives the mechanical lubricators.

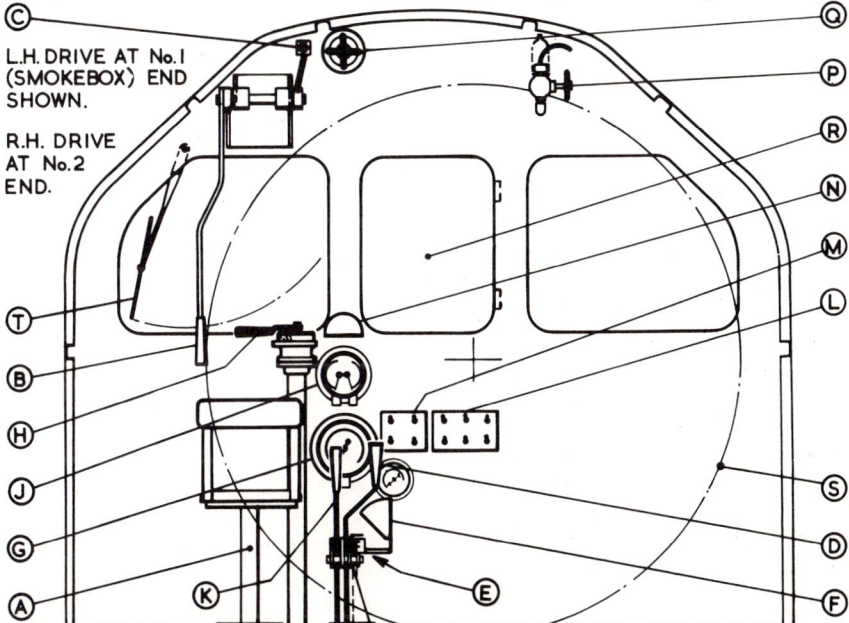

Fig 41 Cab controls in No. 36001.

A Driver's chair
B Regulator
C Regulator connecting rod
D Steam reverser control lever
E Steam reverser quadrant & indicator
F Steam reverse light
G Steam chest pressure gauge (no boiler gauge)
H Driver's brake valve
J Duplex vacuum gauge
K Cylinder cocks
L Switches for route indicator lights
M Switches for cab light and light over drawhook
N Light for gauges (lowest gauge indicates train heating)
P Whistle isolating valve. (One whistle each end)
Q Cab light
R Window opening outwards
S Indicates position of front ring of offset boiler
T Windscreen wiper

141

Missenden had gone to British Railways HQ but the new Southern Region boss, John Elliot, was equally patient with a complex development project even when colleagues went on about the growing costs. He used Missenden to generate similar patience at HQ.

Theoreticians who shudder at starting manufacture before all the drawings are to hand would have had the shudder of their lives with the "Leader." Welding offers the two-faced facility, that you can so easily burn bits off and weld new bits on, at a cost, if design changes emerge. And they did emerge, ranging from later and brighter ideas to errors and fouls caused by hurry and by the side-effects of other changes. There were moments of great exasperation in the Drawing Office and the Works when alterations seemed to come in as fast as they were issued. This was taken later as the main excuse by the Drawing Office for the engine coming out so much over weight.

There were also problems from the advanced techniques. For example, the two triple cylinder blocks warped slightly after finish machining, due either to insufficient relieving of welding stresses or to being strained during welding to the bogie frames, or both, and the result was serious trouble in driving the sleeves. It is not likely that temperature differences in operation caused distortion and so the second "Leader," fabricated in less of a hurry and with the experience of the first, would probably have had markedly better valve operation.

The boiler behaved as expected of an all-welded vessel at its hydraulic test, being entirely free from weeps. Then the first bogie was completed and supplied with steam from a nearby shunter. It started at only 8psi pressure and ran smoothly and sweetly, "like a sewing machine." This was the climax to a long, long design struggle by the drawing office, and draughtsman Doug Smith admitted to a feeling of stupendous relief. But then unfortunately someone on the Works reversed the engine while it was running and buckled several rods and links in the motion. "So Joe (W.H. Hutchinson) and I had to go and tell Mr Bulleid. We went in some trepidation though it was not our fault. He was very nice about it," recalled Doug Smith, adding that "he was always very persuasive — no matter what ideas you went in to see him with he could steer you round to his way of thinking . . . We all felt that, had BR not come about, and Mr Bulleid been a younger man, he would certainly have made something of the "Leader." "

Thanks to final Herculean and round-the-clock efforts by Brighton Works, the first "Leader", No. 36001, steamed away on its trials in June 1949. Bulleid described its novelties and made these comments on the first trials to the American Society of Mechanical Engineers in New York four months later:

"The first of these new engines has run about 4,000 miles. Steam locomotive development has always been handicapped by the absence of proper testing facilities. We have to build the complete locomotive before we can try it and the trials can only be made out on the road. As is to be

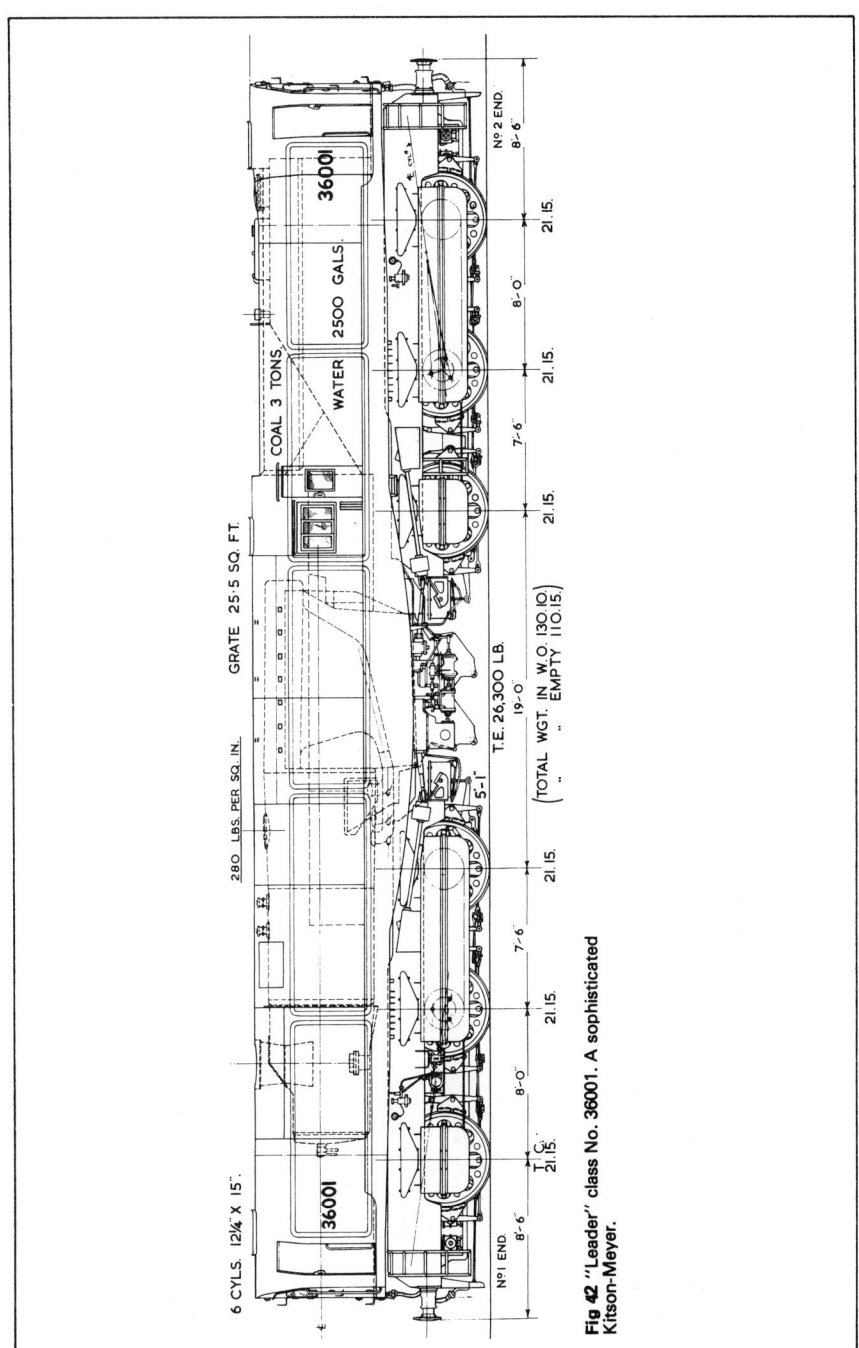

Fig 42 "Leader" class No. 36001. A sophisticated Kitson-Meyer.

expected some troubles have arisen, such as broken ends to the sleeve valves and spalling of the firebrick casing of the firebox, troubles which are being overcome. The engine has shown already the advantage of a double bogie locomotive as regards freedom of running, ease in taking curves, and the great value of having the total weight available for traction and braking."

There were, however, three forces tending to separate Bulleid from his engine: first, the knowledge that British Railways could never abide so much novelty; second that retirement might be only a year or two away; and third a strong plea for his services in Dublin by T.C. Courtney, Chairman of the Irish National Railways, Coras Iompair Eireann. This last had culminated at the CIE Board meeting on April 26, 1949 when Mr O.V. Bulleid was appointed Consulting Mechanical Engineer at a salary of £2,000 per annum "to take effect as soon as Mr Bulleid can become available."

Though not quite sure it could happen without him, Bulleid was quite sure the "Leader" was a viable proposition and he therefore decided that an appropriate date to retire from British Railways was September 30, which was accepted by the Chairman of the Railway Executive. And with his confidence in the "Leader" still growing as tests proceeded, early in September he finished a detailed paper for the Institution of Mechanical Engineers entitled "Stages in the Development of the Steam Locomotive to Restore it to its Supremacy as the Ideal Railway Traction Unit." This was duly accepted for presentation in London on April 21st, 1950. (Appendix 7)

But as the days of September ticked away, with many tributes and presentations to the retiring CME, and with the good and bad points of the "Leader" coming more into perspective, R.A. Riddles realised that the project could not possibly succeed without the presence of Bulleid who, after minimal lobbying, agreed to continue in charge of it till the year end. The arrangement was formalised in Missenden's letter to Bulleid dated September 23; and his reply of the same date welcomed the arrangement, said he did not expect any great difficulty in getting the "Leader" in service by the end of the year as he would have all the help he needed from the old department, and added "I only ask that any information as to what is going on will be obtained from me only."

This was followed by the usual exchange of letters to the several departments concerned arranging the necessary support; one from Bulleid to the new Mechanical and Electrical Engineer, S.B. Warder, specified the main helpers — "Mr Granshaw the Locomotive Works Manager at Brighton, Mr Attwell of the Test section and Mr Hutchinson of the drawing office" — and added that "I will come backwards and forwards from Ireland as necessary. I will keep you informed of all developments and feel sure I can rely on every support from you in seeing that these engines are developed quickly so that they can be put into service." To this Warder sent a very co-operative reply.

144

In November it became clear to Riddles that, however successful the trials, something drastic would have to be done to make the fireman's job acceptable; and since this could involve major changes and high costs he gave instructions for work to be stopped on the second to fifth engines. Then in December it was realised that a further three months' help from Bulleid would be necessary and to formalise this Riddles wrote to C.P. Hopkins, copy to Warder, on January 3, 1950, extending the previous arrangement until the end of March 1950 and reminding him that full assistance must be given "and the usual reports sent in to me as before as to the progress and extent of the alterations etc. that are requested."

By March 8, 1950 the engine was in what one might call a usable state. The trim was better, the bearing springs working, the firebox stokeable by an asbestos-clad fireman and the steaming good. Bulleid, getting very busy in Ireland and beginning to envisage some fundamental improvements to the "Leader" concept, notably an interchangeable engine detachable from its bogie, wrote rather optimistically to Missenden and Riddles on March 8 after failing to get them together for a meeting. He went through the main technical tasks outstanding and concluded:

"I am quite satisfied the engine can be made a useful and valuable locomotive and Mr Granshaw, the Locomotive Manager at Brighton, with the help he is receiving from Mr Jarvis, the Chief Draughtsman, can be relied upon to see that this is done.

I shall always appreciate deeply having been permitted to follow the development of the "Leader" engine so far, as it has given me much valuable information for future work.

I would like to add my acknowledgment of the help I have had from everyone concerned and especially the courtesy I have always had from Mr Riddles.

As I do not think my services are necessary any longer and as I feel I may well be an embarrassment, I shall be obliged if I can be released from the arrangement made last September. I shall be available for consultation if desired and if I can be of any help at any time I shall always be only too pleased to give it."

Only two days later a balanced but less optimistic report on the "Leader" was issued to Riddles by R.G. Jarvis, who had taken over from Cocks at Brighton. He reported:

"LEADER CLASS LOCOMOTIVES

"I have been asked by Mr Warder to express my views on this experiment as the Regional Chief Technical Assistant responsible for design. No personal criticism is inferred in the remarks which follow, and the views expressed represent my views which may well be at variance with those of the designers of the locomotive, on the basis that if doctors can differ, so may engineers."

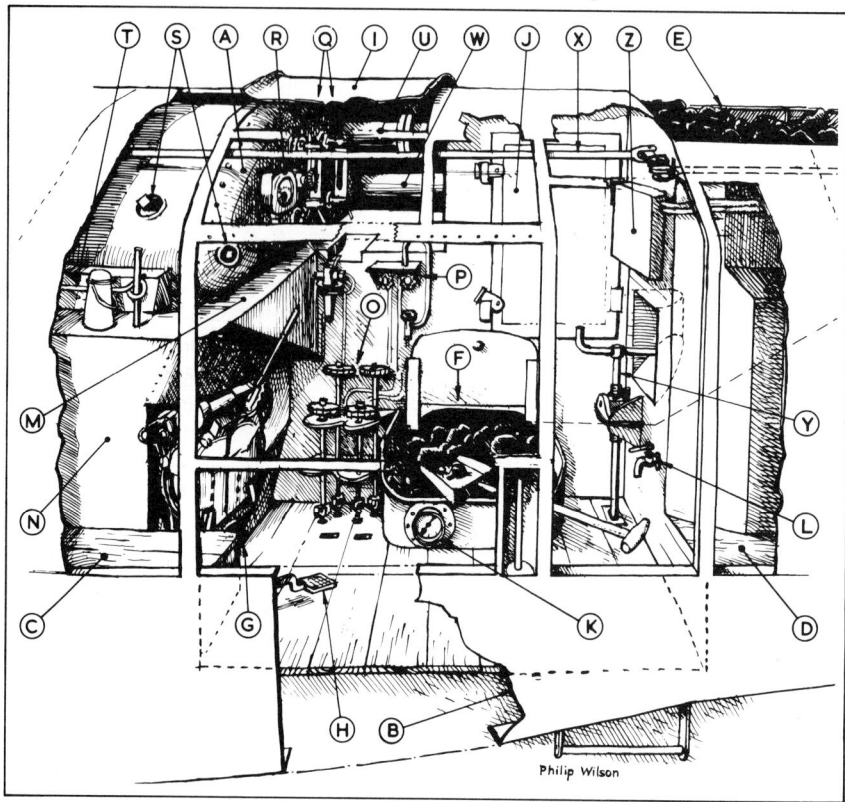

Fig 43 The fireman's position; a major disadvantage in the coal-fired version of the "Leader."

The fireman's cab, half the width of the locomotive, was behind the firebox drum A and had a wooden floor below the main frame B and the corridor C leading to chimney (No. 1) end and D leading to rear (No. 2) end. The bunker E delivered coal to the shovelling plate F. The "Ajax" steam-operated firedoor G was controlled by pedal H. The cab ventilator is shown at I and J is the access door to the bunker. Gauge K indicated water level in the tanks and tap L was also fitted. The tank system was continued round the cab via the "mantlepiece" M to the thin tanks N surrounding the firebox. The controls for the two

"Monitor" injectors are at O and the coal watering controls at P. The boiler had two Klinger reflex-type water gauges Q and was T.I.A. fitted with 3-way cock and recorder R. S indicates wash-out plugs. Fireirons T were parked in a channel over the tank and secured over a post. The blower control was just above the mantelpiece.

The fireman's cab had a window and sliding door on the corridor side. The main steampipe U to the rear bogie and the exhaust pipe W from it passed behind. The regulator rod X from the rear cab passed overhead. Handbrake Y acted on the rear bogie. Fuse box Z covered all electric lighting on the locomotive. There was said to be no problem in keeping tea hot.

146

Then after listing the main aims of the project Jarvis listed the main shortcomings, viz:

(1) The weight will restrict route availability.

(2) The enclosure and lubrication of engines, axleboxes and springs is very unsatisfactory.

(3) The increased steam chest volume and port areas, and the reduced clearance volumes, may only have a minimal effect on thermal efficiency judging by recent tests at Rugby Test Plant.

(4) Replacement of firebox water-legs by firebricks is not successful.

On detail design, Jarvis reported that "the disappointing progress made with the locomotive to date is to a much greater extent attributable to the detail design than to the broad conception." He went on to point out that self-aligning axle bearings were essential, that the fireman's confined space was very unsatisfactory and dangerous in the event of a blow-back on entering a tunnel, and that the valve gear was unsatisfactory on three counts: the out-rigger drive to the valves, the bad effects as wear developed, and the fear of thermal distortion in the fabricated cylinders. He would also have preferred smaller wheels. In conclusion he reported:

"The design has certain attractive features, it has many problems to solve, and it has some fundamental defects.

That the locomotive could be made to work I have no doubt, but a great deal of experimental work will be necessary. It all depends upon how much money can be permitted for the modifications which will entail virtually a complete re-arrangement."

It was quite obvious from this report that, however successful the "Leader" might prove, the chances of the steam locomotive developing this way were remote, having in mind the absence of any money for experimental work and the entrenched conventionality of the LMS-slanted CME Department of British Railways. So, logically, Marylebone withheld permission for the presentation of the Bulleid paper (Appendix 7) and he formally withdrew it on March 17, 1950.

In 1950, those members of the Great British Public who travelled on their Railway saw posters on every station illustrating the twelve new standard engines. Riddles, Chairman Missenden, and in fact all seven members of the Railway Executive were unanimous that steam must continue, except for shunting and perhaps multiple sets, till electrification could be afforded.

This decision was logical and fully supported by the existing locomotives, existing building and repair facilities, and use of home-grown fuel. It was also Hobson's choice — there was no money for anything else. The 1950 comparative figures gave eloquent support:

147

Locomotive Type	Capital Cost	Starting Tractive Effort	DBHP 1-hour Rating	Cost per DBHP
Class 5 4-6-0	£16,000	26,000lb	1,200	£13
1,600hp Diesel-Electric	£78,000	41,000lb	1,300	£61
C C Electric 1,500 V	£37,000	45,000lb	2,100	£18

This was why Riddles decided to proceed with the design of twelve standard engines, combining the best of existing Regional features. It was also why he, unlike his more convergent-thinking colleagues, supported further trials on the "Leader," seeing a steam future for any successes that might emerge. So on March 24, quoting a detailed and accurate but pessimistic report prepared by R.C. Bond, he wrote to his colleagues on the Railway Executive giving them the full current story including the alarming costs:

Estimated cost in September 1948	£100,000
Total expenditure at end of January 1950 on:	
Materials	76,000
Wages	54,000
Workshop Expenses	41,000
Supervision	5,000
TOTAL	£176,000

He went on to say that the engine was being prepared for dynamometer car trials, and that if these showed significant advantages consideration would be given to further work on the engines. This work would have to include attention to the weight and its distribution. The present total weight of 130 tons with maximum axle loading of 24½tons compared with estimates to the Civil Engineer of 110tons with 19tons per axle, and there was also a side-to-side variation of about 10 tons, though it was admitted these figures would probably improve when the free movement of the axleboxes was improved. There were also murmurings that the engine had "spread the track", but these were never substantiated.

When his decision to proceed with dynamometer car trials was endorsed by the Railway Executive, Riddles told the Southern Region Chief Officer, C.P. Hopkins, who told Warder, who issued a staff instruction to Granshaw, copy to Jarvis. This made the main points that Riddles had assumed direction of the project after March 31, that Granshaw remained the man in charge, and that Jarvis would be giving all possible help including taking charge of the coming dynamometer car trials.

There were many technical and other adventures during the trials of the "Leader," and many people learned a great deal and had exciting experiences ranging from exhilarating high-speed runs to just sitting watching

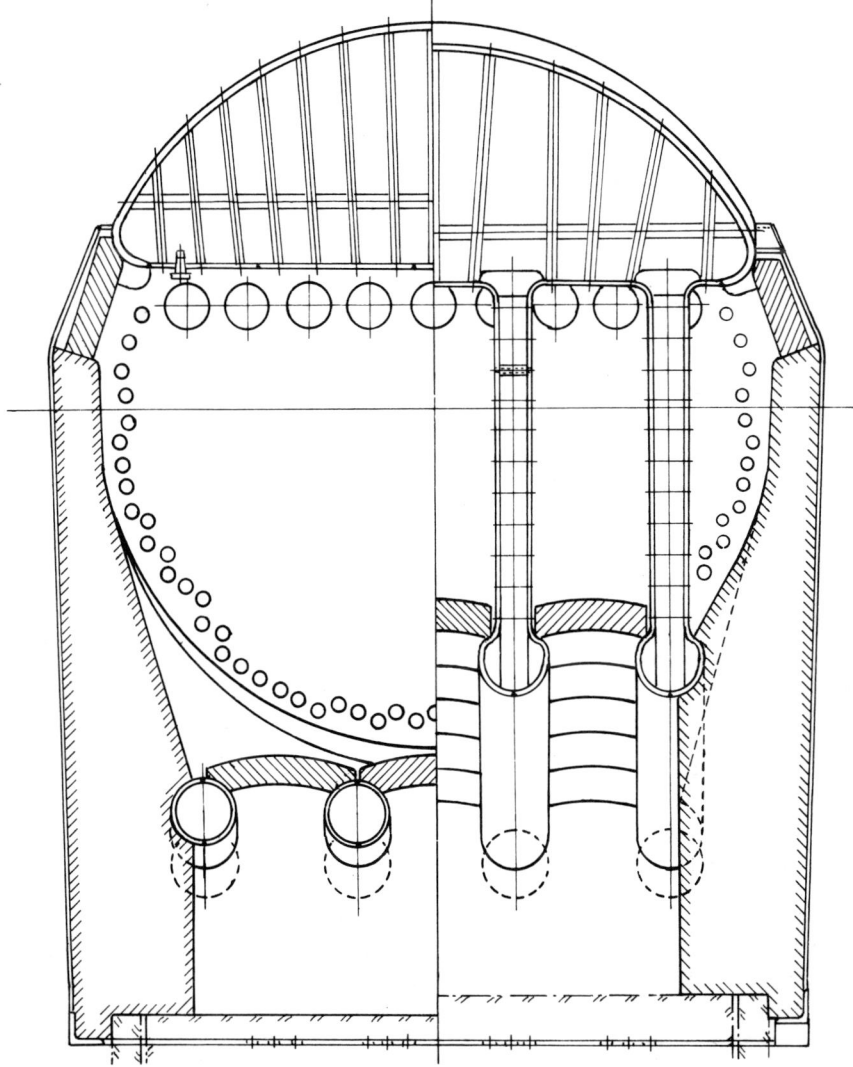

Fig 44 Cross-sections of the "Leader" firebox after
the rocking grate was locked and thicker firebrick
walls built on it. Compare Fig 37.

149

for any malfunction of the valve-rods. On one occasion six draughtsmen were nearly suffocated when a partial vacuum was created by freak circumstances on entering Crowborough tunnel. The engine certainly achieved one record by carrying up to 18 footplate helpers at a time. It also attracted many distinguished visitors, including Bulleid's old friend A. Chapelon, who was keenly interested in many of the innovations, particularly the sleeve valves and the boiler arrangement with four syphons. He could see their potential.

The chief early modifications to get the engine "on the road" were:

Weight: more clearance given to axlebox pedestals to ensure free response of springs. Ballast later added along one side to correct trim.
Firebox: brick lining considerably thickened. Grate area ultimately reduced to 26sq ft.
Sleeve valves: clearance in liners doubled to 0.036in and back ring removed.
Valve gear: oscillating gear removed.

The last two items stopped the breakage of sleeves, whose lugs had snapped off with a sharp crack if a sleeve jammed. Once during the later tests after these modifications Attwell was riding alone in the rear cab when suddenly came *crack — crack — two* sleeve failures, it seemed. Yet there they were, still working correctly. The engine had simply passed over two fog-signals.

The problems met during the trials and the corrective actions taken were:

Poor steaming after grate area reduction: Size of blast pipe nozzles reduced, but this caused excessive fire-throwing.
Fire-throwing after grate and blast modifications: Brick arch added, but this caused flames to lick round firehole door, worsening the fireman's position.
Rocker-grate malfunctioning: It was removed and a drop-grate fitted.
Over-travel of valves: Maximum cut-off was reduced to 65% but this caused poor starting.
Cylinder relief valves blowing: This was due to weak springs, but the valves were simply blanked off.
Cylinder cocks inoperable: They were successfully modified.
Water in oil sump: Improved by disconnecting the oil circulating pipes around the bogie bearing segment containing the exhaust steam passage.
Corrosion of motion pins in oil bath: A suitable inhibitor was discussed with the oil supplier, but the main cause was leaving the engine standing with water in the sump.
Coupling chains lengthening: Clearances were improved and a skid designed but never fitted. Probably caused by water and abrasive impurities contaminating the oil.
Tendency to prime: This was due to the water level being too high in the boiler, partly attributable to a rather restricted steam space.

Brake release time too long: Simple modification needed, under discussion with manufacturer.

Circlips breaking: This allowed motion pins to fall out. Discussion with makers started.

Oil wastage: Mainly due to the unsatisfactory drive to the circulating pump, and a redesign was started.

As Jarvis had pointed out, a great deal more work would have to be done to eliminate all these shortcomings, though none presented an insuperable problem. Inevitably, the failure to do any more than patch some of them up and suffer the others led to unsatisfactory dynamometer car trials and poor results. So the trials finished rather despondently, with all the honours going to the competing old hand, Class U 2-6-0 No. 31630, as shown in the summary of the official report, Appendix 6.

The report was issued in December 1950, and in March 1951 the decision was taken to scrap the project. With the amount of development expenditure needed to retrieve five usable engines, and in the 1951 climate of electrification hopes but mounting diesel pressures, it was the only possible decision. But typically, with that touch of the imp bred of the designer or of steam engine tradition, and with "no one watching", No. 36001 "Leader" had made a notable last trip on November 2, 1950 after the dynamometer car had gone back home to Darlington. Loaded to its taste with a 480ton train it accelerated purposefully and ran without hesitation to its permitted 50mph, holding the sectional timings to Basingstoke and dropping a broad hint as to what could have been done.

17

The Irish Scene

In the latter half of 1948 Bulleid made several trips to Eire as one of the advisers to Sir James Milne's Committee which duly issued its report in December 1948. Broadly, it recommended sprucing up the railway, using engines more efficiently, building modern carriages and wagons, delaying a switch to diesels for express services, buying diesel railcars, and — most important — placing rail, canal and road public transport under one body, Coras Iompair Eireann.

This was accepted by the Irish Government early in 1949 and Mr T.C. Courtney was appointed Chairman of the new CIE Board, to take over the railways on January 1, 1950. He wasted no time on his groundwork and got Bulleid appointed Consulting Mechanical Engineer at the April 1949 Board meeting, the starting date being left open. Neither Courtney nor Bulleid had the slightest intention of the job remaining like that, of course; the strategy was to get this experienced hustler into the CME job and the tactics were to do it gently, to avoid nasty confrontations and to "let the people decide."

Meanwhile there was no CME, so when Bulleid started at Inchicore on October 1, 1949, and took his turn in the famous office with Ivatt, Aspinall, Maunsell, Bazin & Co. over the mantelpiece, no one on the railway was surprised that he took charge. Despite knowing roughly what to expect he had been a bit shaken by his 1948 visits. More than 25% of the engines were normally out of service on repair; the carriage situation reminded him of the Great Eastern in 1923; workshop and shed equipment included archaic items; and the will to get more efficient had gone flabby in the long absence of a CME. Yet here was a nice small compact railway, just waiting to be livened up — comparison with the Southern was only depressing in the ratio of vehicles to route miles, showing up the sparse traffic:

	Southern Railway in 1946	Coras Iompair Eireann in 1948
Staff employed, CME	10,000	4,600
No of locomotives	1,847	491
No of carriages	8,068	1,325
No of wagons	36,500	11,900
Route mileage	2,178	2,028
Ratio: vehicles/miles	22	7

A columnist in the *Irish Times* grumbled quite wittily about the "foreign importation . . . too old to work for British Railways . . . but qualifies to be the big boss at Inchicore." He got the title and salary wrong but the prognostication right. The *Sunday Independent* welcomed the newcomer as likely to decide the right type of engines which, it thought, would not be diesels for main line work. At a press conference and a Radio Eireann interview Bulleid began to outline the Courtney-Bulleid plans:

Electrification had already been turned down by CIE on account of the low traffic density. The five 487hp Brush diesel-electric shunters were satisfactory though hard to utilise fully. Sixty 250hp railcars were to be ordered. Two 915hp Bo-Bo mixed traffic Sulzer locomotives were being constructed at Inchicore, but their high cost suggested it might be better to retain coal-fired steam engines, possibly with types of greater availability such as the "Leader." Meanwhile the existing steam engine availability was being improved and stock reduced from 491 to 350. Fifty wider, modern carriages would be built in 1951. Inchicore, employing 2,000 and the largest Works in the Republic, had great potential and there would be work for all. The new power station at Portarlington, fuelled by machine-cut turf (as the Irish persist in calling peat) was a challenge to provide a peat-burning locomotive for CIE.

These were popular views, liked by almost all, and Bulleid was formally appointed CME of CIE in February 1951. Domestically he was well settled in a comfortable house at Foxrock nearly opposite the new church, and there was a handy golf course at Carrickmines.

By the middle of 1953 the railcars were proving quicker and cheaper to run than the steam trains they replaced, and the price of coal was going up and up. Diesel sales pressures were growing; vested and other interests kept saying they would lick steam, and four American experts visited CIE and advised buying American diesels. Besides, there were scant signs of the aged CIE steam holding its own. So in 1953 the Government accepted the CIE Board's recommended dieselisation and voted the necessary £10½ million to cover the diesels, additional railcars, maintenance facilities, carriages and wagons, and 50 steam engines. These were mainly for the seasonal peak freight traffic and were to be suitable for burning turf or oil.

Though he would never admit it, Bulleid appreciated the massive paradox of the notorious steam advocate undertaking a near-100% dieselisation project. He could see the pro-diesel arguments still gaining force and he was amused to be the Irish pioneer of a technical change which he was certain would spread to British Railways.

The early to mid-1950s were accordingly a very busy time for Bulleid. Apart from deciding on the diesels, preparing for their maintenance, designing the auxiliaries, designing and manufacturing carriages and wagons, not to mention turf-burning, he had to coax increased performance from the Works and improved maintenance from the Running Sheds. He also had the Brake Problem.

After much cogitation and close enquiry he decided on the Oerlikon air brake for the new diesels. He then felt that it should also become standard throughout CIE replacing the vacuum brake, as was then understood to be the intention of British Railways. Davies & Metcalfe were manufacturing the Oerlikon brake system and Bulleid offered them a workshop at Inchicore so that they could manufacture locally for CIE. But then British Railways flabbergastingly decided to retain the vacuum brake so the project fell through.

Not to be deterred, Bulleid thought out an improvement to the vacuum brake by electro-magnetic control (Appendix 8). This naturally interested Davies & Metcalfe, specially when Inchicore equipped a whole train and it worked satisfactorily. But it was not an economic proposition, and Richard Metcalfe characterised it as "a very brave attempt at modernising the vacuum brake and typical of Bulleid's ingenuity."

The volume of work, the interesting experiments, the flow of visiting overseas technical experts, all added to Inchicore morale. Output in 1954 was easily the largest since the Works opened in 1846, pleasing the Works Manager V. O'Neill and the men as much as it pleased Bulleid himself — who might have some strange ideas but surely brought in the work. The activity also delighted the Chief Draughtsman, Paddy Mulvany, despite O.V.B.'s tiresome insistence on an effort-causing, discipline-forming register of drawings — 50 years overdue.

All this Inchicore effort was conspicuously successful, and after their teething troubles all the diesels gave a generally satisfactory performance. By the end of 1957 they were operating three-quarters of the train miles run, clocking up 7million miles a year, and saving nearly £1million a year on fuel and £¼million a year on wages, all diesel units being single-manned. The accelerated timings and the new carriages were extremely popular. There were also economies from reduced freight train mileages, because increased train loads and incidentally faster running were achieved by the diesels, whose low axle loads of 14½tons gave them wide availability, bringing increased power to branch lines and restricted sections.

It was certainly a big project that CIE were pulling off, and through it all strode the perennially energetic Bulleid figure, usually a step ahead of his accompanying colleagues, often more than a step ahead in a discussion, somehow always seeming more physically and mentally alert than his juniors. Once in 1957 he reached the top of the Inchicore water tower so fast that a colleague, not ignorant about racing, thought a handicap was needed. But back in the office, inclined to sit too still when concentrating, he often complained of feeling cold which momentarily made him feel his age; and to counter this everyone took pride in seeing that the room was maintained at the prescribed temperature of 80°F.

Despite or because of the good progress on railway modernisation, the Irish Government decided in 1956 to set up another Committee, under Dr J. Beddy, to re-examine internal transport. There were plenty of good reasons: nearly eight years since the Milne report; considerable relevant changes; an unbiased view of the current situation needed; and noisy whispers from everywhere that railways should be ousted by roads. The Beddy report was published and adopted in 1957. It called for commercially viable internal transport, advised cutting the railway route mileage from 1918 to 850 miles and the stations from 194 to less than 50. Most of the recommendations had been expected in 1956 and a diminishing of the railway foreseen. Courtney later handed over to Dr Andrews as Chairman of the new Board, and Bulleid was happy to retire (again) in May 1958, aged 75½, his Turf Burner (Mark I) duly completed.

News of this second retirement brought another batch of tributes from all quarters. Of them, Bulleid was specially pleased by an appreciative note from John Elliot and an unexpected salutation from Brighton:

Brighton, 24/7/58
"Dear Sir,

May I wish you a long and happy retirement, accompanied by the best of Good Health.

I would also thank you for the courtesy you gave to my fellow workmates and myself in our all too brief association with you as our CME.

Your name will always be associated with that of the ideal Chief (always fair and impartial) in the minds of us all here at Brighton.

On behalf of the workshop staff of the now almost defunct Railway Works at Brighton, I am,

Yours sincerely,
J. Spencer
late chargeman of the building of Engine No. 21C101 etc."

Did Bulleid enjoy his time in Eire? Indubitably. He had all the satisfactions of an important job well done, of doing it after normal retiring age, of doing it without technical interference, of extending his remunerated professional career, and of being allowed to pursue his marginally useful but rather expensive hobby on the side. After he had agreed my chapter about him in *Master Builders of Steam*, which covered his Irish episode in one short paragraph, he must have pondered a bit about it because he wrote to me soon after, in February 1963, saying:

"I believe your chapter on me ends with my service on the Southern Railway.

"CIE, however, was a unique experience. To change over from steam to diesel traction at one step was not frequently done. I replaced carriages and wagons. Built the first three-level diesel repair shop at Inchicore. Re-arranged the running sheds retained in use (intending to have only Inchicore, Cork, Galway and Limerick ultimately). I reduced the establishment by many hundreds of men — 20% or so. The changeover was sufficiently profitable to make CIE an earning system and it was only the ill-conceived wages increases given by the Irish Government that put CIE back into the debit side. The new design carriage in laminated prefabrication aluminium-covered wood was a marked lightening as were the triangulated wagons with box section members and all welded."

18

CIE Diesels

The 1953 dieselisation decision came as no surprise to the CIE technical staff, nor did it find them ignorant about diesels. They had done well with the five diesel-electric shunters since 1948, the two mixed traffic locomotives since 1951, and the new railcars. But the complete changeover would not be simple because a complete stud of reliable locomotives had to be provided with assurance of continuity for spares together with a comprehensive maintenance and fuelling set-up and a massive staff training programme for drivers and mechanics. I think some amiable non-technical friends still wonder why railway engineers could not simply go to a shop, order so many diesels for delivery the next day, and then just fill them up with fuel, attach them to their trains, and get going.

Bulleid's key problem was what to buy. He was not short of conflicting suggestions among the 30 tenders received, all well documented, and he was exploring alternatives which British Railways were only starting to explore five years later. Should the transmission be electric? hydraulic? mechanical? Should the engines be high-speed or medium-speed? How many types were really essential in addition to railcars and shunters? What were the political, financial and delivery complications to be weighed? and the reliability for spares? and for technical follow-up for any problems? The decisions were duly taken and the entire fleet ordered by mid-1954 for delivery between mid-1955 and March 1958.

The performance characteristics and the quick deliveries required by CIE made diesel-electrics the inevitable choice despite Bulleid's instinctive preference for diesel-hydraulics, which was demonstrated by his enthusiasm in designing and building the 19 Maybach-engined Class E locomotives, completed at Inchicore in 1955.

The B class locomotives were formulated by Bulleid to utilise Sulzer engines and Metro-Vickers electrical equipment bought in 1946 and stored; two were built at Inchicore and twelve contracted out, all the Sulzer engines being hotted-up from 915 to 960hp by fitting new turbo-chargers.

The main burden of the work was to fall on the A and C class locomotives: (see table overleaf)
Bulleid placed the manufacture of the vehicles and electrics in notoriously safe and reliable hands; and though he did the same with the engines, he was attracted by a not-so-well-tried design, the valve-less, comparatively

Quantity	Class	Type	BHP	Maker or main contractor	Engine	Transmission	Working weight (tons)	Top speed (mph)	Year placed in service
60	Railcar		250	AEC	AEC	mechanical	40	70	1953-5
6	Railcar		250	BUT & Inchicore	AEC	mechanical	40	70	1956-7
2	B	A1A-A1A	960	Sulzer and Inchicore	Sulzer	electrical Metro-Vickers	80	55	1951
12	B	A1A-A1A	960	BRCW	Sulzer	electrical Metro-Vickers	73	75	1955-6
60	A	Co-Co	1200	Metro-Cammell	Crossley	electrical Metro-Vickers	85	75	1955-6
34	C	Bo-Bo	550	Metro-Cammell	Crossley	electrical Metro-Vickers	57	75	1956-7
19	E	0-6-0	400	Inchicore	Maybach	hydraulic Mekydro	38.8	55	1956-7
3	G	0-4-0	130	Deutz	Deutz	hydraulic Deutz	18	25	1955

5ft 3in gauge diesels for CIE introduced by O.V. Bulleid. (For further details see the paper presented by M.J. Devereux to the Institution of Locomotive Engineers in October 1956, entitled "Experiences with Diesel Railcars.")

Class	A	C
Wheel arrangement	Co-Co	Bo-Bo
Horsepower	1200	550
Maximum axle load, tons	14.5	14.5
Maximum service speed, mph	75	75
Maximum speed on full power, mph	60	60
Minimum speed at continuous rating, mph	15	9
Maximum tractive effort at starting, lb	61,800	43,200
Continuous rating tractive effort, lb	24,000	16,000
Wheel diameter, inches	38	38
Fuel oil capacity, imperial gallons	500	400
Length over buffers, feet	51	42
Minimum curve, chains	4	4

simple, two-stroke Crossley engine. He heard from a contact at the Admiralty that these engines gave no trouble and he knew a lot were on order for the Western Australian Railways, so he would be in high-class company for reliability, service and spares. The larger engines for the A class had 8 cylinders, 10½in bore by 13½in stroke, compression ratio 15.8 to 1, running at 625rpm with maximum horsepower for one hour of 1,320. The pistons were of a special heat-resisting chrome-moly cast iron weighing 178lb, and the mean piston speed was 23½ft per sec. These engines were the main worry in the teething trouble stage; they suffered many piston and consequent cylinder-head failures. One theory was that the continued burning of lubricating oil passing the piston rings maintained the piston heads at too high a temperature, but Bulleid doubted this.

Meanwhile the railcars were settling down well and by the end of 1955 Devereux had nearly 90% of them in regular daily service. They normally operated in four-coach trains made up of two railcars and two intermediate carriages, weighing 140 tons, having a useful 500hp, and with fuel consumption averaging 2½miles per gallon.

As happened to new young diesels everywhere else, stand-by steam engines did a great deal of rescue work and on one occasion a rescue by the Turf-Burner was only averted by dedicated devotion to diesel duty. Nonetheless the diesels firmly took over the trains and the only real regret voiced by drivers was that the C class lacked power. There were stories, some true, of elderly steam locomotives such as the Aspinall 4-4-0s doing better with six-coach trains on the Dublin-Bray service than the 550hp C class could. This must have been due partly to drivers hesitating to use the full available power, and partly to comparisons with the decidedly stronger B class locos which incidentally demonstrated the superiority of the (more expensive) Sulzer engines.

Most of the A class locomotives were available for the 1956 summer traffic and enabled all trains to match the accelerations introduced by the railcars; for example the Dublin-Cork non-stop runs were timed at 3hr for the 165 miles, and 70min were cut from the previous timings on the 206mile run from Dublin to Tralee. The whole travelling tempo was unbelievably heightened, and to some of the older station staff the double change to trains which were a lot faster and arrived on time must have seemed quite bizarre. And not only passenger trains; the Dublin-Cork freight timings were reduced by 80min or more and for the first time ever ample power was available on the branch lines. So everyone took to the diesels which, despite teething troubles, managed to hold an 80% availability rate.

It is not always summer even in the most whimsical reaches of the Republic, so how about train heating, with no more steam engines? Bulleid was not going to muddle Metropolitan-Cammell nor clutter up his new diesels by lumbering them with train-heating boilers; instead he built 41 four-wheeled combined heating and luggage vans. In the summer, when the need for extra van space was greater, the "Spanner" boilers were removed bodily for their annual overhaul, increasing the luggage space by 50%. This commonsense idea worked admirably.

By mid 1957 there was no doubt that the C.I.E. "one-shot" changeover to diesels was a success*, mainly on account of the unswerving attention given to it by Bulleid and Devereux; and the comprehensive re-training of all concerned, particularly the drivers under J.H. Dudley; and to the vital third factor of first class support and maintenance facilities.

Five sheds were equipped to deal with weekly, monthly and three-monthly inspections of each diesel locomotive, and Inchicore was equipped to carry out intermediate repairs at 50,000miles and heavy repairs at 100,000miles, based on makers' advice. Full general repairs, with the engines removed from the locomotives for complete overhaul, were expected to be needed at 300,000miles.

Bulleid sought and obtained the best current American advice on these maintenance facilities, with the result that the boiler shop at Inchicore was converted to the best diesel repair shop in Europe. Four three-level bays were provided, each piped with fuel and lubricating oils, distilled water for batteries, chromated water for engine cooling systems, and compressed air. Adjacent rooms were equipped for servicing fuel injectors and pumps, instruments, and air filters. The necessary water-treatment and oil-recovery plants were nearby, and there was a spray-washer to clean the silver-painted locomotive in a matter of minutes. Similar treatment was available for the railcars but on a reduced scale; their engines were replaced by reconditioned engines every 60,000miles, this being the quickest way to return the railcars to service. At 60,000miles the 125hp engines needed a top overhaul and piston ring inspection, and at 120,000miles the bores were honed and new rings fitted, this coinciding with the routine shopping of the vehicles and overhaul of transmission equipment.

* Summarised in a paper by T.C. Courtney to the Institute of Transport Congress in Dublin on June 4th 1958, reproduced in *The Railway Gazette* for June 6th 1958.

In all this procedure Bulleid followed the text-book and instilled the essential maintenance discipline into Inchicore. "Without it, they will not keep going, like steam engines would," he rightly insisted. And that is why, when he left them in 1958, the only steam engines remaining in service were those few kept for seasonal peak traffic. Paradoxically, it is also why CIE completely lost interest in turf burning.

19

CIE Carriages
and Wagons

Although both the Southern Railway and CIE owned about 2,000 route-miles of track, CIE in 1949 had only 1,325 carriages compared with over 8,000 on the Southern and about 300 of them were unfit for use — including some built before 1900. CIE's wagons were in better shape, average age about 30 years and 750 built within the last five years. Bulleid advised immediate inspection and realistic withdrawal of archaic stock, with a five-year plan to build at least 30 carriages a year at Inchicore in addition to items already on order, which comprised 150 cattle wagons, 15 brake vans, three Travelling Post Office vehicles and 25 main-line composite carriages — the first since 1937.

What prevented Bulleid getting off the mark as sharply as he would have liked was the shortage of materials, the aftermath of the 1947 crisis, which had even longer repercussions on exports from the UK so that, for example, the British Government refused to allow some of CIE's steel requirements to be exported to Eire; the steel was needed for UK exports of finished products, naturally enough. So CIE suffered the delays and expense of shopping further abroad including North America and Belgium, for steel and other supplies. This meant that carriages and wagons ordered before 1948 were not completed till 1951. But by then there were signs of Bulleid influence in the welding generally and the all-steel welded bodies of the brake-vans in particular.

The 1953 dieselisation programme included also plans to build about 35 carriages annually, and with these Bulleid went to 61ft 6in length and 10ft width, provided triangulated underframes, kept the tare weight down to 26½tons for 70 seats in main-line carriages and 76 in suburban composites, and introduced an interesting novelty by constructing the bodies from Mallinson aluminium-faced plywood panels. These dispensed with exterior painting but invited and received the nick-name "Tin Coaches." The material proved light and durable, and a further refinement was rubber cushioning between the body and the triangulated underframe which rode on Commonwealth bogies. Sixteen of these carriages were built in 1956 and 15 in 1957-8. By their light weight, low cost, handsome appearance, ease of construction and effective interior fittings, these carriages paid tribute to a designer who had never stopped thinking since setting out to liven up Doncaster carriages in 1920. They were duly appreciated by all concerned.

162

One important co-operative step in the constant quest for improvement was the mock-up carriage available in the Inchicore carriage shop. On it could be tried any bright idea, affecting either amenity, or safety, or appearance, or ease or cost of construction. Sometimes Bulleid would visit this mock-up first thing of a morning, before looking in at his office, to verify some over-night inspiration. Then the effective Inchicore tracking system of the internal bush telegraph would go into action, reporting the location and actions of "your man" and sometimes gloomily forecasting Himself wanting some new and inconvenient modification.

For the 41 heating vans to go with the diesels, and for parcel and Travelling Post Office vans totalling about 66 in the period 1956-7, Bulleid also adopted the aluminium-faced plywood panels, mounted on laminated wood pillars, and the triangulated underframe and Hoffman roller-bearing axleboxes. These vehicles were all four-wheelers, 30ft long by 10ft wide, wheelbase 18ft, and subject to a speed limit of 70mph. The tare weights were 16½tons for the heating vans, fuelled, and 10¼ tons for the others.

Bulleid would have liked a width of 10ft 6in for all these vans and carriages but was doubtful about clearances: the Irish specified the loading gauge well enough but they could be casual about throw-over — that is, the amount by which the ends or centre of a long bogie vehicle transgress the loading gauge on a curve. It depends of course on the sharpness of the curve and the accuracy of the track alignment and whether there is another wide vehicle on the adjacent running line at the critical moment. This last item happened on the sharp curve in Dalkey tunnel when two carriages "rubbed" and thereby gave a practical demonstration of the risks in going wider.

Even more serious than "rubbing" is the problem of carriage behaviour in a collision. Back in 1911 the Board of Trade was pushing proposals to prevent telescoping, and designers including Gresley and Bulleid favoured the adoption of strong couplers and strong underframes, to hold the train intact and reasonably in line after a collision, independent of the comparatively weak carriage bodies be they wood or steel. This matter got a renewed airing after a collision between two railcar sets at Dundrum, when one ran into the rear of the other and its driver was killed in the ensuing telescoping. Bulleid had ample underframe strength, particularly in the later triangulated underframes, and for automatic couplers he had for some time greatly liked the Fischer type. He had previously demonstrated these successfully in staged wagon collisions at Inchicore and when the Government sought reassurances after the Dundrum accident he staged a 40mph collision at Thurles with Fischer couplers on two strong but aged carriages. Standing dangerously near, the alarming crash of the impact must have reminded him of his full brake application on the fitted freight at Holme thirty years before. A huge dust cloud blotted out the result of the collsion and into this Bulleid disappeared, to see with delight that the couplers had locked together so there was no hint of telescoping despite considerable underframe damage to one carriage and a major shift of its body.

Braking improvements also reduce collision damage and Bulleid introduced an improved 15in diameter vacuum brake cylinder for wagons. This was designed by Stabeg of Vienna, based on their air brake cylinder with its patent moulded seal, and manufactured by Davies & Metcalfe under licence. Five hundred were duly supplied to CIE and gave highly satisfactory performance, all resulting from Bulleid's initiation of three-cornered meetings with Stabeg and Richard Metcalfe.

Then always there was the question of riding — of both new and overhauled carriages. Bulleid fully retained his agility and senses of balance and perception of riding qualities, and continued his long-held practice of checking the riding of a vehicle by standing over the bogie and either writing or just thinking. If he could later read the writing the riding was at least passable. It has been reported that he wrote thus always on the backs of envelopes; this is not wholly true — he sometimes wrote on their fronts — and it fails to explain that these envelopes with their contents made almost as firm a writing base, and a far handier one, than those boards and clips so beloved by the post-war wave of data-takers.

An experiment which involved much riding and writing was the fitting of a bolsterless bogie, generally similar to that designed for the SR Inspection Saloon, to one of the 1950 carriages. Possibly disliking the wider gauge, it never ran well enough to tempt Bulleid away from the Commonwealth bogie, but he persevered with it to the end, making a run to Thurles in 1958 hauled by the equally persevering Aspinall/Ivatt 4-4-0 No. 62.

It was always a problem to ensure a balanced work-load for the carriage side at Inchicore, and one aid to this was the building of the bodies for the last six railcars. They were a straightforward and effective job, though no beauties.

Bulleid's all-steel, all-welded 12ton standard open wagon represented another advance in design development. The triangulated underframe was improved by being fabricated from 3in by 2in welded steel box section, one eighth of an inch thick, giving greater strength for even less weight. Buffing stresses were well distributed, whether applied normally or at one side only as on a curve. The wagon sides were of ribbed steel. Inchicore production of the wagons ran at 12 per week. Two of them were involved in destructive testing at Kilfree near Sligo when an A class diesel hauling 20 wagons overran siding buffers and jumped down a steepish bank followed by all the wagons. It was lucky that no one got hurt. Bulleid hurried to the scene (by car) and was pleased to find, among the formidable pile of debris, two comparatively undamaged triangulated underframes.

Carriage and wagon construction was up-to-date and soundly based when Bulleid retired from CIE in May 1958. It was seen and appreciated by visitors from the Institution of Locomotive Engineers and the Institute of Transport in their June visits when all the main items were on display, labelled with their Drawing Office descriptions — Diesel railcar, Buffet car, Main Line coach, Heating van, Post Office bogie, Covered wagon, Open wagon, and Cattle wagon.

20

The Turf Burner

The use of turf, his home-grown fuel, has naturally always interested the patriotic Irishman, who wondered why the Railways made all that fuss about using it. Aspinall pinpointed the difficulties in his 1885 Presidential Address to the Institution of Civil Engineers of Ireland:

> "It will not stand the punishment in the firebox to which ordinary coal is subjected when burning in a locomotive drawing a heavy train. If, however, the turf is compressed and well dried it makes a fairly good fuel but no efforts to produce it in this form have been commercially successful."

These compressed turf briquettes were available during World War II and their use contributed to keeping at least some engines running. The chief difficulties were maintaining steam pressure, getting enough turf on to a tender, and putting out fires caused by spark-throwing. Turf had about 2½ times the bulk of coal and half the calorific value so you needed nearly five times the tender volume.

This re-proved inability to use turf was still rankling with CIE when Bulleid arrived in 1949, and he at once entered the age-old contest, but making these new fixes:

(1) A special type of locomotive was needed with fan-controlled draught dispensing with the conventional blast-pipe, and with ample bunker space for the large volume of turf needed.

(2) Such an engine would be the ideal replacement for stock badly run down during the war.

(3) It would be cheaper than a diesel engine and so would be more appropriate either for general use or for stand-by to cover the seasonal peak traffic.

(4) Under changed circumstances it could equally well be oil-fired, reverting to turf in a time of emergency.

Superimposed on these admirable desiderata he naturally envisaged the ideal steam locomotive, the improved "Leader," for which he had acquired such useful data from those Southern Region experiments. Patriotically appealing to the Irish by using the local fuel, saving them from buying expensive diesels, and incidentally providing the ideal modern twin-power-bogie steam engine — what could be a better and more challenging proposition? So without difficulty he got CIE sanction for an immediate start on turf-burning experimental work, judiciously seeking also the moral support of Bord na Mona, the Irish Turf Board.

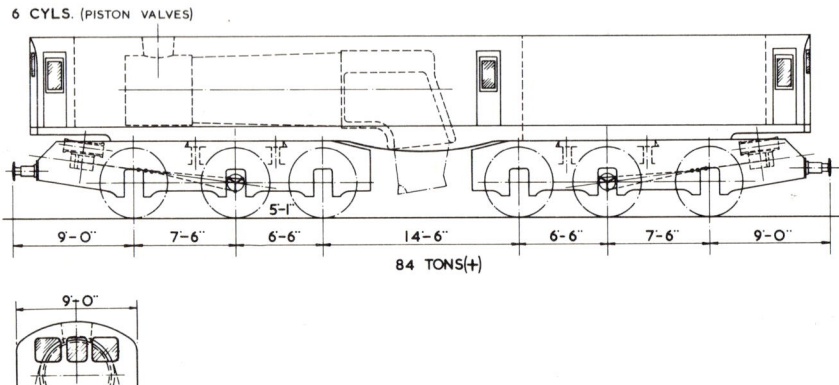

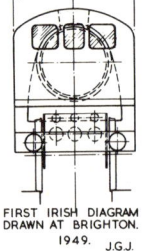

FIRST IRISH DIAGRAM
DRAWN AT BRIGHTON.
1949. J.G.J.

Fig 45 First thoughts for Ireland, with plenty of space for peat, drawn at Brighton in 1949.

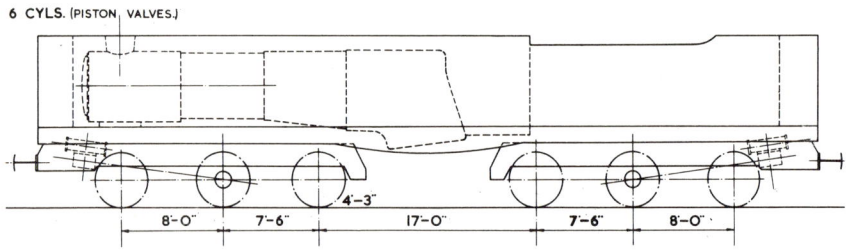

COMPARATIVE NOTES ON
THIS DIAGRAM WERE:-

IRISH.		LEADER.
84	TOTAL WGT. TONS	114
14	AXLE-WEIGHT	19
6	COAL. TONS	4
5000	WATER. GALS.	4000

SECOND IRISH DIAGRAM
DRAWN AT BRIGHTON.
1949.
J.G.J.

Fig 46 Second diagram for Ireland, another piston-valved C-C, with comparative weights.

166

The first aim of the experimental work was to understand and then cope with the essential differences between burning coal and turf, which required a larger grate area and more air inlet space and an even draught, and made some clinker and much fly-ash, and presented a serious spark-throwing problem because the cinders went on smouldering. Moreover, except when in briquette form, turf contained nearly 25% water, which had to be evaporated off in the firebox.

The experimental rig at Inchicore, about which many words were spoken, consisted of two old locomotive boilers, one with its smokebox removed, the other with its chimney blanked off, placed front-to-front and bolted together. One was fired from a 10ton bunker of turf placed in the tender position, and the exhaust was taken through a chimney fitted to the firehole door of the other. The forced draught was from an electrically-driven fan.

Data from this experiment guided work on the first experimental turf-burning locomotive, the much-modified 1903 2-6-0 No. 356. It was fitted with a mechanical stoker and a forced-draught fan driven by a steam turbine. It was duly visited by Dr. C.S. Andrews, Managing Director of the Turf Board. After recounting the advantages of replacing by peat the 200,000tons of coal used annually by CIE he reported:

"The experiments observed briefly on June 28 1951 at the Inchicore Works of the CIE through the courtesy of O.V.S. Bulleid, consulting mechanical engineer to the railway system, showed promising results. A mechanical stoker had been applied to a locomotive of grate area 28 sq ft. It consisted of a screw to feed the broken sod peat from the tender to a

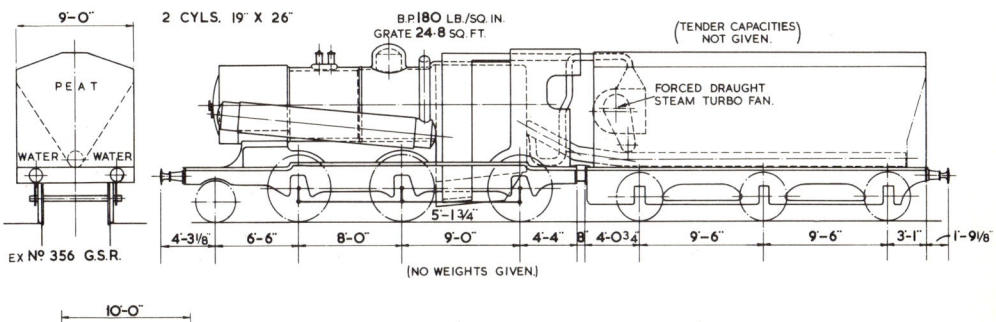
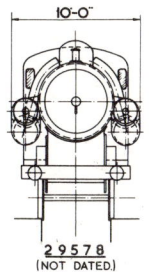

Fig 47 First Inchicore diagram for the converted 2-6-0 No. 356.

167

table plate inside the firing door and jets of steam to distribute the peat to the grate. The flat grate had been replaced by a series of perforated inverted V-shaped plates running lengthwise of the firebox. Thus the area for air admission had been increased."

Then after several technical suggestions Dr. Andrews concluded:

"The development of methods for the application of peat to locomotives is in good hands under the direction of Mr. Bulleid and his associates."

The main trouble with this first rig on engine No. 356 was that the steam turbine driving the fan was not properly matched to its duty, and its efficiency was therefore so low that it consumed most of the steam generated. This was got over by adding a four-wheel truck behind the tender, carrying the fan driven by a diesel engine taken from an old CIE omnibus and controlled by a string passing over the tender. To regain some heat from the exhaust, a Crosti type feed-water heater was fitted on each side of the boiler using the exhaust steam and the flue gases before they passed, via a festoon of ducts and through the tender tank, to atmosphere behind the tender.

Then it was realised that forced draught, with its serious snag of a pressurised firebox from which acrid fumes escaped, was not acceptable and that a change must be made to induced draught with its serious snag of the fan having to handle hot exhaust gases. Water-cooled bearings being impracticable, further effort was essential to reduce the exhaust

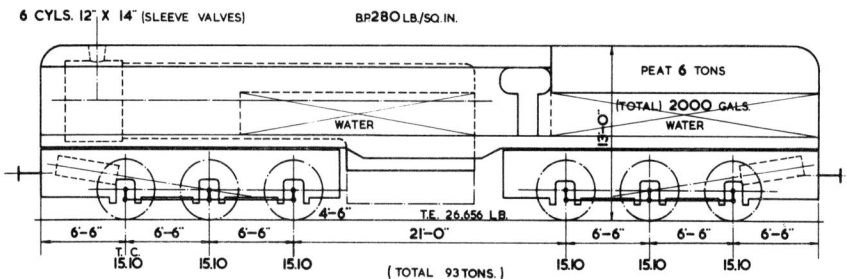

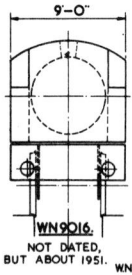

Fig 48 An optimistic Inchicore diagram of a C-C sleeve-valved Turf Burner, the equal axle loading shown being clearly unattainable with the heavy boiler end and light turf end. By early 1952 the drawing office was convinced that a symmetrical fore-and-aft arrangement, as shown on the next diagram, was essential to balance axle loadings.

temperature, and so the Croski pre-heaters were replaced by banks of light-alloy heat exchangers adapted from a Ricardo design.

Most of the year 1952 was thus spent on steaming trials and refining the equipment at Inchicore. The work lacked urgency because political opinion was swinging strongly towards diesels, Courtney keeping Bulleid closely informed on current CIE Board thinking. In 1953 the move to diesels was decided, but with sanction also to build 50 new steam engines, for peat or oil.

In these new circumstances, with the big diesel workload on his shoulders, Bulleid limited trials on No. 356 to a few runs, including a successful run to Cork, and then, with the lessons learned, set about the serious design work for the prototype of what might ultimately be 50 Turf Burners.

In recognising and announcing that the Turf Burner would take its place with the coming fleet of diesel-electric locomotives, Bulleid had set himself the same ambitious design criteria as for the "Leader." It would be of 1,000hp and would carry 12tons of turf and 3,000gallons of water, giving a range of 200 miles between refuelling. He stuck to his intention to use two power bogies. Faced with the really serious problem of finding 1,200cu ft of hopper space for the turf without upsetting the weight distribution, he finally decided, regretfully, on a peat hopper at each end and a new type of boiler with the firebox in the middle. Thus the shape of the Turf Burner was decided and attention turned to detail design.

The boiler was an unconventional all-welded job designed to avoid using pressings and to permit simple local construction. It consisted of two box-form "barrels" 4ft long, 4ft 8½in wide and 7ft 11in deep, mounted each side of a firebox 6ft long. The barrels were stayed by ½in rods at 4in centres and by the 720 smoke tubes, 1in outside diameter by 11swg, all welded in. This large number of small tubes was suitable for turf which contains no tar nor, for that matter, sulphur. At each end, a smokebox and a superheater header with regulator were welded on. Equalising pipes connected the three boiler sections. The ashpan was a separate assembly, brick lined, a shallower version being planned for easy substitution when converting to oil-firing. Messrs Laidlaw-Drew found the firebox ideal for oil-burning and designed equipment to suit. There was some correspondence with H. Holcroft on the subject of a pressure-condensing system, as had been thought of for the Southern Pacifics in 1945, but in December 1955 Bulleid wrote to Holcroft that "at the moment I am not proposing to fit the first locomotive with condensing as I feel there are already enough unknowns to be perfected. I will do so later, so am anxious to be kept informed of any good ideas which can be incorporated in any such scheme."

The vehicle itself was almost completely symmetrical. Driving either way the look-out was good, alongside the turf hoppers. Though the driving compartments backed onto the smokeboxes, the fuel and the draughting method greatly reduced the cleaning-out disadvantage suffered by the coal-fired "Leader."

Each driving cab had one door only, on the driver's left, the normal platform side. As the driver sat, arm on window sill, the four main controls were comfortably to hand; a pull-out regulator handle connected by linkage to the header regulator in the smokebox just behind, notching-up and reversing control operating the Hadfield steam reverser, the conventional driver's brake valve controlling the vacuum brake on engine and train, and — decided luxury — in line with the diesels, an Oerlikon air brake with its own steam-driven compressor.

The buffers and draw-gear were attached to the main frames. And the whistle? When Bulleid heard that the Western Region were fitting their own whistles on the "Britannia" Pacifics, he wrote to Smeddle begging for one of the three-tone chime whistles that were being removed. But in the event it sounded far too subdued and mellow and had to be replaced by a Great Southern and Western ear-piercer in the interests of safety. The Turf Burner moved so quietly that neither cattle nor anyone else took any notice unless warned peremptorily.

A Sturtevant radial-bladed, shrouded-impeller induction fan was mounted at each end of the locomotive, driven by a single-stage radial-flow steam turbine, designed to give 50hp at 2,600rpm with steam supply at 250psi. Each fan drew the exhaust from one smokebox through a bank of light alloy heat exchangers in a duct passing through the water space.

Originally the fans discharged straight to atmosphere, but ducts were later added with exit just in front of the driving cab. This gave three advantages: the longer ducting helped to extinguish sparks, the smoke-lifting was improved in conjunction with fitting deflectors, and a trap was added to return any larger particles to the firebox, via a steeply-falling 3in pipe. This was a bright Bulleid idea, made possible by the pressure in the duct being slightly higher than in the firebox.

Fan draughting also allowed the full steaming rate to be maintained irrespective of regulator position, so a quick boiler recovery could be made after a spell of hard working up to a summit, coasting with regulator closed.

The turf hoppers were designed with top doors and drainage gullies. The water spaces were on both sides of these hoppers, and all four tanks were interconnected for equalisation. Two Weir feed-pumps drew water from a strainer near the firebox and passed it into the boiler via the heat exchangers, with due provision for interconnection and isolation. TIA water treatment was fitted.

Turf was carried from the hopper by a cast steel feed screw into a chamber below the driving cab floor, whence it was conveyed by a short, faster-moving screw just short of the firebox. Both screws were gear-driven by a specially arranged "Berkeley" stoker steam engine. A set of fabricated steam jets distributed the turf evenly across the grate area.

The bogies were of conventional riveted construction, with 1 in frames and a front stretcher of box form which carried the front bearing segment and included an exhaust chamber connected to the engine. The two side bearer segments were carried on angle brackets riveted to the frames. Each of the

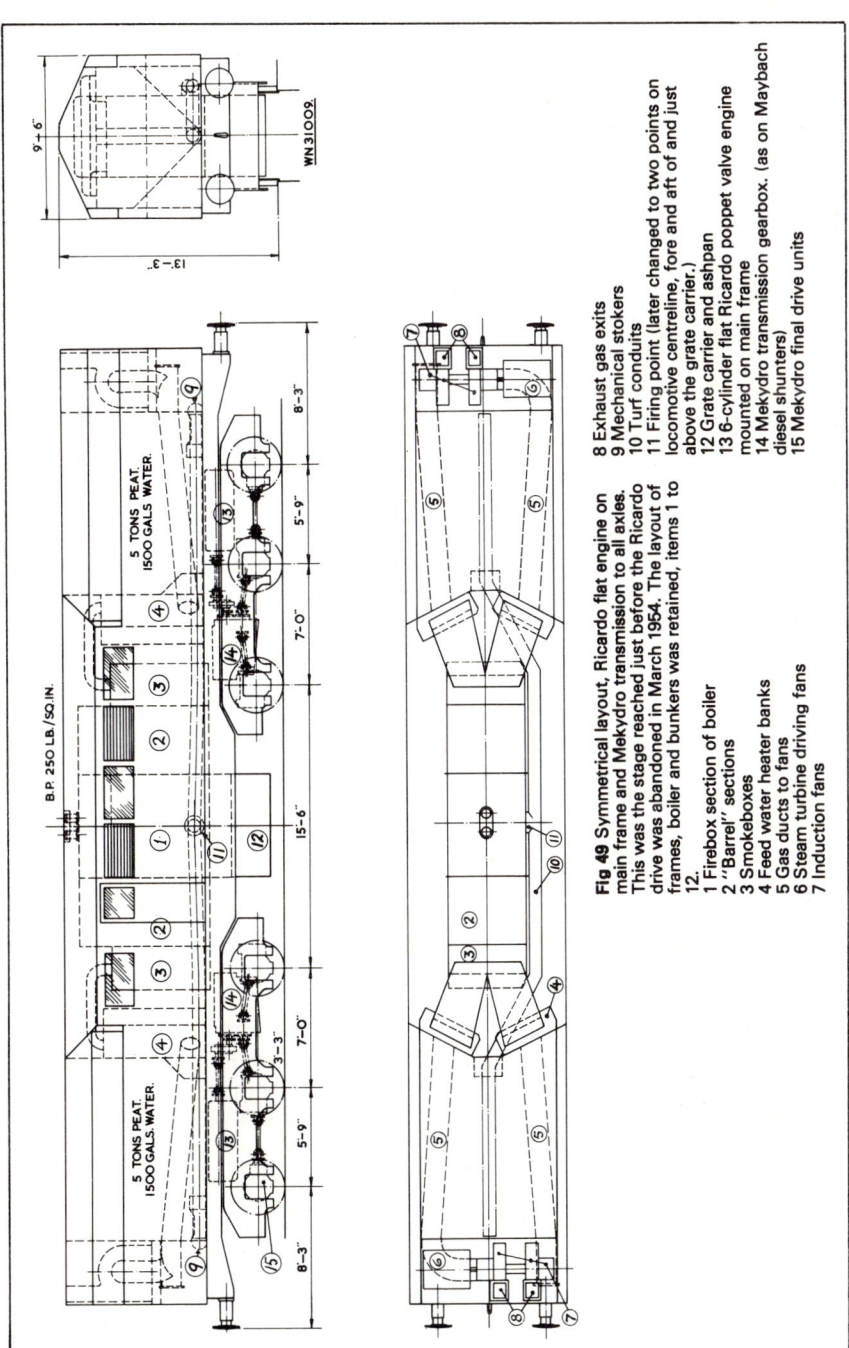

Fig 49 Symmetrical layout, Ricardo flat engine on main frame and Mekydro transmission to all axles. This was the stage reached just before the Ricardo drive was abandoned in March 1954. The layout of frames, boiler and bunkers was retained, items 1 to 12.

1 Firebox section of boiler
2 "Barrel" sections
3 Smokeboxes
4 Feed water heater banks
5 Gas ducts to fans
6 Steam turbine driving fans
7 Induction fans
8 Exhaust gas exits
9 Mechanical stokers
10 Turf conduits
11 Firing point (later changed to two points on locomotive centreline, fore and aft of and just above the grate carrier.)
12 Grate carrier and ashpan
13 6-cylinder flat Ricardo poppet valve engine mounted on main frame
14 Mekydro transmission gearbox. (as on Maybach diesel shunters)
15 Mekydro final drive units

5 TONS PEAT. 1500 GALS. WATER.

B.P. 250 LB./SQ.IN.

8'-3" 5'-9" 7'-0" 15'-6" 7'-0" 3'-3" 5'-9" 8'-3"

9'-6"

13'-3"

WN 31009.

three bearing segments had bronze liners on the vertical thrust faces and the horizontal bearing faces, the side pair lubricated from surrounding troughs but the front segment relying on oil in the exhaust steam.

The detachable engines were secured by fitted bolts to brackets riveted to the bogie frames.

Throughout the preliminary turf burning experiments Bullied had kept actively in his mind the thought of a compact, probably sleeve-valved, three-cylinder balanced engine, to be readily detachable from its power bogie. When, late in 1952, it seemed probable that the Turf Burners would be sanctioned in addition to the diesels, he arranged a consultancy agreement between CIE and Ricardo & Co. He outlined the project to Sir Harry Ricardo in January 1953, seeking in general small multi-cylinder steam engines and in particular their application as substitutes for the six 11.3litre diesel engines in some AEC diesel-mechanical locomotives he was then considering. Sir Harry's notes on the visit reported that four engines each of 150hp seemed appropriate, that he advised six-cylinder single-acting engines with comparatively short stroke, that steam supply was to be at 300 psi with moderate superheat, and that Bulleid proposed to use the same Mekydro gear boxes as on the diesels but would accept a different final drive ratio. From this emerged several schemes with four or six in-line single-acting cylinders and four-throw or six-throw crankshafts, similar in outline to an internal combustion engine. A gear-driven camshaft operated poppet admission valves and exhaust was through a circle of ports opened by the piston near the end of stroke. Flow of steam to the admission valve chests was controlled by a piston valve working in a sleeve connected to the steam supply. Helical ports allowed steam entry and cut-off was altered by twisting the piston valve so that helical grooves in the valve uncovered these ports earlier or later in the stroke. The six cylinders proposed were 6½in diameter by 7½in stroke.

Similar though considerably smaller steam engines had been successfully proved and they offered many attractive features; but many items had to be bought out, costs were far higher than a conventional steam engine, and furthermore the result would fall short of Bulleid's steam-power-bogie ideal, being merely a diesel "copy". So he wrote to Sir Harry Ricardo on March 27 1954:

"When the engine and transmission had been developed to the stage of obtaining prices for gears, delays of the delivery of the equipment and the estimate costs were such as to make it impracticable with proposed arrangement for a high speed single-acting engine with gear drive. As engine must be completed at the earliest possible date, I had no option but to revert to steam locomotive practice.

You will appreciate this decision is arrived at with a great deal of reluctance and regret.

Dictated and not signed by O.V.B."

Thrown back to the less-unconventional, Bulleid finally decided on a

172

two-cylinder engine, 12in diameter by 14in stroke, with 7in piston valves. The block was fabricated and then fitted with cast iron cylinder liners and conventional valve liners.

The crankshaft, connecting rods, crossheads and spiral gear drive to the valve gear were totally enclosed for pumped lubrication from a sump. The connecting rods were 2ft 1in long, and the crossheads circular, running in cast iron liners. The crankshafts were of the welded, built-up type and about 67% of the reciprocating weight was balanced.

The jackshaft carried a 6in chain sprocket each end, one driven from the crankshaft and the other driving the bogie rear axle, with both chain drives enclosed and lubricated from the sump.

A compact version of the Bulleid/Walschaerts gear was designed. It avoided any multiplying linkages, had the minimum of pin-joints, and was actuated from one valve gear shaft, gear-driven from the crankshaft. This was one of the most elegant features of the Turf Burner. It was grease-lubricated.

When considering 4ft wheels for the bogies Bulleid rang Jarvis at Brighton to borrow the patterns from the Stroudley 0-6-0 "Terrier" tanks. But interestingly there were no such patterns because they were wrought iron wheels made by the Canalside Ironworks, Derby. Each spoke had been forged with its share of hub and rim and balance weight and crank throw, after which they were assembled together and smith-welded with much heat and hammering into the complete wheel. Bulleid had had one of these

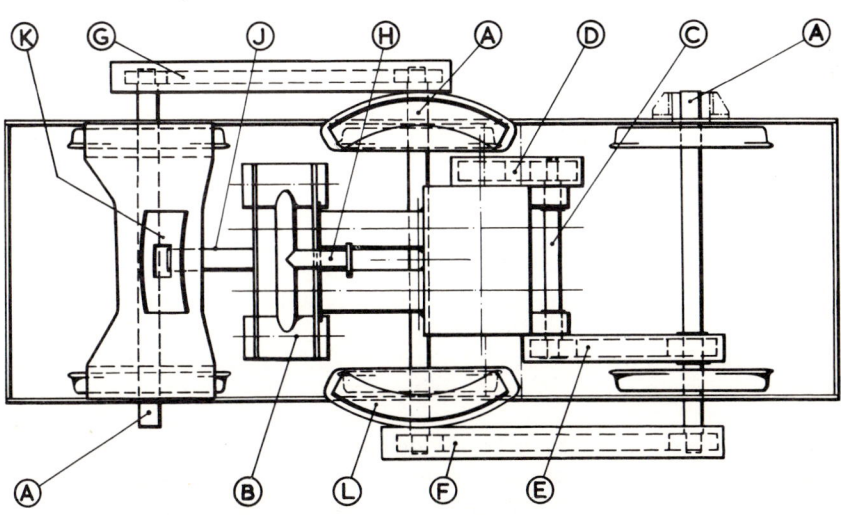

Fig 50 Plan view of a Turf Burner power bogie. The axles A are carried in bronze outside bearings. Drive from the crankshaft of the engine B is to layshaft C by 8 inch chain D and thence to inner axle by 8 inch chain E. The inner and central axles are coupled by 6 inch chain F and the outer axle by 4½ inch chain G. H is the steam pipe to the engine and the exhaust passes through pipe J and a slot in the bearing surface K which, with the two sectors L, supports the main frame of the locomotive.

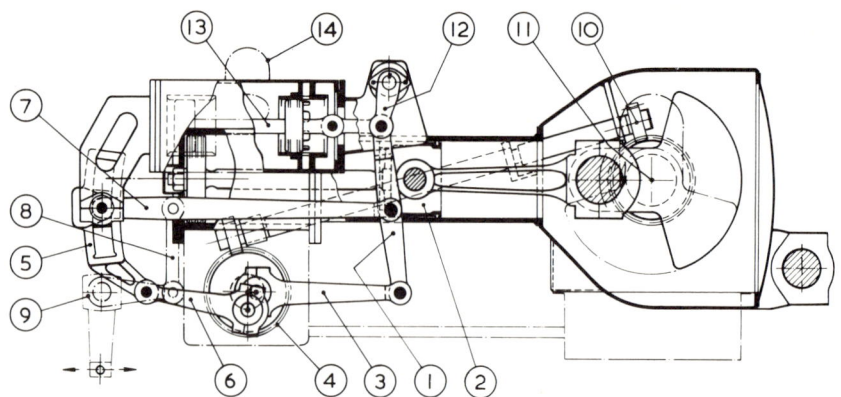

Fig 51 The Turf Burner valve gear. Combination lever 1 is driven in phase with crosshead 2 by the link 3 from a pin on the valve gear shaft 4. The expansion link 5 is driven 90 deg out of phase from a second pin on shaft 4 via the link 6. For reversing and notching up the slider attached to valve rod 7 is lifted or lowered in the expansion link 5 via lifting link 8 from weighbar shaft 9. The valve gear shaft 4 is driven by gears 10 from the crank axle 11. A swing link 12 supports the combination lever 1 which drives the valve spindle 13 to suit inside admission from steam pipe 14.

engines repainted in LBSC livery to serve Brighton Works, he and Jarvis sharing an affection for them and other past splendours. But the Turf Burner duly got conventional wheels of 3ft 7in diameter.

Flexible Aiton pipes, 5in bore, ran from the superheater headers, over the driving cabs, under the turf hoppers to the flanges on the cylinder blocks, accommodating the movement of the bogies. The exhaust was led from the outer bogie bearing segments by pipes with exits adjoining the exhaust gas exits.

There was a nonchalance about work and a tendency to picturesque explanations for not doing it in the Emerald Isle, extending even to Inchicore. It had exasperated a whole line of Locomotive Superintendents and it sometimes exasperated Bulleid. But more serious to him was the lack of quick technical contacts so readily available in London. Typically, when the Ricardo Agreement was terminated in July 1954 he wrote "Consulting Agreement or not, I shall continue to put my problems before you, and would appeal to your good nature to help!"

Though he was well served by Mulvaney and his seniors including Healey, Nolan and Smith, they were all showing signs of fatigue with the project due to a combination of four factors: they had been at it a long time; there was no firm completion date; the inflow of design problems seemed endless; and they suffered that persistent doubt as to whether a Turf Burner was really necessary. So what was needed, Bulleid felt as the year 1955 unrolled, was an enthusiastic young engineer coming fresh and dedicated to the project and determined to get the design finalised and the engine running. Bulleid began to get a bit listless himself, in the local design atmosphere not tuned to innovation and having an abnormal tendency to shade its opinions in line with

174

those thought to be desired by the Chief. He asked H.G. Ivatt to find a keen volunteer or two from Derby, but there were no takers. It chanced that J.G. Click had visited Mulvaney and the No.356 lash-up during summer holidays in 1954 and 1955. His interest growing, he called on Bulleid in November 1955 for what turned out to be a full day's discussion on the project, which led to him suggesting that he and a colleague, A.R. Pocklington, could help to complete the job. Bulleid took this up with E.S. Cox and R.C. Bond who amiably agreed to second the pair from Rugby Test Plant to CIE, starting mid-March and mid-May 1956.

Bisecting their arrival, in April 1956 a question about progress on the Turf Burner was raised in the Dail. In reply the Minister said that "based on the first experiment (No. 356) design work had been begun at the end of 1955 and was now more than half completed. As design and construction were running concurrently it was not possible to indicate precisely when work would be completed but he understood that it was hoped to have a prototype constructed by the end of the present year. CIE considered that when completed it would take at least a year in trials to ascertain whether or not it would be suitable as a locomotive for ordinary working."

Helped by their one year time limit, the two young English experts were well received by Inchicore, Click in overall charge and operating mainly in the Works and Pocklington originating some and helping with others of the outstanding design tasks in the Drawing Office. They found that a lot of the locomotive had been manufactured including the boiler, frames, turf hoppers, water tanks, and structures of the steam engines. The boiler had been successfully tested. But there was a great deal of design work still to do. No superheater had been designed and it was said that "Mr Bulleid is not after making his mind up about superheating." Click had sketched out a smokebox superheater shortly after his arrival in March and had done much persuading about the need to superheat, but Bulleid still hoped it would be unnecessary with the Anderson/Holcroft pressure condensing. So Click and Pocklington met Holcroft in London to get all the supporting data, but found this data far too thin to warrant yet another experimental novelty on the Turf Burner. Pocklington then got out the detail design of the smokebox superheater, utilising spare superheater tubes held in stock for engines then being withdrawn, and came up with a successful arrangement not unlike H.A. Ivattt's 1911 patent for a spark arrester and steam drier/superheater, but making far better use of the hotter gases from the short-barrelled boiler.

As Bulleid had hoped, local enthusiasm for the project was restored by the presence and confidence of Click and Pocklington, though they took rather a dim view of the duplication of turbines, smokeboxes, hoppers, feeds and controls, despite fervid assurances from the Drawing Office that only by such an arrangement could the total weight of the locomotive be uniformly distributed along its length. Click saw clearly from the perspective of the Works that these existing design fixes must be held if the Turf Burner was ever to be completed, but Pocklington in the Drawing Office grew increasingly exasperated, so much so that he in turn exasperated Bulleid by

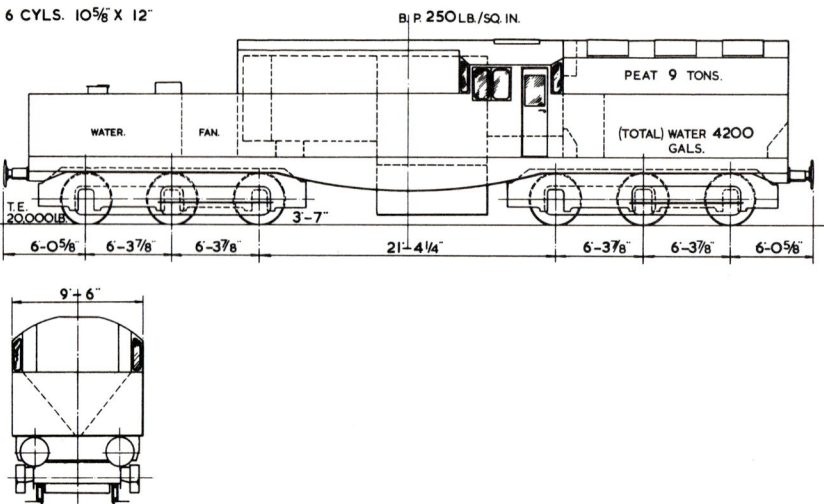

6 CYLS. 10⅝" X 12"

EXERCISE TO SIMPLIFY
DESIGN.
AUG.'57.   A.R.P.

Fig 52 A too-late suggestion for balancing the weight of a turf-burner without duplication of boiler ends, draughting and turf conveying.

producing a feasible diagram of a simpler, single-ended turf burner. Bulleid suffered three-fold irritation on seeing this: it achieved what had previously been considered impracticable; it had the twin attractions of being notably cheaper and simpler for the 50 follow-up engines without jettisoning the attractive features; and it came too late. If the present design was not completed Bulleid well knew there would be no second try. So he told Pocklington, with perhaps slightly chilling politeness, not to bring up new designs at this stage but to get the present design running.

Though Inchicore had not built a new engine since 1939, the skill and tradition was still there. The machine shop was adequately manned and equipped, there were many good fitters, and the welding was up to normal standards. But it was not up to Southern Railway standards, so when Bulleid arrived he recommended welding classes and was agreeably surprised at the ready response. This paid dividends all round, but particularly on the Turf Burner; such good progress was made with the boiler, tanks and hoppers that they were assembled to the main frame in good time to act as a full size mock-up for deciding much of the detail design, including the brake gear, positioning of equipment, and pipe and duct runs. Important dimensions were of course properly set out and checked in the Drawing Office to prevent fouls — careful work which was vindicated when, in the quiet of a Saturday afternoon, J.G. Click and Chargehand George Riley cautiously lowered the locomotive onto its two bogies. It sat snugly home first time. G. Riley was especially surprised and delighted, recalling the anguish and the excuses in 1939 when the boiler of E.C. Bredin's 4-6-0 no. 800 refused to take up its intended position until several fouls had been cleared.

176

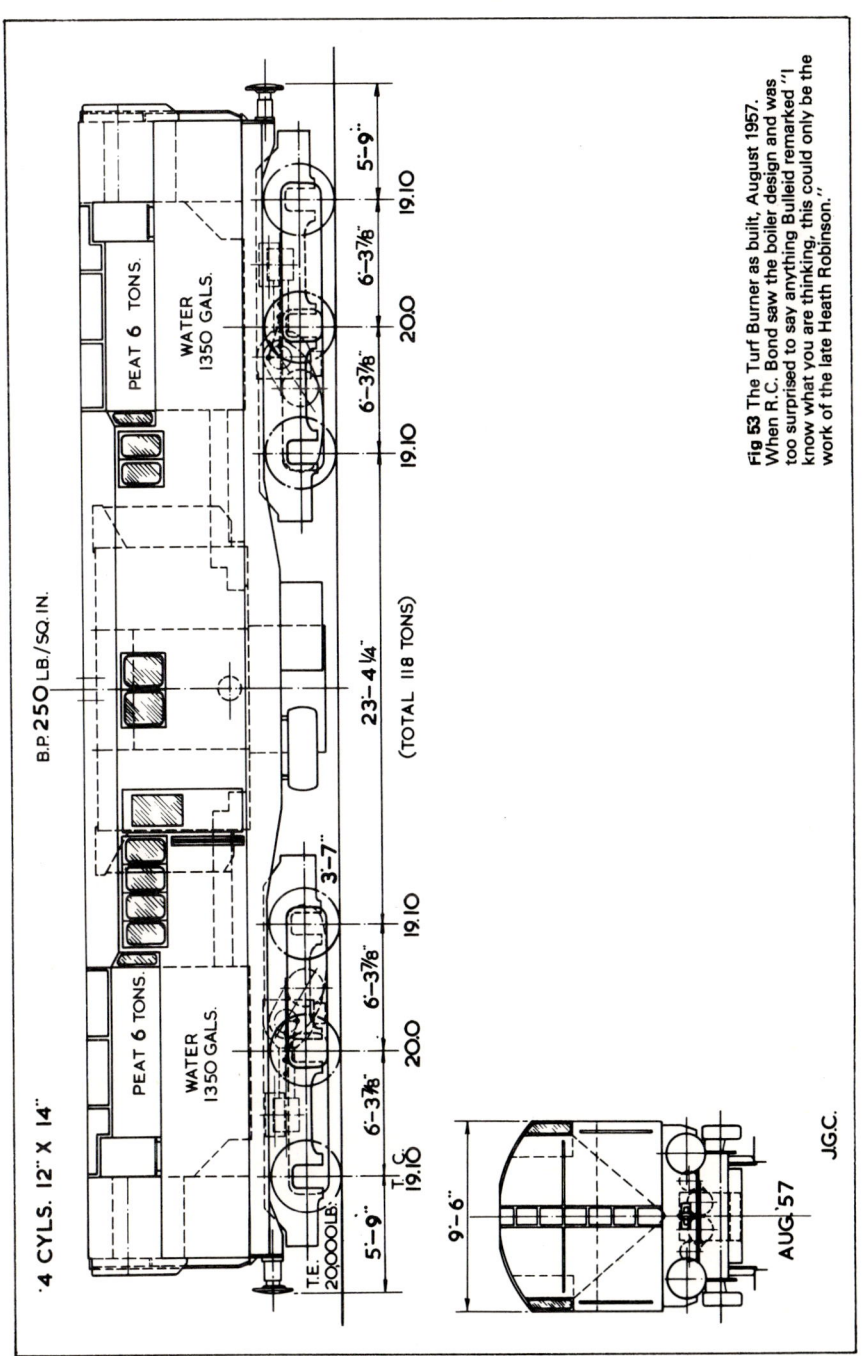

Fig 53 The Turf Burner as built, August 1957. When R.C. Bond saw the boiler design and was too surprised to say anything Bulleid remarked "I know what you are thinking, this could only be the work of the late Heath Robinson."

4 CYLS. 12" X 14"

B.P. 250 LB./SQ.IN.

PEAT 6 TONS.

WATER 1350 GALS.

PEAT 6 TONS.

WATER 1350 GALS.

T.E. 20,000 LB.

(TOTAL 118 TONS)

5'-9" · 19.10 · 6-3⅞" · 20.0 · 6-3⅞" · 3-7

23-4¼"

19.10 · 6-3⅞" · 20.0 · 6-3⅞" · 19.10 · 5-9"

9'-6"

AUG '57

J.G.C.

177

The engines were another token of Inchicore craft skill. On test before fitting to their bogies they ran at speeds from 20 to 300rpm (about half-speed) and Bulleid held that this gave the bearings a useful no-load running in. They certainly ran very sweetly, and starred in a short technical film. The boiler also behaved well on test — reassuringly tight and steaming freely from a fire of soft turf fed by pitchforks, using a ring blower in each exhaust.

The expected good riding qualities of the locomotive were confirmed before final completion by towing it at various speeds along the main line to Cork as far as Kildare, 28 miles. When the question of numbering came up Click suggested CC101 or, as you might say, follow the "Leader." "Now that's rather naughty," Bulleid countered quickly, "What's the matter with CC1" And then he unexpectedly added: "Paint it in orange on the front in honour of the black North." This was duly done, albeit with slight difficulty because the colour orange was often euphemistically referred to as gold or yellow, south of the border.

Static steaming trials were started on July 23, 1957 and the procedure for steam-raising was prescribed: after lighting-up and careful hand firing the boiler began making steam in about 1¼hr after which. with the help of the ring blowers, working pressure was reached in a further half hour. At 80psi the mechanical stokers were started and at 100psi the turbo fans were started, the ring blowers shut off, and the covers replaced on the lighting-up chimneys. Some types of turf formed clinkers in the troughs of the fire bars, but these were cleared when the bars were rocked during disposal. When the locomotive had to stand by for a period both stokers were run forward to clear smouldering turf and then reversed, to prevent burn-back into the hoppers.

The first opening of the Turf Burner's regulator was on August 6, 1957, late in the afternoon, and nothing happened. This technical hitch was due to an assembly error preventing full gear being reached, and after correction the engine moved casually under its own power for the first time, watched with pleasure by the designer and, among the others, M.J. Devereux, who was the first with congratulations. But the next day the Turf Burner collided slowly but forcibly with a C class diesel, giving both a "good test" which the Turf Burner won on points, suffering only stove-in buffing gear which was repaired in time for the visit of Armand on August 9. He and Bulleid were both delighted by a 30mph trip on the long siding. "I feel more confident about it than I ever did," Bulleid confided, and started thinking about a third, reserve, power bogie but with a sleeve-valve engine. He also disliked the "wasted" exhaust and considered directing it through the turf hoppers to act as a drier and preheater.

The Turf Burner's first main line journey was a return trip to Sallins on August 13. Bulleid was delighted by the riding, by the fire "as hot as a GN Atlantic," and above all by the regularity of the exhaust beat — "I would like Master Cocks to hear it." For C.S. Cocks had criticised the short connecting rods and valve rods, though he had later done some calculations

178

which showed the effect would be small, as it duly proved. He had a ride on the Turf Burner on September 6 and heard for himself. In fact the 2ft 1in connecting rod with 14in stroke (ratio 1.8 to 1, compared with 5 to 1 on a GN Atlantic and 3 to 1 on a "Claughton") was uncomfortably short and militated against starting torque. Even so starting trials, loaded with 11 bogie carriages, were successful on August 15 and again on August 21, when they were watched by the Chairmen of CIE and the Turf Board.

On September 25 the Turf Burner ran light to Cork, returning without incident the next day; and a week later it repeated the trip with a 165ton train, attaining its maximum speed of 70mph. The main line was very busy at the time with trial runs of the new A class diesels, and even more so with repeat trials after they had broken their cylinders. At Portarlington on October 8 the Turf Burner noticed one of them standing ominously still and asked whether it would care for a tow back to Dublin? "Oh no, we're just filling in time," came the reply so CCI set off for home — only to pass, a few miles later, another A class diesel dashing to the rescue. The diesel people were not, repeat not, going to be rescued by that ludicrous turf steamer.

During these trials, totalling 2,000miles, corrections and improvements were of course made, covering the brick arch, firebars, steam firing jets, and general improvements to steaming. A maximum rate of 14,000lb per hour was achieved, indicating a grate area (22.8sq ft) adequate for oil firing but too small for turf. Spark-throwing remained a problem, two wooden coaches suffering.

The three test runs that showed evaporation to be the limiting factor were made along the continuously climbing 28 miles from Inchicore to Kildare:

Date	Load, tons	Time, minutes	Turf consumption, lb per mile
4.9.57	160	42	N/A
5.9.57	225	49	84
6.9.57	255	55	99

The return journey on September 6 with the 255ton train was run at an average speed of 47½mph, start to stop. Average operating temperatures throughout these runs were:

Smokebox	820°F	Fan exit	500°F
Duct entry	660°F	Feed water	190°F

Steam pressure to the turbines was between 100 and 110psi and the smokebox vacuum 2in.

J.H. Dudley, who was in charge of the drivers and was ready to settle for any conventional, easy locomotive, preferably a popular diesel, rather than an experimental novelty, accompanied Bulleid on a trip to Portarlington and was soon explaining at some length how no one could be expected to work CCI in its present complicated condition. Bulleid, rather regretting that the good, quiet riding encouraged such critical conversation, waited for him to finish and asked "Is there any good about it?" Dudley seemed to be thinking but did not answer. "Well," asked Bulleid, "doesn't it ride well?" "Ah, yes." "Does it run well?" "Oh, yes, for sure." "Does the driver like it?" "He seems to." "Does it pull a train?" "I don't know yet. I haven't seen it do so," said Dudley, referring to the meagre three carriages whirling behind them. "Does it steam well?" Bulleid persisted. "Yes, it did today." "Well, then, it seems it has some points in its favour. Everybody, including you, said a turf-burning locomotive couldn't be made. Yet here it is." This was Bulleid the great persuader being too much for Dudley who turned the conversation by complaining he had a fragment of turf in his eye. If he expected any sympathy he didn't get it. Bulleid merely enquired: "Did you never get a fragment in your eye on an ordinary steam locomotive?"

Keener riders a few days later were H.G. Ivatt and R.C. Bond on a 40-mile round trip to Straffan, returning with a 65mph flourish and without incident as far as the eminent visitors were concerned but with all the metal run out of one axlebox and three valve rings broken. These were discreetly not mentioned, in the very best tradition of the London & North Western and the Midland railways.

At the end of October Bulleid got J.G. Click to compile a report on the Turf Burner and its trial runs, and to start assembling data for a descriptive paper. The report was issued in November 1957 and the draft paper was ready early in 1958, but on reflection Bulleid decided not to present it. Though by any standards CCI ranked as a successful prototype it would undoubtedly need a great deal of development to become a challenger to the diesels, and the political and technical climate was utterly against such development. Where would the money come from? Would a turf burner ever be completely practicable? Could fires be prevented? Or, summing up, was it worth the trouble? They *had* the diesels and, after May 1958, they would *not* have O.V. Bulleid. Besides, who *wanted* to use turf? They had moved to oil for their transport fuel, and would build their own refinery, and why trouble to use the oil any other way than in diesels? Inchicore had considerable pride in achieving its first prototype Turf Burner, but absolutely no ambition to use it.

On the classic premise that it is better to be looked over than overlooked, the Turf Burner had its brightest hours in May and June 1958, when it was visited first by the Institution of Locomotive Engineers and later by the Institute of Transport. It behaved just as a good prototype should, giving them nice rides without any shows of temperament, to prove that everything worked properly and that it possessed all the design ingredients on which to base an appropriate production model. It was all excellent fun, Bulleid couldn't help thinking, and if no one used the information, that was their lookout.

180

21

Retired

If you continue to be an active innovator and department head up to age 76, then retirement brings an inevitable reaction because the activity has surely also been the hobby, and suddenly both are gone. Bulleid saw this problem and set out to counter it in three ways: he would retire to Devon, near the peaceful and nostalgic North Tawton of his forebears, and enjoy the country; he would be near his daughter's farm which would make a focus for country interests; and he would keep up with his old railway friends, and abreast of current railway news.

All three rather let him down. His house at Belstone looked south to the dark and forbidding moorland slopes of Hangingstone Hill, down which one could imagine chilly air forever flowing. Some aspects of the farm he found frustratingly inefficient but impracticable to improve. And he found railway news from his friends depressing and from the papers positively idiotic, with dieselisation rampant, steam being actively denigrated as official policy, and steam engines scrapped in their prime.

Despite cordial receptions at functions in London such as Smeatonian Society dinners and despite a consultancy arrangement with Davies and Metcalfe, he felt himself redundant — a keen mind full of ideas with no outlet. He was always feeling cold and out of sorts. And then his wife had to have a biggish operation and in December 1960 they went to Exmouth to recuperate. Impressed by the notably milder climate they bought a house in Fairfield Close, added central heating and a small conservatory, and settled in with sighs of relief in June 1961.

That move was a real tonic. Bulleid resumed his normal flair for doing everything with relish. He stopped excusing himself from London visits and he started frequent travels to the Continent, typically meeting many old friends at the June 1962 International Railway Congress in Munich and extending the trip to visit Oerlikon at Zurich and Fischer at Schaffhausen and others. His resulting article on Automatic Couplers and Compressed Air Brakes appeared in the April 1963 *Railway Gazette*. The trips always had a business basis but he took his time and freely indulged his pleasure in visiting and photographing local items of historic interest.

An aggravating jolt came later in 1962 when he was involved in a very minor car accident. Having verified that there was nothing coming from behind and switched on the rather dim trafficator, he pulled out from a parking space and was immediately grazed by an overtaking car. The total physical damage was some rubbed paint, but mental upset followed; the other party was a police car which for various reasons decided to prosecute. The AA said, in effect, "pay up and forget it." The family said the same. Both annoyed clean-licence Bulleid, who was certain he had not lapsed and felt that, if this was justice, he might acquire further penalties for future driving. It was only a few days from his 80th birthday. So he went and handed in his driving licence at the police station — rather a wasted gesture, really, as there was an inadequate audience.

It was pretty obvious to everybody by 1963 that the change to diesels on British Railways could have been done better: the number of failures and the smell in the stations and trains had to be experienced to be believed. Political pressures, excessive haste, and anti-steam propaganda were the main causes, the last apparently blinding those concerned to the attractive alternative of running at least one region on oil-fired steam engines. Bulleid wrote to the *Telegraph* in July, adding logic, facts and figures to the despairing and doomed debate on the diesel debacle. He was goaded to write by gloomy stories from friends in the United States, who all said that diesel economies had been over-claimed, both because the life of the locomotive was shorter than estimated and because it was so difficult to work the whole fleet the desirable and assumed 20hr per day. Bulleid enjoyed these letters and their jokes, particularly one by his friend T.T. Taber of New Jersey who was on the footplate of Class A4 Pacific No. 60008 *Dwight D. Eisenhower* one day in 1962 when some GIs boarded the train at Huntingdon. On arrival at Kings Cross he got off the engine and asked one of them what he thought of it. "We were standing on the platform at Huntingdon watching the train come in," the GI replied, "and someone hollered 'Holy smoke! Look at the name on that engine!!' Were we surprised! Mister, I worked for the General for quite a while, but this sure is the first time he ever worked for me."

It must be fairly flattering to have your biography written (and published) whilst you are still alive and flourishing, and Bulleid enjoyed this flattery one-and-a-half times. The half started when he agreed with my proposal to write six interlinked CME biographies including himself, Stanier and both Ivatts. He co-operated quite enthusiastically, despite some fear of family-type debunking, and he nobly approved the less flattering comments in the chapter about himself wherever he knew them to be true. But he obviously found deeper delight when Sean Day-Lewis, following up a *Telegraph* article on the Pacifics, proposed a "proper" full-length biography. For it he went to additional pains to check and complete the information handed over, and he also sought help and verification from his old colleagues.

The publication of my book in late 1963 and the other in early 1964* brought Bulleid a surge of correspondence, mostly very flattering and all very interesting, from relatives, friends, ex-colleagues and strangers. A

---

* *Master Builders of Steam* and *Bulleid, Last Giant of Steam*. See Bibliography.

surprising number deplored diesels, or British Railways, or modifying the Pacifics, or all three, and these certainly entertained the ex-CME. So many copies of the book came in to be autographed that I was tempted to point out that un-autographed copies would become rarer and therefore more valuable. Interest in steam was soaring and O.V. Bulleid was *the* steam stalwart. An interview with him was published in *The Chartered Mechanical Engineer* for February 1965; writing to me about this interview in a letter dated November 17, 1964 my father typed:

"I spent an interesting afternoon yesterday with Mr Rex Wailes and his tape recorder though I could not but feel what I said compared very badly with other interviews. He however seemed to be satisfied. He took two flash exposures of me sitting casually in my easy chair without any previous warning which was just as well.

Thinking over his comments on some reminiscences, I wish I were in better form these days and able to sit down and put on paper everything I could remember of all the interesting people I have known, and details of the many entertaining situations in which I have found myself.

The Inst. of Loco Engineers is having its annual Dinner-Dance on the 10th of December, but I feel I cannot manage to go this year: a pity as I always enjoyed meeting such a crowd of old colleagues and friends."

He added a handwritten note: "Typed by himself, the errors being a clear indication of the health barometer."

Though still very fit at 82 he increasingly felt the cold and he was worried that the house and the garden were proving too much for my energetic mother. And so, after an enjoyable modernisation operation including the Perspex-enclosure of a South-facing balcony (which turned it into a furnace) they moved, early in 1965, to a first-floor flat overlooking the sea (and the Dawlish line diesels). The only worry was space, but I received a triumphant letter just before they moved in saying "I discovered a few days ago that there was a spare storeroom in the basement. We shall be given its use at a small fee which will be well worth while as it will give the sadly lacked junk room so necessary in any home."

Bulleid was well suited by the spacious but compact, warm flat and he began devoting a lot of energy to helping his daughter to move to a larger farm house near Hatherleigh, to making improvements on the farm, and to preparing modernised, self-contained quarters in the farmhouse as a final old-age retreat. House improvements had become quite a hobby, to be relished in tremendous detail, seeking many views and weighing many alternatives, and often preferring a hopeful novelty to a previously tried successful solution. And there were still railway topics, some increasingly controversial and a few rather irritating, such as Dr Tuplin's notes on the "Leader" in the *Railway World* for November 1965. They irritated when they listed shortcomings in a Bulleid design but omitted to indicate similar or worse shortcomings in the conventional design it replaced. Then there were matters of semantics. I had chosen my words with reasonable if not extreme care when I captioned the "Leader" diagram in my book "A sophisticated Garratt." It means "A Garratt deprived of simplicity." My father grumbled faintly when he read it and said he did not know what I meant. He was unmoved by my explanation and I wished I had taken Churchward's advice, 'never explain'. Then along comes this Tuplin and writes in the above-mentioned article "The description by H.A.V. Bulleid of the 'Leader' as a sophisticated Garratt is a good one." This provoked my father to write to a friend: "It is odd that my son's irrelevant remark about a 'sophisticated Garratt' should be quoted as it was very stupid at the best. The word 'sophisticated' has become objectionable." 'Stupid at the best' is blame indeed, and a real Bulleidism.

These were trivial teases in the flow of railway topics and were dwarfed by a great new interest of 1965 — preservation. Several railwaymen at Nine Elms distinctly preferred the original Pacifics and one of them, Alan Wilton, hit on the idea of buying one to preserve it. With a few colleagues he founded the Bulleid Pacific Preservation Society and in January 1966 persuaded O.V.B. to become its first President. The ensuing success brought much amusement and pleasure, particularly as Wilton always expressed his opinions, which were invariably favourable to the original design, in forthright and colourful language.

Then yet another nostalgic pleasure arose, this time in the form of letters from an enthusiast not on the railway, George Harrison. He quite often wrote in quoting comments by Salisbury drivers that they preferred the Pacifics before the modifications. Bulleid savoured these as others might savour the finest brandy; and after a string of them he asked, rather typically, if they were just talk, or did they really mean it? Enough, for instance, to write it all down? This idea appealed irresistibly to George Harrison. He tracked down all the Salisbury drivers who had reasonable pre-modification driving experience, so that their views would be based on first hand knowledge — quite an undertaking for someone not employed by the railway. They duly signed agreement to a statement prepared by driver E. Pistell who, accompanied by Harrison, handed over the 33-signature testimonial to Bulleid on September 17, a couple of days before his 84th birthday. He was highly delighted. And then the idea caught on. Why not Exmouth Junction drivers? And why not Nine Elms? Why not indeed. So Harrison pressed on. He and others found that interest in steam, both direct and nostalgic, was growing. The BBC caught the feeling and filmed a TV interview with the steam giant at Exmouth.

Meanwhile there were other portents of interest for the year 1967. The new University of Bath decided to confer on Bulleid an honorary degree of Doctor of Science in recognition of his outstanding contributions to the steam locomotive. The preservation of another Bulleid Pacific, No. 34051 *Winston Churchill*, seemed assured. Modelmakers were enquiring after drawings and details of the Pacifics, the "Leader" *and* Q1, and soon photographs of their excellent work were pleasurably received. But despite all this action Bulleid felt he needed a new adventure. It was cosy enough *in* the flat, but outside the English winters were very cold. They had a good *pied-à-terre* on the farm at Hatherleigh so why not use it in the summer and spend winter in the sun? Gibraltar or perhaps Malta?

After much discussion the Bulleids planned a four-week test trip to Gibraltar in June/July 1967 and meantime thoughtfully obtained permits to reside in both. In the midst of all this planning, and acting as a booster, there was quite a bad fire at the flat caused by a glass ornament focusing the June sunlight on to a curtain. This was within days of the Gibraltar trip and on their return, having by then decided to go to Malta and as soon as possible, there was a fine rush to get everything installed at Hatherleigh and this new address notified to all. Nor was there ever a dull moment, because early in August the *Observer* came to interview "the last of the great steam locomotive designers" and gave him a wroughty write-up; and — perhaps the climax of his steam pleasures in this country — he was presented with the testimonials signed by the Nine Elms and Exmouth Junction drivers in a ceremony at the Exmouth Junction Staff Club on August 2. He wrote to me a day or two later:

"There was a good gathering of drivers, many retired, and it was interesting to listen to their reminiscences of really startling exploits. It is a great pity some one has not compiled these men's recollections* as they would make entertaining reading specially if expressed in their original language."

And he added:

"We are more or less ready to go to Malta. I have cleared away a lot of papers, but think I might as well leave much in case we do come here in the summers. Then too the Executors† ought to be left something to do when we have died . . ."

Early in September 1967 everyone noted yet another Bulleid address, the Osborne Hotel, Valletta, and wondered about the next. It came only a few weeks later, when they moved into a small cottage at Birzebbugia, town of **irresistible mispronounciation**, after adding a bathroom. It had the usual two down and two up plus Maltese flat roof for sunning and drying and collecting rainwater. My father might have been just momentarily abashed when I asked what had happened to the arguments proving that they must have a flat. The real answer was that he thoroughly enjoyed making the improvements and then sampling the new abode: but when, only eight

---

* Someone has. Appendix 5 and Chapter 15.
† My brother and I.

months later, they moved to the far more convenient Balzan he triumphantly anticipated any comment of mine by saying "I could see you didn't approve of the cottage."

Unfortunately the new house proved incurably damp, and so a final and very successful move was made (after due improvements) to a superior single-storey residence in Balzan in April 1969. It was quiet, had a tiny, sunny garden with covered patio, and was handy for Church and the bus to Valletta. Bulleid was very happy there, relishing occasional technical tributes, keeping abreast with correspondence, studying Solar Heat systems, reading and commenting on papers: of the J.G. Jones description of the "Leader" for the Mechanicals* he wrote "It could hardly be bettered."

My wife and I took H.G. Ivatt over on a visit in October 1969 and my father demonstrated a complex arrangement of electric pump and valves he had coaxed the local plumber to rig up, to pump the well water to either a tank, a garden sprinkler or a service pipe. It worked perfectly and George Ivatt was suitably impressed. The two ex-CMEs, ages 87 and 83, had much enjoyment from their reminiscences, spiced by a dash of controversy.

Early in 1970 I suggested a new Bulleid biography, with an eye on all the unpublished material. He compiled many notes but then showed fatigue and we called it off — at least until it could be talked over when he returned to England, to Hatherleigh, as planned for the early summer.

I was surprised at the warmth of the tributes received after his death in April 1970; and surprised again at the same warm sentiments expressed by those who have helped me with this biography. Not just a few, not only a dozen, but very many have said how much they appreciated working for and with him — some with growing appreciation as their own careers developed. And several added how fortunate they had been to work for a CME like O.V.B., rather than for one cast in the more conventional mould.

* "The Steam Locomotive — an Historical Review" by H. Holcroft and J.G. Jones.

Appendix 1
Mrs Bulleid's
Chapter

My "life on the railway" started in January 1888 when I was born within the sound of the trains of the GSW Railway of Ireland. My father H.A. Ivatt was Loco Superintendent at Inchicore and we lived in a big, old-fashioned house belonging to the railway at Island Bridge. Part of the garden looked down on the railway lines below. My two brothers and I could watch the Northwall Express dash through, or stop as it sometimes did, and there were many cattle trains which often seemed to be held up near our territory. We were forbidden to climb over the railings on to the line, but this had great attractions for us, and when some minor rail work was in progress we couldn't resist climbing over for a word with the gaffer and his men. Unfortunately my elder brother picked up a few undesirable words from these men, and using one in my father's hearing was asked how he had picked it up. My three older sisters pretended to be horrified. From then on a firm stop was put to our little expeditions.

When my father joined the GNR and we came to Doncaster in 1896 life did not seem so amusing and carefree as it was in Ireland and my sisters grumbled a bit. Bicycles were then a novelty and I was taught to ride on a boy's solid-tyre bone-shaker. I could not reach the pedals from the saddle, so this was taken off and a small cushion tied on in its place — not very comfortable.

My elder brother died when he was 14 and the funeral had to be on my tenth birthday so it was a sad day. I believe he was a very gifted boy and my parents were shattered by his death. My mother told me years later that my father never really got over the loss of his elder son. My second brother George and I had a governess till we went to boarding schools. He got bored with the governess and whittled away at the table till he had cut out quite a big wedge. When mother saw it she exclaimed: "You bad wicked boy! Put it back this instant."

An engine I remember well is No. 990.* My father took my sister Dorothy and me to the station to see her first run through. We stood on the main up platform near the bookstall. "Here she comes!" father said; and a tall slim silver-grey engine with a very long train swished *quietly* through the station, from our right, coming from York. It seemed ghost-like, somehow, to me at

---

* Preserved (in green) at York.

10. No noise to speak of and grey instead of green. My father explained later that it was her "workshop coat." Mother was not there: she had not gone out much since Campbell's death. To help take her mind off her sorrow, Father urged her to learn to ride the bicycle. She was taught by Brown of Bennethorpe who had invented a method of teaching his older clients by fastening a broad leather belt round their middles. This belt had a grip at the back which Brown held as he ran nimbly by the side of the learner! Every now and then he would let go, to see how his learner was progressing. Mother and I used to get up at daybreak, to go for a ride before breakfast, because she was shy about being seen on a modern bicycle. A local church dignitary had recently declared he "would rather see his wife in her coffin than on one of the new machines of the devil."

Mr Earle Marsh, who often came to see father, called one day with a friend, a Mr Cockey. Later, mother remembered meeting a Revd. Cockey and his sister, friends of her parents, and made a note to ask Mr Cockey if they were relations. "Better not mention the sister," we advised, always on the look-out for accidental puns. Sure enough! They were related. "Ah yes," said mother reminiscently, "I felt positive there was a Miss Cockatoo."

My parents were hospitable to the young men in the Works, and they often came to the house. Of course they were all over 18 before we first saw them, and they spent their time with my elder sisters. They seemed to me very grown-up, even Mr Bulleid and Mr Talbot who were younger than Mr Bazin. There was some alarm when Mr Talbot came out in spots and Mr Bulleid, who shared rooms with him, spent some time rubbing in ointment. Then Dr Clark, the Plant doctor (that sounds silly but they always called the Works "the Plant") diagnosed smallpox. The house was sealed and no one allowed in or out. The neighbours kindly left them food outside. Luckily no one else caught it. Poor Mr Talbot was killed in the accident at Grantham. Father was terribly worried that it might have been due to a fault on the engine, but afterwards it was found to have been all right.

Mr Gresley was one of my father's assistants. I remember him when he first came to Doncaster as a young man of about 28; we saw a good deal of him and his wife. He was a tall, slim man — nearly as tall as my father who was 6ft 2in — and a good dancer.

Like my three sisters, I went to a finishing school in Brussels — about the same time as George started at Crewe — and after a year Fate led me to persuade my parents to let me go to a school near Paris for a year before coming home, and it was there that I improved upon the Anglo-French we picked up in Brussels. I felt much more grown-up when I was home for the holidays and began to see more of Mr Bulleid, who did not now seem to be as keen on one of my sisters as I had thought. It was also much nicer at home because we had moved to Avenue House on Thorne Road; I had a bedroom to myself, and there was a better garden, and a tennis-court — also a billiard-room (empty) for impromptu dances. My elder sisters were a good musical trio, but not very good at games or on bicycles.

Soon after I came back from the convent outside Paris, a bachelor friend of the family (to me an oldish man) asked me to go for a bicycle ride, me on my brand-new Raleigh three-speed and he on mother's old bike. We stopped after a bit and one thing and another got rather embarrassing for me, so I murmured "there is someone else." He was very nice I must say and just said shortly "It's young Bulleid isn't it?" And that was that.

Though Oliver Bulleid was worried by his small salary on the GNR we knew we wanted to spend our lives together and we became informally engaged in 1907. It was a bit difficult because I was only 19, my three older sisters were not engaged and Oliver did not have a particularly good job. But my mother championed us throughout — there had also been a lot of family opposition when she and my father wanted to become engaged. Then, early in 1908, Oliver was offered a job in Paris at £240 a year and on father's advice he accepted it. He left for France on Monday, March 2, and I so well remember getting up early to say good-bye to him before breakfast. Luckily things went well in France, and we were allowed to announce our engagement in April. And so at last, on November 18, 1908, H.A. Ivatt led his youngest daughter up the aisle of Christ Church, Doncaster to marry O.V. Bulleid. I must have been a good deal more hardy all those years ago, because I went off to the Church at 8.45am attired in a cream-coloured satin dress, with ne'er a wrap of any kind! The church was lovely and warm, and the sun shone through on us, as we stood together before the altar . . . very sentimental, but then I *am* "old-fashioned" and still sentimental!

Our honeymoon at Folkestone — en route to France — was short but sweet. Then we had a very rough Channel crossing and poor Oliver felt awful. I was the only passenger on deck and a sailor said it might be too rough to dock, but luckily he was wrong. When the French Customs asked if we had anything to declare we said "Trousseau de mariage." Nothing to pay, just hand-shakes and congratulations from Customs.

After about a year Oliver got a better job, as Engineer to the Exhibitions Branch, Board of Trade, and we proceeded to live in my old school town of Brussels — quite a thrill for me! My daughter was born there, and we had a very nice maid, Fanny Vanderkelen. When Oliver was posted to Turin for the next exhibition we asked Fanny if she had a sister or friend who would come with us. "I'll ask my mother," she said, and came herself.

We had much fun in Italy — parties, balls, opera and many friends among the English and American women married to Italian officers, and we got our first car, a small second-hand Ford.

Oliver once dared to criticise his chief, who had told an un-varnished lie about some work he had told Oliver to do. I remember Oliver being upset at the time because the blame fell on him, the innocent party. Later he told me how foolish he had been to speak out, when he should have said nothing. Oliver's was the only name put forward by the Italian government for a decoration, but this was suppressed by higher authority. Oliver also said it was the reason for him not being asked to stay on with the Board of

Trade. Anyway, we left Turin in December, said sad goodbyes to Fanny in Paris, and went home to Haywards Heath, where my father had by now retired, till Oliver's job was fixed definitely for Doncaster. Then we wrote to ask Fanny if she would come too and luckily for us all she jumped at it!

We were hard up in 1912 and could not afford a car, so father very kindly gave us his Cadillac. It was a long, long drive from Haywards Heath, the back loaded with luggage and veg, and we had a breakdown en route, when all had to be removed to get at the engine! We left at 8 in the morning and got to Doncaster just after midnight. There was no wind-screen; our poor eyes were blood-shot after the journey. Our eldest son was born two days before Christmas, and Fanny kept running to tell me that the turkey had not come.

Oliver joined up early in the War* and my eldest sister came to live with and help me. I remember pathetically short leaves for Oliver and the misery of good-byes. Then just before the end of the War he was moved to Richborough, to my relief and his disgust. Mr Oliver Bury wanted him for a job in Brazil, but it fell through, to our parents' great relief. Instead we came back to old Doncaster; rather dull after our experiences, and the fogs seemed to be worse than ever. One evening Fanny only found her way home with great difficulty to Victorian Crescent, and when she entered the garden gate three people following her were very indignant to be told they were no longer on Thorne Road!

A colonial customer left a long stock-whip for repair with Frost the saddler in Scott Lane, and word got around that no one in Doncaster could crack this whip. Oliver said he would have a go; he had been taught the trick in NZ. I was rather unbelieving because he could never crack the dog's whip as well as I could. However, he took the stock-whip, stood in the middle of the road, whirled the lash around above his head and then, giving a sudden jerk, crack! a loud pistol-shot rang out. Quite a crowd had collected and applauded loudly. I was so relieved and proud.

In 1923 we moved to Hadley Common, where our two younger sons were born. Oliver was assistant to H.N. Gresley, known in railway circles as "The Great White Chief," whom he liked and respected for his great abilities. I think my husband served him very well, staving off many worries and anxieties, and also learning a lot from him. Someone once said to me that "Gresley is very lucky to have Bulleid to devil for him."

I met Sir John Aspinall again at an Engineers' outing not long after my father died in 1923, and he said he thought father's illness had been coming on for a good many years because he so often complained of a feeling of tiredness, quite unusual for him. It was easy for mother to visit us at Hadley Common and sometimes I went back with her to Haywards Heath. Once as we got on our train at Victoria station I said: "Are you sure this is the right carriage?" "Of course I am, dear," she replied, "this is my line and I know

---

*He enlisted early and Mrs. Gresley, who was sometimes a bit impulsive, said to me "I shall never forgive Mr. Bulleid for going off to the war and leaving Tim."

190

this train well." When we raced madly through Haywards Heath I looked back out of the window and saw, trailing behind, the slip carriages in which we should have been sitting. Mother gave a sigh and said; "If I had £5 to spare . . ."

Sir Henry Fowler once said that "O. Bulleid and W. Stanier are both very promising young engineers." The Fowlers were always very kind on Railway Congress meetings. In Vienna we had all attended a wine-tasting ceremony and reception out in the country with picnic supper. A band struck up *The Blue Danube*, our favourite waltz, so we took to the floor (grass!) and danced till we realised we were the first couple to do so. We felt shy and sat down — amidst loud applause! At a later Congress, Oliver got up and said the interpreter was giving an incorrect translation from the French and so Sir Henry engaged him as a translator; later still he became a member of the Permanent Commission. I taught myself to type; he used a dictaphone and I typed from that, the extra income being very handy.

In May 1930, en route for the Madrid Congress, our trunk was left behind after the Customs at Irun, near San Sebastian. We saw it on the platform as our train ran out of the station. In it were all our evening and party clothes! I think Oliver gave the alarm somehow, but anyway the very first thing I spotted on the station at Madrid was *our trunk*. We never found out what magic got it there before us. At a reception held in the Royal Palace, Oliver and I were the two chosen from the British contingent to be presented to King Alphonso and Queen Ena and two of the princesses. I think we were chosen because Oliver was well liked by all the Congress Officials. He was always polite, and "had a way" with foreigners, never looking down on them as, alas, many English were inclined to do.

In the spring of 1931 Oliver contracted erysipelas on the head, a dangerous and often fatal illness. Mr Alec Spencer phoned and said I should get a specialist. I nervously asked our doctor and to my relief he jumped at the idea and got a specialist immediately — an odd-looking little man, not English. He told me it was very serious but capable of treatment, and not to be alarmed if Oliver's head became very inflamed and swollen. He recommended two nurses, well up in such cases. Oliver received the last Sacrament and was unconscious for ten days. Our doctor said to me "His brain may be affected — he may never recover properly." The poor man was worried over the case and forgot to whom he spoke. One of the nurses was reassuring and told me that "after a bad illness, the patient is often "re-made" and becomes generally better in all-round health." Fanny was a tower of strength and people kept ringing up with kind enquiries. H.N.G. called one day while Oliver was unconscious. I understood he was on the phone. In tears at the time, I went to the study to answer it and there he was, reassuring and a great comfort.

We moved to Mackerye End in 1935, renting a nice old manor house. From there, Oliver was offered the post of CME on the Southern Railway. This came as a great surprise, for like so many clever men he had a very modest opinion of himself. We bought a big house, Boxhurst near Dorking, which needed a lot of doing up, and moved there in November 1937.

Oliver made a point of seldom talking shop when at home. He liked to forget the stresses and worries when he got back to me. But I remember he was very worried and "put out" when the Civil Engineer of the Southern Railway was difficult about the weight of Oliver's engines — thought them too heavy and demanded drastic lowering of weight which Oliver said was unnecessary, and almost impossible to achieve in keeping with his designs.

The Second War gave us an anxious and difficult time at Boxhurst. Fanny and I coped on our own. Bombs fell nearby and we lost several windows. We were once fired on by an enemy plane while mother and my eldest sister Henrietta were getting into the old Crossley in front of the house. Mother, who was then over 90, said "He couldn't have been firing *at* us — just his bit of fun." I later found a bullet in one of the bedrooms. Oliver was working very long hours, and driving himself long distances, sometimes to the three Works in one week. He got overtired and once fell asleep at the wheel. Then the railway supplied a chauffeur, and so he was able to do quite a bit of work in the car.

We moved to Steyning in 1946, to a smaller house and one more convenient for Oliver than Boxhurst. When he heard that he was to be awarded a CBE in the 1949 New Year's Honours list he took the news very calmly and with his usual modesty. With a friend's chauffeur to sit beside Oliver's driver, Hills, we drove in state to the Palace entrance and were conducted to the Ball Room. I was given a good seat at the front and Oliver joined those waiting to be invested. HM King George VI arrived quite soon and in due course Oliver was presented to him and handed his award. He quite often wore the medal afterwards with his four miniature World War I medals. That same year we moved temporarily into a flat in Brighton owned by Miss Billinton whose brother had been on the Brighton line.

Also in 1949 we flew to New York for Oliver to be made an Hon. member of the ASME. At the dinner before the ceremony Oliver made a very popular speech. The President then stood up and said: "Mrs Bulleid is also here tonight, will she please stand up for everyone to see." This I did, feeling a little confused, but everyone very kindly cheered and clapped. Upon leaving, we were asked to stand by the way out, with the officials, and to shake hands with all the hundreds of members and their wives. I now understand how tiring this must be for Royalty; my poor right hand was nearly shaken off.

Oliver much disliked the nationalisation of the Railways, though he liked Mr Riddles, and was glad to accept the job in Eire where he would be left more on his own. There, in the land of my birth, which was convenient because a house could be bought in my name, we lived very happily until Oliver decided the time really had come to retire.

Back in England, he never really settled down. I think he greatly missed the day-to-day activity of his Railway work. Also, he felt the cold very much as he became older. Though we still grieved for our youngest son who was killed in a road accident in 1938, the other three children were happily settled. So we decided to try life either in Gibraltar or Malta. Then Gib. became a bit involved with Spain and Malta was the choice. We had two very happy years there and celebrated our diamond wedding in 1968. Oliver was so well whilst we were there, it was quite unbelieveable that he should die so suddenly, after a mercifully short illness, in 1970.

Urged by my eldest son, I wrote these notes about the railway part of my life (and love) in 1974.

M.C. Bulleid
Hatherleigh,
Devon. 1974.

Appendix 2
The CME's Talk to
Locomen at Feltham

Let us review the origins of the Q1 design. The order to build 40 new 0-6-0 tender engines was issued in 1941. An engine was needed that would run over as much of the system as possible, that is to say, over all the lines other than the unimportant branch lines. The Chief Engineer advised me he could accept an engine not exceeding 54tons (actual weight 51¼tons) over some 93% of the track and this figure was adopted as the limiting weight. The tender weight too was restricted to 39tons 10cwt (actual weight 38tons).

The Q Class met these limitations of weight. This class of engine had been giving good service. It had shown, however, that larger boiler capacity would be an advantage. Its motion could be improved, furthermore the cylinder design left something to be desired. We have here a good example of difficulties of standardisation. The easy course would have been to build a further 40 Qs exactly like the others and this would have commended itself to the works, though hardly to the shed repair staff. A locomotive has a life of some 40 years and obviously when improvements can be made they must be even at the cost of some additional increase in the number of types with the resulting increase in the stock of spares, but if attention be paid to the detail fittings to ensure they do not vary or are interchangeable, the drawbacks of additional types are minimised.

Having a maximum weight fixed, the next question to be settled is the boiler.

The locomotive is a coal-burning machine and given reasonable design and an average fireman it may be said that the work done depends on the coal consumed. In other words, the boiler should be the largest that can be fitted, so that the engine can do as much work as possible. The evaporative capacity of a boiler is dependent on the grate area and the firebox heating surface and volume. A large volume is needed to ensure the gases have time to burn as the flame is extinguished as soon as it enters the tubes. A large heating surface is necessary to ensure the maximum heat transferred to the water. A point to remember is that no work is required to ensure the transfer, whereas any transfer through the tubes involves work in that the gases have to be drawn through the tubes. The largest firebox as regards width at the top we can fit inside the Southern loading gauge is that of the "Lord Nelson." We had the press blocks required to press the various plates.

I therefore adopted this design of box, the only dimension remaining to determine being the length of grate and it was fixed to give 27sq ft of grate.

The wheel base was to be the same as the Q and the cylinders to be in the same position. These factors determine the overall length of the boiler and it was found that the distance between the tube plate would be 10ft 6in.

The preliminary design of the boiler showed that the boiler would weigh 21¼tons in working order leaving only 32¾tons for the rest of the locomotive. "Was it possible?" was not the question raised, but "how are we to do it?" It was quite obvious we could not follow precedent but had to do some independent thinking. The first thing was to see what parts could be lightened and the second what could be eliminated.

Starting from the rail upwards, we adopted the BFB centres which are about 10% lighter. The frame was lightened wherever possible and fabricated details introduced instead of steel castings, as for example the dragbox.

The boiler being lagged with Idaglass, a separate casing was designed following the "Merchant Navy" arrangement. The shape was determined for convenience in manufacture, the curves being true curves so that the main members can be rolled from cold strip 8SWG thick.

By supporting the casing off the frame, the usual crinolines were not needed and weight was saved by using 20gauge sheet in place of the usual lagging.

The footplate and splashers were abolished as representing weight that must be saved; moreover they are survivals of early practice and obstruct access to the engine as well as requiring frequent attention by the repair staff.

The shape of the fabricated smokebox was determined by the arrangement of the superheater header and the steam pipes with the object of giving access to the steam pipe flanges and leaving the nest of tubes unobstructed. The bottom was made flat: this improves the joint with the cylinder block and makes the machining easier. The smokebox was fabricated and so weight was saved here.

A clipped door was used as being lighter than the dart type.

The cab, like the casing, was fabricated from thin sheet and thereby much weight saved. The arrangement of the cab received close attention to make everything as easy for the driver as possible.

Steam reversing gear was fitted as it occupies less room, is lighter, and as it obviates unnecessary physical labour.

The ashpans were made of 3/16in and 1/8in thick plate.

The result was an engine having a light weight of only 45tons 18cwt.

By fabricating and by using thin plates, the weight of the tender was reduced to 16tons.

An engine and tender of normal design would weigh about 14tons heavier, so on 40 engines, 560tons of weight has been saved equal to about 700tons of materials, equal to about nine engines and tenders.

The completed engine consequently complied with the Engineer's limitations.

The design too lent itself to prefabrication of parts, with the advantage that the work could be distributed over more shops and works.

The external appearance of the engine has been determined by practical considerations and to use the language of the day, is functionally correct. It has evoked much interest and favourable and unfavourable comment.

The motion is a modified version of that used on the Qs, the valve events of which could be better.

Certain mechanical improvements have been made to facilitate examination and repairs.

The big end brasses have only 1/32in of white metal. The engines are the most powerful 0-6-0s in the country and the following table gives a comparison of it with the WD 2-8-0 as regards hauling capacity.

	SR Q1	WD 2-8-0
Tractive effort lb	30,000	32,438
Weight of engine and tender	89T. 5C.	125T. 3C.
Engine and tender resistance, lb per ton	12	12
Grade resistance 1 in 50, lb per ton	44.8 + 12	44.8 + 12
	56.8	56.8
Grade resistance 1 in 100 (22.4 + 12)	34.4	34.4
Grade resistance 1 in 200 (11.2 + 12)	23.2	23.2
Wagon resistance, lb per ton	6	6
Total resistance 1 in 50, lb	5070	7106
1 in 100, lb	3070	4305
1 in 200, lb	2070	2904
Available tractive effort behind the tender		
1 in 50, lb	24,930	25,332
1 in 100, lb	26,930	28,133
1 in 200, lb	27,930	29,534
Equivalent No. of 12 ton wagons at 16 tons gross		
1 in 50	31	31
1 in 100	59	62
1 in 200	101	107

These figures illustrate the effect of engine weight

In designing these engines, I had always in mind the convenience of the enginemen as far as was compatible with the War effort.

When first built, a number of suggestions were made in order to improve the engine or to make them more comfortable.

Some of them have been adopted, some will be and some will not. Now we are more familiar with the engines, we can appreciate their good points and tolerate their bad ones, knowing that as the engines pass through the shops for general repair the bad points will be remedied.

To the unreasoning critic I would quote the Arabic proverb:

"The dogs bark, the caravan proceeds on its way."

C37 is available for inspection and incorporates certain modifications.

I have indicated the reasons for many of the outwardly apparent innovations.

Let us now consider a few technical points of the design.

The boiler has a Belpaire box and as we build both Belpaire and round top fireboxes, we know there is so little difference in the cost that the type selected is determined on technical reasons. The outstanding merits of the Belpaire box are three: greater steam space, larger water surface, better staying.

The volume of the firebox is 167cu ft and the area no less than 170sq ft.

The water surface is 96sq ft. and the steam space 150cu ft.

If you refer to the cylinder drawing, you will notice the straight ports, moderate clearance volume and the direct passage. The inside exhaust ensures free escape of the exhaust steam and the back pressure is kept low. The multiple blast pipe again helps as less pressure is required for the blast. An interesting feature is the blower as it is fitted inside the exhaust cavity. The object is to enable the driver, by opening the blower valve when the regulator is shut, to prevent a vacuum in the cavity.

Appendix 3
The War-time
Railway Executive

A good description of the Railway Executive was given in Bulleid's Presidential Address to the Institution of Locomotive Engineers in December 1939:

In wartime the national importance of the railway industry is admitted even in the most antagonistic, and may I say, interested circles. A transport system using home-produced fuel, having its own system of roads, and with almost limitless capacity, compels recognition. There is no other organisation in the country which serves its users, and the country, with greater loyalty and selflessness. There is no other organisation with more skilled and more conscientious staffs.

The organisation of the railway services in wartime was considered long before the outbreak of hostilities, and preparations made to meet all foreseeable contingencies. The rolling stock was kept in good repair, the tracks properly maintained, and stores accumulated within reasonable limits by the companies themselves. The lessons of the last war were remembered, and preliminary arrangements were made for the control of the railways in wartime.

At the outbreak of war, the Minister of Transport, in accordance with the Defence of the Realm Act of 1939, took over control of the railways, and by an Order in Council entitled "Emergency (Railway Control) Order, 1939," he appointed an Executive Committee consisting of:

Sir Ralph Wedgwood, CB, CMG (Chairman)
Sir James Milne, KCVO, CSI (GWR)
Sir Wm Valentine Wood (LM&SR)
Mr C.H. Newton (LNER)
Mr Frank Pick (LPTB)
Mr Gilbert Savill Szlumper, CBE (Southern Rly), with Mr Cole Deacon as Secretary, to be his agents for the purpose of giving directions under this order.

On the appointment of Mr Szlumper as Director-General of Movements and Transportation at the War Office, Mr Eustace Missenden was made General Manager of the Southern Railway, and took Mr Szlumper's seat on the Railway Executive Committee.

This Railway Executive Committee is a co-ordinating Committee to a large extent, and decides all questions of policy. In turn, this Committee appointed the following Sub-Committees as follows:

Solicitors.
Goods Managers.
Passenger Superintendents.
Mineral Managers.
Operating Superintendents.
Accountants.
Statistical.
Staff.
Civil Engineers.
Mechanical and Electrical Engineers.
Signal and Telegraph Engineers.
Docks.
Stores.
Police.
Surveyors.
Publicity.
Road Transport.

The Chairmen of these Sub-Committees are selected from the chief officers of the various railways.

These Sub-Committees deal with all matters referred to them by the Executive Committee, as well as questions raised by individual members of general interest, which it is felt should be handled on uniform lines. The decisions of the Sub-Committees are, of course, subject to the approval of the REC. Orders given by the REC are carried out by the respective General Managers, who, whilst seeing that such orders are made effective, retain in all essentials the managerial operation of the railways with freedom in local matters.

The Sub-Committee in which we are most interested is the Mechanical and Electrical. This Sub-Committee is under the Chairmanship of your Past-President, Sir Nigel Gresley, and could not be in better hands. Its other members are:

Mr Stanier ⎤
Mr Fairburn⎦ (LMSR)
Mr Graff Baker (LPTB)
Mr Richards (LNER)
Mr Collett (GWR)
Mr Raworth and myself (SR)

I should like to make it clear that this Sub-Committee has no executive authority over its members as, so far as each Railway Company is concerned, each chief mechanical and electrical engineer remains responsible to his general manager for his department.

The evacuation of 3,000,000 civilians from London and the other large centres of population was a triumph of railway organisation; everything to the smallest detail had been thought out, nothing went wrong.

Mr Hore-Belisha, speaking in the House of Commons on the 11th October, referred to the magnitude of the task accomplished by the railways in transporting overseas in the first five weeks of the war 154,000 men, 25,000 vehicles, including the largest and heaviest tanks, and the immense quantities of supplies needed to maintain them in the field. A wonderful achievement indeed, and a tribute to the equipment and staff of the railways.

Armies in the field represent a concentration of large numbers of men and great quantities of equipment in a small area, and demand large scale transportation to feed them. Due to the armies being collected over wide areas at home little relief as regards rail transport is given when they have gone overseas, whilst the supplies needed by them in the field add materially to the burden on the home railways.

How are these additional demands to be met? They can only be met by making greater use of the rolling stock, or by the provision of additional equipment. Here again the locomotive engineer is called upon, and we are proud to say he meets the demands.

It will be appreciated from these few remarks how essential it is the railways should be maintained in the most efficient way, not only for war purposes, but so that they may be able to meet peace conditions when hostilities cease; and how they must cover such maintenance work even before they can undertake munitions work.

We locomotive engineers know that a prosperous railway industry, one of the greatest of the country, means prosperity to many towns and trades and to the 600,000 people directly employed by it. It is no exaggeration to say that the country cannot be prosperous if the railways are not. The services rendered to the country in peace time are great: the assistance given would have been greater in both men and material but for the economies imposed on the Companies in peace time by the failure to ensure equitable treatment: we may hope this will not be allowed to occur in the future.

The railway staffs are giving of their best to ensure efficient transportation and thereby help the State.

The terms of compensation to the Railway Companies for the great railway organisation systems taken over are now under discussion, and we have no doubt but that they will be generous and just.

These are stirring times, and we should rejoice we have our share in them.

We are a race experienced in war; once all steps to ensure peace have been unavailing we do not fear war — rather we find it stimulating; nor are we depressed by thoughts of the sufferings and losses involved. Still less do we depreciate the many benefits resulting from the application to peaceful ends of the energy and intelligence devoted to the achievement of victory.

When we contemplate our daily life and its environment since the 1914-1918 war, we are compelled to admit great progress in all directions in major part as a result of it. Think of the progress in surgery and medicine; in locomotion there have been great advances whether we consider sea, rail, road or air transport by steam, electric or diesel power. Do not these advances in science, and the art of living, demonstrate the greater power of good than evil, and may we not look forward with confidence to the future?

Many of our members are now serving in the armed forces; the reputation of the Institution is safe in their hands; they will show the versatility, resourcefulness and phlegm expected of the locomotive engineer. They have our best wishes for success in all their undertakings and a safe return.

Author's note: Although these arrangements only became formal at the outbreak of war, there had been preliminary meetings. The Mechanical and Electrical Engineers Sub-committee first met in October 1938. They took decisions on details like the black-out of railway carriage windows and the protection of glass, and on materials such as deciding they must be allowed copper for fireboxes but could use home-grown timber for wagon repairs. They later agreed total building programmes including, for example, 25 4-6-2 locomotives by the Southern Railway at their meeting on January 15, 1941. They allocated scarce materials, logged war damage and coped with requisitioned privately-owned wagons until these were de-requisitioned in May 1946. Stanier took over as Chairman in April 1941, and Bulleid succeeded in January 1946.

Their last major task was to cope with an urgent Government request dated June 19, 1946 to report how many engines should be converted to oil-firing to match an expected availability of 12,500 tons per week of heavy fuel oil. They advised, there and then at the July 2, 1946 meeting, that 625 engines and at least 10 sheds should be equipped. They gave the cost at about £600,000 for the engines and £100,000 for the sheds. They also pointed out that this extra work would delay and unbalance their repair and building programmes and reminded the Government that the Great Western had already converted 11 out of a planned 44 engines to oil firing.

The wartime Railway Executive Committee was wound up in 1946 and the nationalised Railway Executive was formed in October 1947 to take command on January 1, 1948.

Appendix 4
Modifications to
the Pacifics

Abridged extracts from the Report on the Proposed Modifications to the "Merchant Navy" and "West Country" Classes of locomotives, which was issued by the Chief Mechanical & Electrical Engineer's Office, Brighton, in January 1955:

The locomotives, when hauling the principal express trains of the Region, have demonstrated their ability to run to time with an ample margin of power, due to their excellent steaming properties, and free running characteristics.

From availability and maintenance points of view, however, the locomotives are less satisfactory, whilst their consumption of coal, water and oil is high in relation to other modern locomotives.

Specially kept records show that the number of weekdays lost to service on account of engine defects at sheds in 1953 for the 140 locomotives from all causes was 5501 or 39.3 days per engine. Of these the following totals were attributed to individual causes:

	Days	Days per engine
Valve gear	1021	7.3
Valves & Pistons	251	1.8
Steam & Exhaust pipes	423	3.1
Grates & Ashpans	215	1.54
Steam reversing gear	50	0.36
(remainder	3541	25.2)

The proposal now put forward will virtually eliminate the principal troublesome features and will bring the running costs into line with those of the other principal express passenger locomotives without impairing their performance in any way, and increase the availability, whilst reducing the maintenance in Shops and Motive Power Depots.

The proposal involves the retention of the boiler, frames, outside cylinders, wheels, axleboxes etc. and the replacement or removal of the following existing components:

(1) Special valve gear and rocker shafts.
(2) Inside cylinder.
(3) Smokebox, superheater header, steampipes etc.
(4) Reversing gear.
(5) Piston heads and rods.
(6) Oil bath.
(7) Air-smoothed casing.
(8) Mechanical lubricators.
(9) Regulator.
(10) Ashpan and grate.
(11) Cylinder cocks.
(12) Sandboxes.
(13) Tender; raves, fire iron tunnel, tank sieves, water level gauge and intermediate drawbar.

The main points in the design of the components which will replace the components listed above are given below:

(1) The main purpose of the modifications is to provide the locomotive with three independent sets of Walschaerts valve gear of a type which has been well proved and which is known to give a very good steam distribution. The two outside sets will be similar to those of the standard Class 4 2-6-4 tank locomotives and the inside set will follow the design of the Southern Region "Schools" class.

(2) Forward of the inside cylinder (which will have a piston valve with inside admission), and bolted to it, will be a saddle. These two components will butt up to the existing stretchers and give a very strong construction, which will eliminate the frame fractures which have been experienced at the leading end of the "West Country" class.

(3) A circular smokebox, fixed to the saddle, will ensure a robust construction, which will remove the troubles experienced with the present design of steam pipes and stuffing boxes. The latter will be similar to those on the standard locomotives.

(4) The reversing gear will consist of one shaft for both inside and outside valve gears, operated by means of a screw. This type of gear will enable fine adjustments of the cut-off to be made and will result in the locomotives being worked at an early cut-off with a degree of certainty not possible with the steam reversing gear.

(5) It is proposed to replace the existing type of piston heads, having a coned attachment to the piston rod, by parallel fastened heads of the type on the BR Standard locomotives.

(6) The elimination of the oil bath will make the examination of the inside big end and motion much easier and the trouble which has been experienced of rusting of pins and gear will cease.

(7) The normal type of clothing will be fitted to the boiler which, together with the removal of the oil bath, will eliminate the trouble which has been

experienced of fires occurring in oil saturated boiler clothing mattresses. Many details, particularly pipework, will be far more accessible than heretofore.

(8) Two new mechanical lubricators will be used for the lubrication of the cylinders and axleboxes.

(9) The existing regulator will be replaced by one of the horizontal grid type, arranged in such a way as to give a well graduated opening, in order to reduce the tendency of the locomotive to slip.

(10) Both classes of locomotive will be fitted with new ashpans with hopper bottom doors and front and rear damper doors. The fitting of dampers will improve, as far as the "West Country" class is concerned, the control which can be exercised on the fire in order to prevent blowing off. The ashpans will be self-discharging to a greater extent than those now fitted and will therefore assist in the disposal of the locomotives.

(11) The existing coned plug type of cylinder cock has proved expensive to maintain in a proper state of repair and the poppet type will be fitted in its place.

(12) New sandboxes will be provided and fitted, where possible, between the frames.

The gross outlay involved is £5,615 per locomotive. Coal, water and oil savings agreed with the Motive Power Superintendent are £48,934 per annum for the 140 locomotives taking the annual mileages at 50,000 for "Merchant Navies" and 43,000 for "West Countries." When all 140 have been modified there will be a staff saving of 10 grade 1 fitters and 17 fitters' assistants, £13,650 per annum.

The Regional Accountant has been consulted and a copy of his memorandum setting out the financial aspect of the scheme is attached. This shows that the total estimated net saving up to the assumed date of scrapping of the locomotives (1987), before taking account of the interest factor, is £2,051,402. Allowing for interest charges the saving becomes £850,000.

Anxiety about the increased weight added to the problems of Jarvis and the Brighton Drawing Office as they designed these modifications, and the monitoring steps are shown in the Table opposite.

Marylebone was well pleased with the results reported from the modified engines, and the figures available were sent to Bulleid by C.P. Hopkins in February 1960 as follows:

MEMORANDUM: GENERAL MANAGER.   *5th February 1960.*

"Merchant Navy" and "West Country"
Class Engines-Modifications.

The following figures are extracted from up-to-date records and reports:

Coal and water economies actual:	⌉10% for coal ⌋8% for water
compared with first estimates:	⌈6% for coal ⌊7% for water
Disposal time	Actual savings of £154 per annum per locomotive
Running repair costs	Actual savings of £250 per annum per locomotive
Examinations	Valve and piston examination extended from 30/36,000 miles to 40/48,000 miles.
Consumption of sump oil	Actual saving of 2 gallons per 100 miles (100% as estimated for).
Consumption of lubricating oil	Actual saving of 1.8 pints of superheat cylinder oil per 100 miles. (Not calculated first estimates).
Works repairs	Average saving in works repairs firmly estimated at £550 per locomotive.
Availability	Improved very considerably but cannot be taken full advantage of while modified and unmodified locomotives have to be worked from same depots.

Weights on Wheels in tons-cwts

| | "Merchant Navy" | | | | "West Country" | | | |
	Bogie	Coupled	Truck	TOTAL	Bogie	Coupled	Truck	TOTAL
Diagram	16-14	63	15-1	94-15	15-10	56-5	14-5	86
Actual, average of several weighed at Eastleigh	17-1	62-6	15-16	95-3	15-17	56-10	14-3	86-10
35021 with stiffened front end frame	17-12	62-6	15-12	95-10	—	—	—	—
"Guinea pigs"	17-2	63-19	15-16	96-17	16-8	58-9	14-0	88-17
Estimated wts after modification	17-7	64-15	15-16	97-18	16-11	59-1	14-5	89-17
Actual weight of first loco modified	17-0	64-18	16-0	97-18	17-0	58-6	14-15	90-1

Steps recorded by Brighton Drawing Office in estimating the weights of the Pacifics after modification. Engines having all preliminary mods were referred to as the "guinea pigs." These were three engines of each type incorporating all the 1950-52 improvements devised by Jarvis and Eastleigh Drawing Office, including the balanced crank axle which added 11cwt unsprung weight. The major mods listed in the Report only added a further ton or so.

Appendix 5
What the Drivers
Wrote

The Testimonial by drivers to the Bulleid Pacifics was planned as a set of cards bearing the signatures of all drivers who fitted the specification and agreed with the sentiment of the statement prepared in 1966 by driver E. Pistell:

> We the undersigned, having had considerable experience in working the "Merchant Navy," "Battle of Britain," and "West Country" classes of locomotives, both in their original and modified condition, are in *no doubt* that the best performance and free running were obtained when they were in their original design.

Altogether, 80 drivers signed out of about 150 eligible, and some added comments which, of course, turned out to be the most interesting feature of the entire excercise. Some also added reservations to the Pistell claim:

Shed	Total signed	Signature only	Praise added	Praise and Reservations added
Exmouth Jct	38	7	21	10
Nine Elms	9	—	8	1
Salisbury	33	27	6	—

Here are some typical messages of praise:

> "The performance of the engines *before* modification can be summed up in one word — "MAGNIFICENT"
> "Having worked these engines before and after modification, I consider that in their original design, they were themselves sufficient testimonial to a very fine engineer."
> "I personally thought they were the "Cassius Clay" of locomotives, the greatest thanks again to that great designer Mr. Bulleid."
> "When working a passenger train with a "West Country" engine over the Great Western road to Plymouth, a Motor Engineer paid a compliment by saying that she ascended Dainton Incline (2 miles at 1 in 50) as if she was fitted with a Rolls-Royce engine."
> "These were most economical and one of the fastest that it was my

pleasure to drive. But now in the later years of conversion they have become stifled in the front end, retarding their running."

Some drivers aired their personal dislikes amongst the praise:

"The finest engines that ever ran on rails, the Rolls of locomotion. I've raised many an eye-brow with this remark as you can well imagine. My only complaint — no bucket seat. I must say, to get the true value from these wonderful engines one had to be a driver by nature. I can quite understand your feelings, a 'West Country' class 6 was found to be so good they made it a class 7 then decided they were not economic. What bosh! Perhaps you will have another name. To my regret what's left in my opinion have been sabotaged. I've stated facts as I see them after a life time of railway service — 50 years."

"Best in the original design . . . good all-round engines for all classes of work in the West Country . . . In the modified condition the outlook was better but the screw-reverser was harder work."

"With all the praise for these engines, don't let us forget the snags at maintenance level. And undoubtedly the most expensive piece of machinery any railroad produced. This is no reflection on Mr. Bulleid but on the Management that sanctioned their construction."

"When they were maintained properly they were unbeatable, masters of the job and good riders, also the electric lighting was a boon!"

"My son was a fitter at Exmouth Junction and said failure of non-return valves in the mechanical lubricators was a cause of excessive wear in the inside valve bushes, also ashes being drawn down the blast pipe while coasting on freight trains, so the valve would lose some of its travel and form a ridge against which a valve ring would break and hence the engine became out in its beats. Undoubtedly had Mr. Bulleid remained with us some of the lubrication troubles would have been dealt with . . . Properly maintained the engines were the best I ever rode on and I rode on all the main line types on the Interchange runs between Salisbury and Exeter. During tests with the 'WCs.' over the WR route as between Bristol and Truro with both freight and passenger trains, the WR Inspectors riding with me were astounded at the performance and boiler efficiency which was capable of maintaining the heaviest demands."

Some drivers had a bit to say about the steam reversers:

"They were, in my opinion, one of the finest engines ever built; it is also true that there were one or two faults with them, for example the steam hydraulic reverser, which gave very little trouble if properly maintained; the look-out, yes, bad at times when the wind was blowing the wrong way. All the little faults, we somehow managed to get over; it was the very free running of these engines that was the secret, and if properly managed,

207

they were masters of their jobs — when they were in their *original design.* When they were modified, the Walschaerts valve gear fitted, the very free running was gone! Had to almost steam them into stations — not the same engine by any means."

"The steam reversers were prone to creep. The main reasons for this (especially on 'West Countries') was, in my opinion, incorrect operation of the lever control by persons not understanding the correct way to operate this reverser and, of course, coupled with lack of maintenance when trouble was developing. As is so often the case with new machinery and modifications, no instructions were printed or told to the loco staff on the correct method of using this reverser; it was found by trial and error!"

"The hydraulic cylinder was often a source of trouble as regards to keeping it full, I've seen buckets of oil used on them daily, filling up on leaving shed, and filling again at say Plymouth or Salisbury for the return journey, and the thing useless each way often at that. Starting away with a train at a station was often difficult; they did not seem to take steam and one would have to build the steam chest to full boiler pressure when they would slip at a terrific speed, but this would often do them good as they would often afterwards go away with ease. This I considered was caused by the valves being thrown out to their full distance in the spin and would then take steam better. *Now for the rebuilds.* The screw reverser in one go did away with almost all the trouble as the new gear was 100% perfect as possible to get, the blast on the fire was more even and consequently a saving on coal . . . When an engine will tackle 17 corridor coaches from Salisbury to Exeter as I did, tho' only once, as a young driver on a Saturday prior to August Bank Holiday when traffic was very heavy, it is a good bit of machinery. This was done with a 'Merchant Navy' of course and *prior* to its being rebuilt but in *good nick!* Rebuilding of course robbed them of no power. Am sorry I cannot go all the way with you."

"I preferred them all in their original design for free running, you could run miles on atomised steam in 15% cut-off, they were also much easier in preparation. The steam reverser gave no trouble when hydraulic washers were kept in good order and cylinders topped up."

"They were in my opinion the finest loco ever built — with one exception which was really a bad one, the Driver's look-out window in hazy weather or heavy rain — you just had it, visibility nil. But on going into Shops, that was rectified . . . I had three days learning the road from Exeter St. Davids to Plymouth North Road on *King George V*, the one that went over to the States, and I am fully convinced that the 'West Country' or 'Merchant navy' would have left the 'King' standing! I was all for the steam reverser in preference to the wheel which was a real manual job to notch up against steam. dam hard work."

"The creep was not so much to do with the topping with oil as it was the passing of oil, the washers being worn so badly — there again, maintenance! I was once asked by a gent at Bude how I liked them and I told him about the inside big end and gear being taken out of our hands by the oil bath, and that it took a lot of oil, and that it was a wonderful job. He said it did not matter about a barrow of oil: and *that* we *drivers* found out when they were *modified* — they were the dirtiest job of oiling we had in our lives! Mr. Bulleid's engine was the best I have driven or rode on.''

Several drivers had something to say about speed, and about their regrets at the passing of steam:

''The finest and fastest locomotives I have ever driven. I am only sorry that an official attempt to break the existing steam locomotive record was not made; I should have loved to have had the opportunity, and I feel sure it could have been broken — that is, of course, before they were modified.''

''The pick of the bunch in my experience was 34043 which I had booked to me when I was working in the Ilfracombe passenger link. She was brand new at the time and, in the old loco men's saying, ''She would catch pigeons.'' ''

''Both before and after modification the performance of this class of locomotive was marvellous. On one occasion with a load of seven bogies I started from Axminster and passed Whimple in 15min. One performance that is worth recalling is that of driver Hamilton. With a load of six bogies he started from Salisbury and passed Yeovil in 33min.''

''I have enclosed a running by me of the 'Atlantic Coast Express,' which was taken unknown to me.'' (The timings include passing Yeovil in 36min 20sec and passing Axminster in 54min, from Salisbury; engine No. 35014, tare load 435 tons.) ''Also when the paper train used to run non-stop from Salisbury to Exeter, I have done it in 1hr 15min, which I think speaks well of the free running of these engines.''

''In appreciation of the Pacifics which in my opinion could have beaten *Mallard's* record.''

''I am only too pleased to testify to the supreme qualities of Mr. Bulleid's Pacifics. Those engines would outrun, and outpull any steam engine I have ever handled. My experience of steam engines is wide and varied, from the old L&SWRly Sharp's and Adams' high-wheelers down to the last of the steam engines, including the famous *Mallard*. Now that I am retired I can tell you that the record put up by the *Mallard* has been broken — unofficial, of course — many times by these engines of Mr. Bulleid. I would be speaking tongue in cheek if I didn't say that these engines had some drawbacks, notably poor lookout, and the steam reversing gear was often at fault, but overall they were the most capable engines I have ever handled.''

"The riding of the suspension under the footplate was immaculate to the other engines that had gone before it; there was also complete absence of axlebox knock with these engines running at all speeds. It is my firm opinion that this rebuilt machine lacks freedom in its running and due to this alteration these engines lack potency in power output, and both the riding and general axlebox and valve motion knock has deteriorated its performance."

"When the 'West Country' class came to Exmouth Junction, Driver R. Dawe and myself had No. 10, which was named *Sidmouth*, to ourselves, early and late turns of duty on the run Exeter to Ilfracombe, and what a grand and reliable engine to have had, and what a lovely ride. Everyone really admired those engines; what a great pity they were ever taken out of service."

I have quoted about half the drivers who sent in comments, and on average extracted about half of what they wrote, taking great care to give the views they expressed proportional representation! The originals are lodged in the Library of the Institution of Mechanical Engineers.

Appendix 6
Extracts from
"Leader" Test Report

M & E Engr's Dept
Southern Region
Brighton
1950

Mechanical failures during running:

Period ending	Cumulative mileage	Mechanical Failures No	Description
July 1949	378	4	Valve rods and one sleeve valve
Sept. 1949	1356	3	2 sleeve valves broken and one motion pin fell out
Oct. 1949	2625	4	2 lubricating pump drive failures
			one sleeve valve broken
			cast iron firebox lining failed
Dec. 1949	5076	6	one valve rod broken
			one motion pin fell out
			2 lubricator drive failures
			one valve gear chain drive sprocket shifted, putting valves out of beat
			one bogie union link broken
	(No running between Dec. 1949 and June 1950)		
29/6/1950	5938	1	one crank axle broken (the other was badly flawed)
21/8/1950	6088	1	drive to mechanical lubricators failed
2/11/1950	6997	1	smokebox door white hot due to having been improperly closed

(In addition there were six failures due to shortage of steam)

The dynamometer car tests were done between Eastleigh and Woking, with train loads between 240 and 325 tons, on four double trips each with the "Leader" and a Class U 2-6-0. A summary of average performance is given in the table overleaf.

Comments on the results:
The high consumptions are the results of the waste of fuel and power due to the high smokebox vacuum and exhaust pressure.

Notes on the final run:

The fact that Mr. Bulleid intended that the locomotive should be capable of handling trains of 480tons, whilst the loads so far hauled amounted to no more than 325tons, prompted the request that tests should be made with heavier loads.

The dynamometer car, having been returned to Darlington on September 28, 1950, was not available for these further tests and, for that reason, no accurate figures are available of the actual drawbar pull, work done, etc.

On October 17, 1950 a load of 13 bogies, weighing 430tons, was assembled at Eastleigh, and a test was made over the same route and to the same timings as the dynamometer tests. The engine ran satisfactorily and, whilst some time was lost on the easier sections, this could have been avoided by slightly heavier working. The steam pressure and water level were fairly well maintained, but steaming was not entirely satisfactory during the heaviest working conditions. The performance of the locomotive was such, however, as to indicate that a trial could be attempted with 480tons . . .

A test run with 480tons was made on November 2, 1950, the train being

Summary Showing Comparative Performance Based on Average Results Obtained. Eastleigh - Woking

	Engine No. 31630 Class U	Engine No 36001 'Leader' Class	% Difference Class U = 100%
Boiler pressure lb/in	187	240	28.3 greater
Steam chest pressure lb/in	167	135	19.2 less
Exhaust pressure lb/in	1.81	7.3 6.0	—
Smokebox vacuum in. of water	2.34	4.00	71 greater
Inlet steam temp °F	478	546 564	—
Exhaust steam temp °F	220	285	29.5 greater
Smokebox A temp °F	570	574	.7 greater
Smokebox B temp °F	578	620	7.26 greater
Trip coal — pounds	1455	2457	68.8 greater
— lb/mile	29.75	50.17	68.7 greater
— lb/ton mile (inc. eng)	.0818	.121	48.0 greater
— lb/hour (running time)	1125	1830	62.7 greater
— lb/sq ft grate/hour	45	71.8	59.6 greater
— lb/DBHP hour	4.01	6.727	67.6 greater
Water — gallons	1245	1850	48.6 greater
— gals/mile	25.44	37.78	48.5 greater
— lb/hour (running time)	9621	13790	43.3 greater
— lb/DBHP hour	34.34	50.66	47.5 greater
— lb/sq ft evap heating surface hour	6.334	5.777	8.8 less
— lb/ton-mile (incl engine)	.702	.912	30.0 greater
Evaporation — lb water/lb coal	8.554	7.532	12.0 less
Boiler efficiency — %	78.29	71.22	9.0 less
BThUs/DBHP hour	53893	90262	67.5 greater
Overall efficiency %	4.72	2.82	40.25 less

Tests with 480ton Train on November 2, 1950

Place	Time Bkd p.m.	Time Act p.m.	Pressure Blr	Pressure Stm Ch	Cut Off (%)	Water in glass (F = 6½)	S'box vac (" of water)	Temp °F Lge tubes	°F Small tubes	Remarks
Eastleigh	6.40	6.40	260	240	67	F	1	500	500	Started without difficulty
—	—	—	270	130	25	F	1¾	600	585	
Allbrook Jc	6.45	6.45½	245	240	10	F	2½	650	620	Pricker & dart used
—		—	260	255	18	F	4	680	630	
Shawford		6.53½	230	225	18	F	6½	730	680	Pricker used
Shawford Jc		—	220	210	18	F	7	730	660	
St. Cross Tunnel			220	210	18	F	7	730	660	Pricker used
Winchester		6.58¾	245	240	18	F	9	750	700	
Winchester Jc	6.59	7.1¾	255	225	18	F	10½	760	710	Pricker & dart used
Wallers Ash Box		7.5	245	220	18	F	10½	750	700	Pricker & dart used
Weston Box		7.7	240	225	18	F	10	750	720	
Micheldever		7.9½	250	235	18	5½	10	785	750	
			260	250	20	5	13½	800	780	Blowing off
Litchfield Tunnel		7.12¼	255	240	20	4	13½	820	800	Pricker used
Worting Jc	7.19	7.18½	—	—	—	—	—	—	—	Sig. stop 1½mins
Basingstoke	7.24	7.26								

213

made up of 15 carriages. The schedule was arranged as before, except that the Operating Dept. allowed 5 additional minutes to pass Winchester Junction on the outward run, as some loss of time on this section had caused operating difficulties on previous runs. Details of the test run are given in the table.

A good start was made from Eastleigh with only slight slipping due to wet rails. The steaming was quite satisfactory and the frequent use of the pricker and dart was to level the fire, which was being considerably torn by the heavy working.

The performance on this test was far in excess of anything previously attained, the estimated power output, corrected for gradient, being of the order of 1100hp at the drawbar.

Appendix 7
Extracts from Bulleid's
Paper on "Leader"

"Stages in the Development of the Steam Locomotive to Restore it to its Supremacy as the Ideal Railway Traction Unit."
This last paper on the "Leader" was submitted to the IMechE in November 1949, accepted for presentation in April 1950 but withdrawn at British Railways request in March 1950.

Bulleid did not over-exert himself in writing it, closely following much of the text of his ASME paper which he presented in December 1949 and which was printed in their Journal, Mechanical Engineering, *in June 1950. The main additional material in the IMechE paper was the following:*

Steam locomotive designs, other than small tank engines, utilise only a small proportion of the total weight for adhesion. A "West Country" engine with tender, weighing 128½tons, uses only 56¼tons for adhesion and 98¾ for braking. In comparison the most recent designs of electric locomotives have total adhesion . . .

There are six stretchers on each power bogie:

(1) *Buffer Beam.* This forms a brace between the front ends of the main bogie frames and is of channel construction with life guards welded into position, a channel cross-tie between the life guards forming an attachment for the brake gear tie rods. Lifting brackets are welded to the top corners of the frames.
(2) *Cylinder blocks.* See later.
(3) *Slide-bar carrier and motion plunger support.* An inverted channel section, with brackets at the foot to carry the front ends of the slide-bars and pierced by cylindrical bushed carriers for the valve motion plunger guides.
(4) *Combined outer bearer and motion stretcher.* This consists of a horizontal top plate with vertical supporting members, the whole carrying the outer bearing segment which contains the radial bearing block on the main frame. On the front side, brackets support the rear ends of the slide-bars, and at the rear, brackets carry the swing links for the valve rods. The cylinder exhaust pipe is welded to the stretcher and an internal exhaust chamber is provided with a rectangular vertical exhaust nozzle.

(5) *Combined inner bearer and expansion link carrier.* Supporting members are similar to item 4 above but the top plate is extended to suit brackets carrying the expansion links and the hand brake lever. Bogie side control gear is carried on this plate, and brackets are also provided for the swing links carrying the valve rods and combination levers. At the lower edge of the rear vertical support a bracket is welded, carrying the valve crank shaft and the intermediate compound sprocket of the valve gear chain drive.

(6) *Rear headstock and brake cylinder carrier.* The main bogie frames are tied at the rear ends by a channel section which carries brackets for the vacuum brake cylinders and brake shaft.

All these stretchers are welded in position, the whole bogie forming a fabricated monoblock structure. The only riveted or bolted attachments are:

(a) the bearing segments
(b) the cylindrical pedestals for the roller-bearing axleboxes.

Some considerations on the use of sleeve instead of piston valves, having in mind that locomotive designers seek to improve thermal efficiency as well as availability:

The "West Country" Pacifics had 10in piston valves, 16⅜in cylinders, area of ports in piston valve liner 36.6sq in, area of cylinder ports 34.7sq in, clearance volume 10%. The cylinder walls were cooled by exhaust steam, the same ports being used by live and exhaust steam. Thermal efficiency may be improved by:

(1) Separating inlet and exhaust ports and steam jacketing the cylinder barrel to reduce condensation losses.
(2) Increasing port areas to reduce wiredrawing.
(3) Reducing the clearance volume to reduce expansion losses.
(4) Providing adequate steam chest volume to avoid drop of pressure during admission.

Sleeve valves met all these requirements for thermal efficiency and for space limitations. Single piece sleeve valves were made of cast iron (Meehanite) machined all over but for lubrication reasons not too highly finished. The sleeve forms a cylinder in which the piston reciprocates and is provided with separate ports for admission and release. The exhaust is arranged outside the live steam ports. The ports are rectangular, separated by narrow bars, all corners and edges having a generous radius. The forward end of each sleeve has extension wings at top and bottom projecting through slots of similar shape in the front cylinder covers to which the driving gear is attached, driven from the valve motion. Cylinder liners, one each end of each cylinder, have ports arranged to suit those in the sleeves. Rings are provided in each liner as follows:

216

2 at inner end to prevent leakage from sleeve steam port and cylinder barrel to the opposite end of the cylinder.

2 at inner side of steam port, the outer edge of the outer ring being the admission cut-off edge.

2 between live and exhaust steam ports.

2 at outer edge of exhaust port, the inner edge of the inner ring being the exhaust cut-off edge.

2 at outer end to prevent exhaust steam passing to atmosphere.

(These 10 rings per liner are shown in Fig. 38)

There are also 4 rings on each cylinder cover to provide a steam seal to atmosphere. All ring joints are of the scarf stepped type. Clearance volume is 7%. Steam and exhaust ports are separate. The port area of the sleeve is 34.14sq in with cylinders 12¼in dia by 15in stroke. A common live steam chest round three cylinders acts as a steam jacket; its volume is three times the swept cylinder volume.

The sleeve valve is in balance; resistance to motion is only frictional. Rings have only sufficient grip to be steam-tight. The working faces of all the rings are on the sleeve.

The cylinders are fabricated complete; one 3-cylinder block complete with liners but without covers, sleeve valves and pistons weighs 1.3tons, i.e., 2.6tons per locomotive, compared with 4.8tons for a "West Country."

Valve gear similar to "Merchant Navy," good events. All details similar for all three sets of gear in contrast to normal three-cylinder locomotive. Cranks at 120 degrees, perfect balance. Connecting rod big ends as on "Schools" and Q1.

Two cylindrical pedestals, bolted to the bogie frames, fit inside each roller-bearing axlebox casting; between each pedestal and its axlebox chamber is an outer steel sleeve fitted over a rubber sleeve bonded to an inner steel bush, providing sliding surfaces between pedestal and axlebox. The whole is flood lubricated, the rubber protected by Neoprene washers on the top and bottom surfaces. The advantages are, compact; free from grit; thrust always taken on both pedestals; thrust taken on rubber; no hornstay required; no localisation of stress tending to frame fractures; easier to manufacture; bearing springs immediatedly above axleboxes in frame, — no spring links, springs loaded by a rubber pad inserted between spring and top plate of frame, a radius plate being attached to the underside of the rubber pad. Springs flood-lubricated and oil fed through them to the axlebox.

The vacuum brake is applied through clasp brakes, compensated throughout. Gresham and Craven auto ejector control system, no small ejector. A vacuum of 25in, created in a separate cylinder, is used to open the steam valve which automatically operates the large ejector to restore the vacuum. When the vacuum in this cylinder is reduced, due to leakage, the air compresses a diaphragm which draws the steam valve off its seating and again permits steam to pass to the large ejector. This cycle is repeated automatically until a brake application is made. When the driver's brake valve is moved to the lap or brake position, the automatic equipment on the engine is isolated from the train pipe by the air disc in the driver's brake valve. The reserve reservoir is immediately charged to 25in vacuum and the ejector is shut down. As little or no leakage can take place with the train pipe isolated, the ejector will remain out of commission until the brake handle is replaced in the "off" position. Air then passes from the train pipe lowering the vacuum in the reserve reservoir and causing the ejector to restart.

Summary. A 100% adhesion steam locomotive with good power and speed characteristics and stable at all speeds has been shown to be a practicable proposition. A new design of this kind, especially when it incorporates features never previously used, cannot be expected to go into service until it has undergone much experimentation. It is hoped that this design will carry locomotive development a stage forward.

Interestingly, it was in the American paper that Bulleid added pointers to the way ahead:

The use of the blast to create the draft should give way to fans so that we can control the production of steam accurately.

The exhaust steam should not be allowed to escape to the atmosphere, but should be returned to the boiler.

Experimental work already done encourages the thought that these two problems can be solved, and I commend them to the young engineers as worthy of investigation.

I shall feel more than recompensed if I have shown that, while the Stephenson locomotive today may in some circumstances be dead or dying, this cannot be said of steam traction itself.

Appendix 8

Patents

Back in December 1911 Bulleid took out a Provisional Specification for improvements to the piston/conn. rod assemblies of internal combustion engines but the idea was overtaken by other developments and was never patented.

The six completed Bulleid patents were:

No	Prov Spec	Dates of Comp Spec	Patent	Subject
547,156	6.2.41	6.2.42	17.8.42	Bulleid valve gear
547,180	6.2.41	6.2.42	17.8.42	Valve operation by rocker in exhaust space
584,858	17.7.44	17.7.45	24.1.47	Triangulated underframe
616,445	2.9.46	7.5.47	21.1.49	Leader type boiler
766,917	23.8.54	16.8.55	30.1.57	Improvements to triangulated underframes
819,493	16.7.56	16.7.57	2.9.59	Brake apparatus

The first two patents cover the valve gear arrangement on the Pacifics.

The third, co-patented with Lionel Lynes, offers increased strength, reduced weight, and use with either side or central buffers, as can be seen at a glance from Fig. 54. Why did no one think of it before? Why is it not in wider use now? Perhaps because nobody could or can be bothered. Bulleid launched a Company to exploit this invention — Triangulated (Vehicle) Frames Ltd., incorporated July 29 1953. It netted some useful royalties before being wound up in 1960.

The fourth patent mainly covers the replacement of the conventional firebox by one having four syphons, no water legs, and three drums forming the firebox top.

The fifth improves the triangulated underframe by the use of welded, box-form sections.

The last Bulleid Patent covered electrically-controlled versions of continuous vacuum or air brakes. Every vehicle would be fitted with its own exhauster or compressor and two electro-magnetic valves controllable by driver or guard from a four-line train cable which would also allow telephone communication. The sole disadvantage was the cost of the electric equipment on every vehicle; the advantages included simpler inter-vehicle connections, instant brake applications on every vehicle, ability to connect through non-fitted vehicles, a choice of refinements based on electrical control, and sundry facilities for shunting, particularly when the brake vans were fitted with electric power supply.

Bulleid also supplied the original idea, and Firth-Brown the manufacturing know-how, for their combined patent of the BFB wheel.

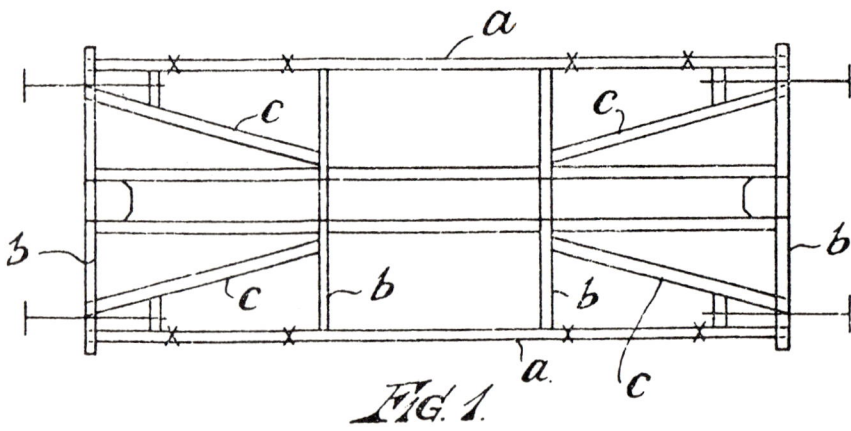

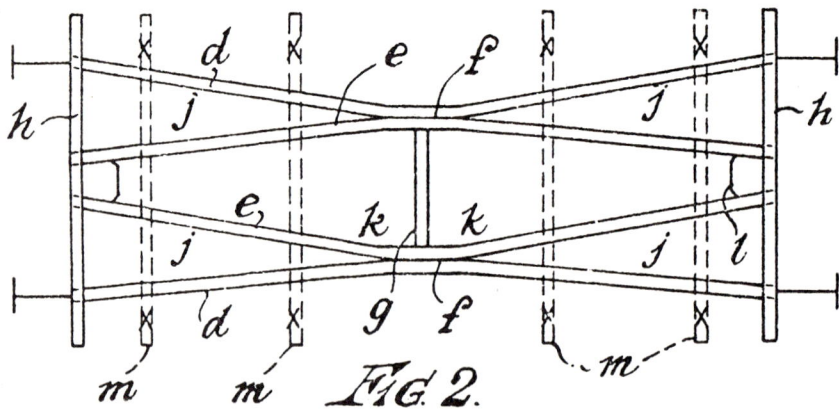

Fig 54 The triangulated underframe patent No. 584,858. The elegance of this development by Bulleid and Lynes is seen by comparing the conventional with the new, Figs 1 and 2 of the patent. The latter is simpler and lighter and takes oblique buffing shocks with less risk of distortion. Transverse member g is an integral part of the design, helping to form the six triangles. Four transverse members m placed under the triangulated frame carry the wheel springs at x - x, so distributing the load to the underframe better than in Fig 1 where it is all carried by the outer members a.

Appendix 9

Preservation

The Bulleid Pacific Preservation Society was inspired and started up by Alan A. Wilton of Nine Elms, with footplate and fitter colleagues, in mid-1965. He persuaded a widening circle of international enthusiasts to contribute and in July 1967 was able to buy from British Railways, for £1,900 in hard cash, No. 34023 *Blackmore Vale*. He and his Committee planned its restoration to original detail and livery as a tribute to the designer. The present Chairman is H.A.P. Browne and Bulleid's footsteps as first President have been stepped into by R. Curl. *Blackmore Vale* lives at Sheffield Park on the Bluebell line and restoration was completed in May 1976.

Others followed this admirable lead and at a count in 1976 there was a preserved team of eleven — five originals and six modified — all but one of which are expected to be put into working order. The twelfth man is an 0-6-0, as listed:

Engine No	Class	Name	Owner
34016*	WC	*Bodmin*	Quainton Rd Railway Society
34023	WC	*Blackmore Vale*	The Bulleid Society
34039*	WC	*Boscastle*	Main Line Steam Trust
34051	BB	*Winston Churchill*	British Railways
34081	BB	*92 Squadron*	Battle of Britain Loco Preservation Society
34092	WC	*City of Wells*	Keighley & Worth Valley Rly
34105	WC	*Swanage*	
35005*	MN	*Canadian Pacific*	Steamtown, Carnforth
35009*	MN	*Shaw Saville*	
35028*	MN	*Clan Line*	Merchant Navy Locomotive Preservation Society
35029*	MN	*Ellerman Line*	Sectioned by British Railways for York Museum
33001	Q1		British Railways

(*denotes modified)

Further information about Preservation can be had from the Association of Railway Preservation Societies.

Bibliography

Allen, Cecil J., *British Pacific Locomotives*. Ian Allan, 1962.

Allen, Cecil J., *The Locomotive Exchanges 1870-1948*. 2nd edition, Ian Allan, 1950.

Allen, Cecil J. & S.C. Townroe, *The Bulleid Pacifics*. Ian Allan, 1951.

Bond, R.C., *A Lifetime with Locomotives*. Goose, 1975.

Bulleid, H.A.V., *Master Builders of Steam*. Ian Allan, 1963.

Chapelon, Andre, *La Locomotive a Vapeur*. J.B. Bailliere & fils, 1952.

Cox, E.S. *Locomotive Panorama, Vol. 2*. Ian Allan, 1966.

Cox, E.S., *Speaking of Steam*. Ian Allan, 1971.

Day-Lewis, Sean, *Bulleid, Last Giant of Steam*. Geo. Allen & Unwin, 1964.

Esau, Mike, *Steam into Wessex*. Ian Allan, 1971.

Hardy, R.H.N., *Steam in the Blood*. Ian Allan, 1971.

Haresnape, Brian, *A Pictorial History of Bulleid Locomotives*. Ian Allan, 1976.

Lynes, L., *Railway Carriages and Wagons*. Loco Publishing Co, 1959.

Nock, O.S., *British Locomotives from the Footplate*. Ian Allan, 1950.

Nock, O.S., *The British Steam Railway Locomotive, Vol. 2*. Ian Allan, 1966.

Reed, Brian, *Merchant Navy Pacifics, Loco Profile No. 22*. Profile Publications Ltd, 1972.

Rogers, Col. H.C.B., *Chapelon, Genius of French Steam*. Ian Allan, 1972.

Rogers, Col. H.C.B., *The Last Steam Locomotive Engineer: R.A. Riddles*. Geo. Allen & Unwin, 1970.

Rowledge, J.W.P., *The Turf Burner*. Irish Railway Record Society, 1972.

Tavender, L., *HMRS Livery Register No. 3, LSWR & Southern*. Historical Model Railway Society, 1970.

Winkworth, D.W., *Bulleid's Pacifics*. Geo. Allen & Unwin, 1974.

Index

Note: Figures in bold type refer to plate numbers

223

225